FAMILY
PRESERVATION
SERVICES

OTHER RECENT VOLUMES IN THE
SAGE FOCUS EDITIONS

FAMILY PRESERVATION SERVICES

Research and Evaluation

Kathleen Wells
David E. Biegel
editors

SAGE PUBLICATIONS
The International Professional Publishers
Newbury Park   London   New Delhi

For information address:

SAGE Publications, Inc.
2455 Teller Road
Newbury Park, California 91320

SAGE Publications Ltd.
6 Bonhill Street
London EC2A 4PU
United Kingdom

SAGE Publications India Pvt. Ltd.
M-32 Market
Greater Kailash I
New Delhi 110 048 India

Printed in the United States of America

Library of Congress Cataloging-in-Publication Data

Main entry under title:

Family preservation services : research and evaluation / editors,
    Kathleen Wells, David E. Biegel.
        p.   cm. -- (Sage focus editions ; 129)
    Includes bibliographical references.
    ISBN 0-8039-3515-3. -- ISBN 0-8039-3516-1 (pbk.)
    1. Child welfare--United States. 2. Family social work--United
States. I. Biegel, David E. II. Wells, Kathleen.
HV699.F317 1991
362.82'8'0973--dc20   90-24568
                                                            CIP

FIRST PRINTING, 1991

Sage Production Editor: Diane S. Foster

Contents

PART II: Conceptual and Policy Issues

Foreword

This volume will prove fascinating for those interested in child welfare policy issues as well as researchers who seek to hone their skills in evaluating the implementation and effectiveness of social programs. The highly significant federal legislation that made it national policy to seek the prevention of unnecessary out-of-home placements of children, the Adoption Assistance and Child Welfare Act of 1980, P.L. 96-272, had as one of its key thrusts the development of preventive and reunification services. These were to be strengthened in a context of an overall national policy umbrella of "permanency planning" related to children at risk of loss of their family ties. Thus the federal government has stood ready over the past decade to increase funds to the states for this purpose while it has strictly limited further contributions to the placement services required for children who wind up in substitute care arrangements.

It is not surprising that considerable research interest has emerged in determining whether the marked growth in child welfare prevention programs in all of the states has been of benefit to children and parents in families at risk of dismemberment. This volume provides the results of important first efforts in this area. The summation presented here is very timely and can strongly influence the disposition of the Congress and state legislatures as they seek to reduce social investments, presumably through the identification of "programs that don't work," in an economically stringent period.

An unusual aspect of the interventive program strategy that receives special attention in this volume, the Homebuilder's model of intensive family preservation services developed in Tacoma, Washington in 1974, is that its use has been very actively promoted by a single philanthropic foundation. The Edna McConnell Clark Foundation has invested considerable funding in the promotion of the model from its very beginnings at various sites in the country. It also has supported training and research efforts to test and strengthen the way intensive family preservation services are delivered to families and children.

The initiative of the Clark foundation has given preventive child welfare services, as envisioned in federal legislation, a much needed thrust and a strong sense of coherence. The efforts of the foundation are responsible for a sense of excitement that now attends this serious effort to make an impact upon a social problem with a service model that is quite well specified.

Ten years after the enactment of P.L. 96-272, a basic question arises: Given its central position among child welfare prevention service, will evaluative research show the intensive family preservation model to be as effective as its supporters have maintained? Is the heavy investment in this area producing some pay-off? There are some who fear that a valid appraisal of programs such as Homebuilders is at risk of being unduly influenced by those who have promoted its use with considerable zeal. The evaluation has to be as rigorous as possible to allay such fears.

An examination of the contributions of the researchers whose chapters are included reveals that the task of introducing evaluative research in agency settings where the Homebuilder's model is being employed can be daunting. A mine field of research methodological problems are identified, and this fact requires surefooted approaches on the part of the investigators. Of course, this is not a new phenomenon and there is a rich literature on the pitfalls that can be encountered in evaluating social programs that followed the anti-poverty social action investments of the Kennedy-Johnson years.[1]

The problems in evaluating the best known survivor of the war on poverty, the Head Start Program, have become almost legendary for researchers in this field.[2] The group of studies reported here builds on the experiences of the 1960s and 1970s and charts a research agenda to be executed in the 1990s.

The investigations shared with the reader are in three main service systems dealing with children in out-of-home placements: child welfare, mental health, and juvenile justice. All have used an intensive family preservation services model with some adhering closely to the Homebuilder's models while others have somewhat altered the basic format. Taken together, these studies represent a first generation effort to answer difficult evaluative questions. Impressively, there are reports of several efforts in the use of experimental and quasi-experimental designs as well as several efforts in the use of descriptive and exploratory investigations. The investigators are painstakingly conscious of the soft features of their research and candid in their cautionary notes.

Given the possible confounding of results introduced by problems of design and measurement specified by each of the researchers whose chapters appear in this volume, the reader might wonder whether the glass is half full or half empty. Despite the if's and's and but's that surround all the discussions of outcomes, enough positive findings have emerged to warrant a sense of optimism, expressed in several chapters, that the general thrust of intensive family preservation services has validity even if the specific elements of the Homebuilder's model remain to be tested.

It is a piece of practice wisdom in child welfare that once a family has been dismembered, it may be very difficult to bring the members together again. An approach, which offers family court judges and others with decision-making responsibilities in protective service cases, an option in which placement can be postponed to permit a thoughtful effort to alter a family's dysfunctional mode of operations, has appeal on the face of it.

The authors have identified many research issues that need to be resolved as part of the future research agenda for those seeking to add to the knowledge base underlying practice in this area. The collaboration between the Bellefaire/Jewish Children's Bureau and the Mandel School of Applied Social Sciences at Case Western Reserve University in the persons of Kathleen Wells and David Biegel has provided a very fine contribution to the professional literature. We are in their debt.

David Fanshel
Columbia University School of Social Work

Notes

1. See, for example: Rossi, P. H., & Williams, W. (1972). *Evaluating social action programs: Theory, practice, and politics.* New York: Seminar Press.

2. McKey et al. (1985, June). *The impact of Head Start on children, families and communities. Final report of Head Start Synthesis Project* (DHHS Publication No. [OHDS] 85-31193).

Acknowledgments

The idea for this volume grew out of a two-day invitational National Intensive Family Preservation Services Research Conference sponsored by the Bellefaire/Jewish Children's Bureau, the Mandel School of Applied Social Sciences at Case Western Reserve University, and the Treu-Mart Fund. The conference, which was held in fall 1989, was attended by 28 leading researchers, policy makers, and practitioners from around the country. It was designed to assess the state of intensive family preservation services research and to develop a research agenda for the next generation of empirical investigations in this field. This volume was influenced heavily by the presentations and discussions at that conference. Most of the contributors to the volume presented papers at the meeting.

The success of the conference and the development of this volume would not have been possible without the combined support and assistance we received from a number of organizations and individuals. Samuel Kelman, Executive Director, Bellefaire/Jewish Children's Bureau, and Richard L. Edwards, Dean, Mandel School of Applied Social Sciences, provided financial support and encouragement. Michael Cole and Ellen Ticktin at the Cleveland Jewish Community Federation helped us to secure funding. Funding for the conference and support for this volume were provided by the Bellefaire/Jewish Children's Bureau, the Commonwealth Fund, and the Treu-Mart Fund.

At the Bellefaire/Jewish Children's Bureau, the Board of Trustees and the Board Research Committee provided support for the conference. Staff members from the Division of Research and the agency's family preservation program, Parents and Children Together (PACT), worked closely with us to identify unanswered research questions that were addressed at the conference and in this volume. We are particularly grateful to the assistance received in this regard from Mario Tonti, former Director of Community Services, Selma Gwatkin, Director of PACT, and Dale Whittington, former Research Associate at Bellefaire. Dale Whittington also assisted in the editorial review of draft chapters for this volume; we are indebted to her for her aid. Shirley Ross, Research Department Secretary, assisted with the arrangements for the conference and the preparation of the manuscripts for this volume; we are also indebted to her for her help.

Finally, we are extremely grateful to the conference participants and to all the contributors to this volume. The contributors worked tirelessly with us in conceptualizing both the conference and this volume. Their willingness to help us critically examine knowledge building in the human services, to analyze the state of intensive family preservation research, and to develop and present an agenda for future research were central to this work. Therefore, this book is truly a collaborative effort between the editors and the contributors. The editors, of course, accept responsibility for any errors of omission or commission.

Kathleen Wells
David E. Biegel

Introduction

DAVID E. BIEGEL
KATHLEEN WELLS

The 1980s were a time of considerable strain for America's families. Increases in poverty, homelessness, child abuse, drug abuse, and alcohol abuse combined to place many families at risk of having their children removed from their homes and placed in foster care, group homes, residential treatment centers, psychiatric hospitals, or correctional facilities. In fact, today growing numbers of children are experiencing out-of-home placements in each of the three major American child-serving systems—child welfare, child mental health, and juvenile justice. The U.S. House of Representatives Select Committee on Children, Youth, and Families estimates that 500,000 children are currently in out-of-home placements in the United States. The Committee projects that by 1995, if no major changes in governmental policies take place, the number of children in out-of-home placements will rise by more than 73% to 850,000 (Select Committee on Children, Youth, and Families, 1990).

These trends, together with increasing concerns that the current child-serving systems are not working adequately or consuming resources efficiently (see Kamerman & Kahn, 1990), has led to a search for new models of service delivery. One such approach is family preservation services, whose aim is to prevent the out-of-home placement of children.

The number of family preservation service programs has increased significantly over the last decade. Although the current number is unknown, the National Resource Center on Family-Based Services listed 20 such programs in their 1982 directory and 269 in their 1988 directory (National Resource Center on Family-Based Services, 1988). During this time the federal government and many state governments (National Conference of State Legislatures, 1989) passed legislation to allow public funds to pay for such services. Private foundations, most notably the Edna McConnell Clark Foundation, have made family preservation services a priority.

Family preservation services enjoy considerable public and professional support because they emphasize keeping families together and because they are believed to be a cost-effective alternative to the institutionalization of many young people. In addition, these services are compatible with the public policy mandates to preserve families (e.g., the Adoption Assistance and Child Welfare Act of 1980), to treat children in the least restrictive environment possible (e.g., the 1975 Education for All Handicapped Children Act), and to keep youths who are status offenders out of institutions in the juvenile justice system (e.g., the 1974 Juvenile Justice and Delinquency Prevention Act).

In view of the potential significance of such services, it is important to determine how and to what extent these policy goals are being achieved. In fact, research has been conducted in this area and has documented a number of positive effects. Current knowledge about family preservation services is due largely to the commitment of developers of family preservation service programs, especially developers of the Homebuilders' program (Kinney, Madsen, Fleming, & Haapala, 1977), to examine their practice. Yet, many questions regarding the implementation, effectiveness, and role of these services remain unanswered. The answers are important if public and private resources are to be spent wisely.

The purpose of this book is to assess the current state of research and practice knowledge pertaining to family preservation services. To focus and clarify the discussion of the scientific literature, we restricted our attention to intensive family preservation services. These services are short-term (4 to 12 weeks), family-focused, and intensive (8 to 10 hours of service provided per week per family) (Child Welfare League, 1989). We present critical issues and newly emerging research findings on these services and evaluate their potential in the child welfare, mental health, and juvenile justice systems. The volume also includes a research agenda for the next generation of empirical investigations.

The idea for this volume grew out of a National Intensive Family Preservation Services Research Conference sponsored by the Bellefaire/Jewish Children's Bureau, the Mandel School of Applied Social Sciences at Case Western Reserve University, and the Treu-Mart Fund. The conference, held in fall 1989, was attended by 28 leading researchers, policy makers, and practitioners from around the country. (A list of participants and an agenda are included in Appendix A.) The conference was designed to assess the state of research on intensive family preservation services and to develop a research agenda for the field (Wells & Biegel, 1990). The agenda presented in the conclusion to this volume was informed by discussions at the conference.

To place family preservation services in context, we will review broad trends with respect to out-of-home placement of children. Then we will describe intensive family preservation services, review the status of research conducted before the work presented here, delineate the organization of the volume, and summarize briefly each of the chapters.

Service-Use Trends in the Child Welfare, Juvenile Justice, and Child Mental Health Systems

The data given below suggest both the extent of the problems of American families and the numbers of children entering placement.

Child Welfare System

In the child welfare system, the number of children in out-of-home placements fell during the 1970s and then began to rise dramatically in the mid-1980s. The number of children in facilities for dependent and neglected children decreased from 60,459 in 1966 to 24,533 in 1981 (Young, Dore, & Pappenfort, 1989). Foster care cases declined by 9% from 1980 to 1985, but increased by 23% from 1985 to 1988. During this three-year period, the number of children in foster care grew from an estimated 276,300 to an estimated 340,300. It is estimated that this number will reach 553,600 by 1995 (Select Committee on Children, Youth, and Families, 1990). The House Ways and Means Committee estimates that 360,000 children were in foster care in 1989, a 29% increase since 1986 (Ways and Means Committee, 1990).

Child Mental Health System

In the child mental health system, the number of children served over the past 25 years has increased consistently. In 1966 there were 13,876 children in institutions for the emotionally disturbed; this figure rose to 20,397 in 1981. Similarly, in 1966 there were 8,028 children in psychiatric facilities; this figure increased to 12,683 in 1981 (Young, Dore, & Pappenfort, 1989).[1] Burns, Taube, and Taube (1990) report that inpatient hospital admissions for children and adolescents (under age 18) increased by 24% from 1975 to 1986. In a narrower time span, the House Select Committee on Children, Youth, and Families (1990) reports a 60% increase between 1983 and 1986 in the numbers of children under age 18 who were in psychiatric hospitals, residential treatment centers, or other residential care settings. The Committee estimates that at the end of 1986 there were 54,716 children in care; by 1995 this figure is projected to grow more than twofold to 123,000 children with emotional problems in out-of-home placement (Select Committee on Children, Youth, and Families, 1990).

Even so, the large increase in children being served in this sector does not mean that currently designed services are meeting their needs adequately. The Office of Technology Assessment of the U.S. Congress estimates that from 70% to 80% of the 7.5 to 9.5 million children and adolescents with mental and emotional problems are not receiving appropriate care (Office of Technology Assessment, 1986).

Juvenile Justice System

In the juvenile justice system, admission rates to public detention centers and public training schools had been declining, but now have increased.[2] Steketee, Willis, and Schwartz (1989) report that admissions to public juvenile detention centers decreased from about 490,000 in 1977 to less than 405,000 in 1984. In 1986, however, admissions increased by more than 60,000. Admission rates decreased from 1977 to 1982, and then increased to 1,799 admissions per 100,000 eligible youths in 1986. Similarly, admissions to public training schools decreased between 1977 and 1982, and then began to increase. The admission rates for both public detention centers and training schools in 1986 were the highest of the decade (Steketee et al., 1989).

The House Select Committee on Children, Youth, and Families reports that the number of youths in public and private juvenile facilities in 1987 increased by 27% from 1979, with a 10% increase between 1985 and 1987. The Committee calculates that by 1995 there will be 119,700 to 130,000 children in custody in the juvenile justice system (Select Committee on Children, Youth, and Families, 1990).

Increasing rates of drug abuse, alcohol abuse, child abuse, child neglect, and homelessness in the American population are major factors in the increasing placement rates of children in all three systems (Select Committee on Children, Youth and Families, 1990).

Description of Intensive Family Preservation Services[3]

Intensive family preservation services are described most clearly by reference to the Homebuilders' program, one of the best-known of its kind (Kinney, Haapala, Booth, & Leavitt, 1990). Nearly all of the investigations reported in this volume were of programs that used the Homebuilders' approach. In the Homebuilders' program, families must meet two criteria in order to be referred for services: first, at least one family member must express the desire to keep the family together; and second, no key family member can refuse the option that the family stay together (D. Haapala, personal communication, January 1990). The goals of treatment are to resolve the crises that led to the decision to place a child outside the home and to teach a family the basic skills they need to stay together.

To achieve these ends, families are seen by a program worker within 24 hours of their referral. After that visit, they are seen as often as needed. Their worker is on call 24 hours a day, 7 days a week to deal with emergent family problems. Workers deal with no more than two families at a time; services generally are provided for 4 weeks; and meetings usually take place in their families' own homes. Interventions are both concrete (e.g., helping families to obtain food or jobs) and therapeutic. Therapeutic interventions include cognitive, environmental, and interpersonal strategies. These interventions are based on social learning theory, crisis intervention theory, and ecological perspectives on child development.

Kinney and her colleagues observe:

> All these aspects of the model—the rapid response to referrals, the accessibility of workers at home during evenings and weekends, the time available for families, the location of the services, the staffing pattern, the low caseloads, and the brief duration of services—produce a much more powerful intervention than one that utilizes only one or two of these components. (Kinney et al., 1990, p. 53)

Status of Existing Research

Not surprisingly, initial investigations of Homebuilders-type programs were modest in scope. Typically they focused on one or two outcome variables, depended on small samples, and employed nonexperimental designs (Hinckley & Ellis, 1985; Kinney et al., 1977). These studies focused on the proportion of children served who remained at home. As Pecora and his colleagues note in chapter 1, early investigations showed that between

40% and 90% of these children remained at home at termination of service or at follow-up.

The existing investigations, however, when considered together, have a number of significant limitations (Frankel, 1988; Magura, 1981; Rosenthal & Glass, 1986; Stein, 1985). These limitations also characterize research pertaining to some other types of children's services. We note them here not to hold intensive family preservation services accountable to a higher research standard than we apply to other services but to identify issues to which the next generation of studies must attend.

These limitations include the following: (a) Few studies employ comparison or control groups, so it is difficult to attribute outcomes obtained to involvement in a program; (b) the flow of clients through programs and of subjects through studies is described poorly; (c) data-collection procedures are not articulated, and the reliability of measures, particularly those relying on clinical judgment, is not addressed; (d) assessments of change rely on single-variable analyses; and (e) problems posed by statistical regression effects are not taken into account.

Organization of the Volume

The material presented here represents an effort to overcome the limitations of the extant literature and to advance our knowledge. This volume has two parts: the first contains previously unpublished empirical investigations in this area; the second is concerned with conceptual and policy issues.

Part I: Empirical Studies

Part I includes five chapters, each of which presents original research findings from recent studies of intensive family preservation service programs. The first three chapters, by Pecora and colleagues, Schwartz and colleagues, and Feldman, use the strongest research designs to date to evaluate the effectiveness of these services. Chapters 4 and 5, by K. Nelson and by Yuan and Struckman-Johnson, focus on important unresolved questions in the literature: Are the families in intensive family preservation service programs less troubled than those in the child welfare system as a whole? What factors are associated with placement?

Chapter 1. Pecora, Fraser, and Haapala report findings from a study of six intensive family preservation service programs. Pre- and post-treatment data were collected from families that received these services. Follow-up data were collected from a subsample of these families. Few children were in placement at the end of treatment; 12 months after the start of treatment, this number increased to about one third of the sample. The authors also obtained a small comparison group of families that were referred to intensive family preservation services but received traditional services instead. They matched comparison with treatment families and compared the placement rates for the two groups. The placement rate was higher for the comparison group than for the treatment group: 12 months after beginning treatment, 85% of the comparison-group children were placed, as opposed to 44% of the matched treatment cases.

Chapter 2. Schwartz, AuClaire, and Harris report on a study of the degree to which an intensive family preservation service program served as a placement alternative for youths who were identified as being at risk of imminent out-of-home placement. The study used a two-group experimental design. The comparison group was randomly selected from a group of cases not served by the intensive family preservation program. The use of all placements by subjects was tracked over a 12- to 16-month period. Youths in the treatment group experienced fewer placements than youths in the comparison group: 56% of the treatment-group children were placed during the study period, as compared to 91% of the comparison-group children. Comparison-group children who were placed also experienced more total days in placement than did all of the treatment-group children. The two groups did not differ, however, in the average number of placements made.

Chapter 3. Feldman uses an experimental design to evaluate the effectiveness of five intensive family preservation service programs. Families who had a child less than 18 years old and who met several other intake criteria were assigned randomly to either the intensive family preservation services program or to traditional community services. Data were collected for up to one year after termination of service. In significantly fewer treatment-group families than control-group families, a child entered placement from one to nine months after termination; the differences between the groups dissipated by the 12th month. The author uses a wide variety of measures to assess family functioning. Results showed improvements on some measures for the treatment group over time, but few differences were found between the treatment and the control groups.

Chapter 4. K. Nelson examines two issues: first, the differences between families receiving intensive family preservation services and families in the child welfare system in general; and second, among families that receive intensive family preservation services, the factors that distinguish those with children who are placed from those with children who remain at home. To address the first issue, the author compared families who received intensive family preservation services with a sample of families in the child welfare system studied previously by Magura and Moses. Children in intensive family preservation services consistently had more problems than the comparison-group sample on all comparable measures. To address the second issue, the author reviewed the case records of families who had received family preservation services to identify a subset of cases in which placement did or did not occur. Predictors of placement for families referred for child abuse or neglect differed from those for families referred for problems pertaining to status offenses and delinquencies of their adolescent children.

Chapter 5. Yuan and Struckman-Johnson further explore variables associated with placement of children served by intensive family preservation service programs. They examine the predictors of placement, with a focus on the degree to which prior placement combines with reason for risk of out-of-home placement to predict placement. Subjects were families in eight intensive family preservation service demonstration projects. The authors found complex interactions between prior placement and reason for risk; the placement rate differed as a function of both the number of prior placements and neglect (i.e., one of the reasons for risk of out-of-home placement). Subsequent discriminant analyses using a large number of both child and family variables confirm the importance of the above variables in contributing to placement, but show that a variety of other variables are important as well.

Part II: Conceptual and Policy Issues

Part II includes six chapters. The first three, by Dore, Tracy, and Jones, address significant gaps in the intensive family preservation research literature. They pertain to the context of family preservation programs, the identification of client populations, and the measurement of outcomes. As a group they are designed to raise issues and to provoke debate that will inform future studies in this area. The next chapter, by Schuerman, Rzepnicki, and Littell, is a window through which one can see the practical dilemmas inherent in conducting research in family preservation services. The final two chapters, by D. Nelson and by Yelton and Friedman, address policy issues pertaining to family preservation services within the child welfare and child mental health systems.

Chapter 6. Dore argues that the character of family preservation programs is determined strongly by the service system context in which programs are developed. Although similarities exist among programs in each of these systems, there are also divergences. Dore believes that these divergences have not been explored fully, and that this lack has prevented a full understanding of the role of contextual variables in research on family preservation services.

Chapter 7. Tracy examines current definitions of the target population for intensive family preservation service programs in the child welfare system and discusses major factors that influence this definition. She discusses a number of conceptual, definitional, and programmatic issues pertaining to assessment of the need for placement, establishment of criteria for program selection, and implementation of referral procedures. Tracy's discussion highlights the difficulties involved in defining "at risk of imminent placement"; these difficulties, in turn, complicate research in intensive family preservation services.

Chapter 8. Jones presents a comprehensive analysis of the nature and measurement of change at the case and program level, and then applies this analysis to intensive family preservation services research. This discussion underscores the complexity of conceptualizing and measuring outcomes. Topics discussed include the dimensions of change (occurrence, direction, magnitude, rate, duration, and sequence), the locus and the level of change goals, and the content of change goals (both child and parent outcomes), as well as types of measures and sources of data.

Chapter 9. Schuerman, Rzepnicki, and Littell provide practical lessons for researchers of intensive family preservation service programs. On the basis of their experiences in designing and implementing an evaluative study of such programs in one state, the authors examine issues pertaining to target populations and outcomes from the perspective of researchers in the process of implementing a study. The chapter includes a discussion of the problems inherent in implementing a program evaluation, particularly an experimental design.

Chapter 10. D. Nelson's chapter is predicated on the belief that we already know a great deal about intensive family preservation services; therefore this knowledge should be applied aggressively to human service policy and practice issues. Nelson believes that such knowledge can be applied in a way that would allow states to initiate and expand cost-effective services. He argues that family preservation services offer a reasonable alternative to placement, which can be used to counter the recent trend to more out-of-home placements. In Nelson's view, lessons learned from family preservation services have wide applicability to human services in general; in particular, they suggest that we need to reexamine the categorical nature of our service delivery systems.

Chapter 11. Yelton and Friedman discuss policy issues of family preservation services within the child mental health system. The authors review the current status of this system and discuss agendas for reform, and then present a framework for understanding the role of family preservation services in the child mental health system. The role they envision is predicated on their belief that these services can be used for four purposes: protection, assessment, treatment, and linkage with other services. The chapter concludes with an agenda for future research into these services.

Conclusion

In the conclusion we summarize the major themes and issues raised by the chapters in this volume, identify unresolved questions for future research, and present an agenda to guide the next generation of studies.

Notes

1. There are two types of mental health facilities included in this study: those for children considered emotionally disturbed, and those providing psychiatric inpatient care for children.

2. A detention center is defined as a temporary preadjudicatory placement facility, while a training school is defined as a postadjudicatory placement facility.

3. This section relies on a paper by K. Wells (in press).

References

Burns, B. J., Taube, C. A., & Taube, J. E. (1990). *Use of mental health sector services by adolescents: 1975, 1980, 1986.* Portion of background paper for Adolescent Health Project, United States Congress Office of Technology Assessment.

Child Welfare League. (1989). *Standards for services to strengthen and preserve families with children.* Washington, DC: Author.

Frankel, H. (1988). Family-centered, home-based services in child protection: A review of the research. *Social Service Review, 62,* 137-157.

Hinckley, E., & Ellis, F. (1985). An effective alternative to residential placement: Home-based services. *Journal of Clinical Child Psychology, 14*(3), 209-213.

Kamerman, S., & Kahn, A. (1990). Social services for children, youth, and families in the United States. *Children and Youth Services Review, 12,* 1-184.

Kinney, J. M., Madsen, B., Fleming, T., & Haapala, D. A. (1977). Homebuilders: Keeping families together. *Journal of Consulting and Clinical Psychology, 45*(4), 667-673.

Kinney, J. M., Haapala, D., Booth, D., & Leavitt, S. (1990). The homebuilders model. In J. K. Whittaker, J. Kinney, E. M. Tracy, & C. Booth (Eds.), *Reaching high risk families: Intensive family preservation services in human services* (pp. 31-64). Hawthorne, NY: Aldine de Gruyter.

Magura, S. (1981). Are services to prevent foster care really effective? *Children and Youth Services Review, 3*, 193-212.

National Conference of State Legislatures. (1989). *Selected family preservation enactments.* Unpublished manuscript.

Office of Technology Assessment (OTA) of the United States Congress. (1986). *Children's mental health: Problems and services—a background paper.* Washington, DC: U.S. Government Printing Office.

Rosenthal, J. A., & Glass, G. V. (1986). Impacts of alternatives to out-of-home placement: A quasi-experimental study. *Children and Youth Services Review, 8*, 305-321.

Select Committee on Children, Youth, and Families, U.S. House of Representatives. (1990). *No place to call home: Discarded children in America* (Publication No. 25-744). Washington, DC: U.S. Government Printing Office.

Stein, T. (1985). Projects to prevent out-of-home placement. *Children and Youth Services Review, 7*, 109-121.

Steketee, M. W., Willis, D. A., & Schwartz, I. M. (1989). *Juvenile justice trends, 1977-1987.* Ann Arbor: The University of Michigan, School of Social Work, Center for the Study of Youth Policy.

Ways and Means Committee, U.S. House of Representatives. (1990). *The enemy within: Crack-cocaine and America's families.* Washington, DC: U.S. Government Printing Office.

Wells, K. (in press). Family preservation services in context: Origins, practices, and current issues. In I. Schwartz (Ed.), *Family and home based services.* Lincoln: University of Nebraska Press.

Wells, K., & Biegel, D. (1990). *Intensive family preservation services: A research agenda for the 1990s.* Proceedings of the Intensive Family Preservation Services National Research Conference. (Available from The National Resource Center on Family Based Services, School of Social Work, The University of Iowa, Iowa City, Iowa 52242).

Young, T. M., Dore, M. M., & Pappenfort, D. M. (1989). Trends in residential group care: 1966-1981. In E. A. Balcerzak (Ed.), *Group care of children: Transitions toward the year 2000* (pp. 11-35). Washington, DC: Child Welfare League of America.

PART ONE

Empirical Studies

1

Client Outcomes and Issues
for Program Design

PETER J. PECORA
MARK W. FRASER
DAVID A. HAAPALA

In response to criticism that children and families in the United States were not being served adequately by traditional child welfare services, social workers and allied professionals in the 1970s instituted a series of program reforms and new service strategies to prevent the placement of children in substitute care programs. These program reforms included changes in child welfare services and statutes to prevent children from "drifting" from one foster home to another without a sense of permanence. Program practices were also modified to encourage the adoption of a variety of children, including older children, children from racial or ethnic minority families, and children who were developmentally disabled, mentally ill, or otherwise handicapped. In addition, policies were changed to promote the adoption of sibling groups of children to prevent the separation of brothers and sisters.

AUTHORS' NOTE: An earlier version of this chapter was presented at the NATO Advanced Research Workshop: State Intervention on Behalf of Children and Youth, Acquafredda di Maratea, Italy (February 23, 1989), and material in this chapter is used with the permission of Kluwer Academic Publishers. We would like to thank the intensive home-based family preservation services (IFPS) therapists and supervisors in Utah and Washington who participated in the research project and helped us interpret the evaluation data. The research for this article was made possible through grants from the Edna McConnell Clark Foundation, and the Office of Human Development Services, Administration for Children, Youth and Families, U.S. Department of Health and Human Services (No. 90-CW-0731/01). Opinions expressed by the authors imply no endorsement by the U.S. Department of Health and Human Services.

More recently, these program efforts have been supplemented by a focus on providing intensive home-based family treatment in order to prevent child placement. This chapter will report the results of a recent evaluation of the effectiveness of one type of home-based service: intensive home-based family preservation services (IFPS).

Resurgence of Intensive Home-Based Preservation Services

During the past 25 years, child welfare administrators and workers have been criticized for placing large numbers of children without providing adequate preventive services. A prominent international foundation recently charged that, in America, "children are separated from their families by default. Too few alternatives are available to help them [families] stay together safely" (Edna McConnell Clark Foundation, 1985, p. 2). In fact, many children have been placed outside their homes not once but multiple times, and in different family, group home, and institutional settings (Fanshel & Shinn, 1977; Rzepnicki, 1987).

To address this problem, a number of policy and program innovations were instituted by federal, state, and local authorities. Most notable among these were Permanency Planning, as well as the related program and fiscal reforms promoted by the Adoption Assistance and Child Welfare Reform Act of 1980 (P.L. 96-272) (Emlen, Lahti, Downs, McKay, & Downs, 1978; Pine, 1986). The Permanency Planning reforms of the 1970s and P.L. 96-272 have been supplemented recently by home-based service programs that are designed to help families remain together safely. These programs represent a refinement and extension of family-based services provided in the 1950s that addressed the needs of the "multi-problem family" (cf. Geismar & Ayers, 1958; Horejsi, 1981). Currently, IFPS programs are being implemented not only in child welfare systems, but also in juvenile justice, mental health, and other systems.

The implementation of IFPS programs represents a commitment of state and local governments to operationalize the principle that we should be willing to invest as many resources in preserving families as might be spent for substitute family care (Lloyd, Bryce, & Schulze, 1980, p. 3). Thus, home-based services were developed to provide a viable alternative to out-of-home placement by improving family functioning, as well as by linking families to sustaining services and sources of support.

The "Homebuilders Model" of Intensive Home-Based Family Preservation Treatment

The more recently designed home-based service programs have many different names—intensive home-based family treatment, family preservation services, home-based services, and family-based child welfare services—as well as different program characteristics.[1] Within the broad framework of family-centered services, there is wide variation in terms of clinical methods, duration of treatment, caseload size, nature or number of concrete services provided, and other program characteristics.

The Edna McConnell Clark Foundation and other child welfare organizations active in this program area have promoted the use of the term "family preservation services" to denote a particular form of home-based service. More recently, the Child Welfare League of America, in its *Standards for Service to Strengthen and Preserve Families with Children,* termed this model "Intensive Family-Centered Crisis Services" in contrast to "Family Resource, Support, and Education Services" and "Family-Centered" types of programs (Child Welfare League of America, 1989).

From the perspective of the Child Welfare League and many program administrators, Intensive Family-Centered Crisis Services or Intensive Family Preservation Service (IFPS) programs must have certain characteristics. Program staff should deliver a variety of clinical and concrete services in the home setting. The service should be of short duration (90 days or less) and should be intensive (a minimum of 8-10 hours of face-to-face client contact per week). Probably the most intensive and well-established IFPS program is Homebuilders, which was founded in 1974 in Tacoma, Washington. This model of family preservation services is the focus of this chapter.

IFPS therapists who use the Homebuilders model are distinguished from other types of family-centered or child welfare workers by the intensity and diversity of services that they deliver. Homebuilders therapists provide a wide range of counseling, advocacy, training, and concrete services to families. They work with families in the home and focus on improving child and family functioning, so that children can be prevented from running away or being placed unnecessarily in substitute care.

Therapists carry small caseloads of two to four families at a time and they use various on-call procedures to provide 24 hour-a-day case coverage. Services are crisis-oriented, intensive and brief. On average, they are provided for four weeks, and it is common for the workers to spend 10 hours a week with a family during the initial stages of treatment and five to eight hours a week thereafter.

The Homebuilders program is based upon Rogerian, cognitive-behavioral, crisis, and ecological theories. The family and its social support system are viewed as the focus of service with an emphasis upon promoting client independence and psychosocial skill-building. In addition to teaching skills, Homebuilders therapists provide or arrange for a variety of concrete services to assist families to obtain food, clothing, housing, and transportation. Other community resources that provide families with food stamps, medical care, day care, and employment training may also be recommended by the worker. Therapists also use a variety of clinical methods, including parenting training, active listening, contracting, values clarification, cognitive-behavioral strategies, and problem-management techniques (Kinney, Haapala, Booth, & Leavitt, 1990; Kinney, Haapala, & Booth, in press).

The Effectiveness of Family-Centered and Intensive Family Preservation Services

To date, research findings for the programs within the broad category of family-centered services and for the more specific family preservation service types of programs have been contradictory. A variety of family-centered programs has been evaluated, but many studies have been compromised by poor research designs, limited measures of child or family functioning, inadequate analyses, and small samples.[2]

In spite of the limitations present in the literature, the emerging mass of research studies with positive findings cannot be ignored. On balance, the data indicate that family-centered programs, and IFPS programs in particular, are successful in preventing placement in 40% to 95% of the cases referred to them.[3] Although impressive, such findings are difficult to interpret because few studies have used control groups. Thus, it is not always clear what proportion of children would have been placed in the absence of family preservation services. Lacking a definitive body of controlled studies, claims of program effectiveness must be viewed cautiously.

To contribute to this literature and to extend research on the Homebuilders model, the Family-Based Intensive Treatment (FIT) study was undertaken to identify: (a) characteristics of the families and children served by this service; (b) types of clinical and concrete services provided by the IFPS therapists; (c) changes in child, parent, and family functioning that occurred during the service; (d) rates of child placement during and subsequent to service; and (e) correlates of service success and failure. In this chapter, the research design, outcome measures, placement prevention findings, and their implications for program design are summarized.

Method

Research Design

To identify changes in child and family functioning, as well as the factors associated with treatment success and failure, a quasi-experimental design ("one-group pretest-post-test") with a partial 12-month follow-up period was employed (Cook & Campbell, 1979, p. 99). This design is also known more precisely as one using "reflexive controls" because it uses the pre-treatment observations of the clients as a "control" or comparison for the post-treatment observations (Rossi & Freeman, 1989). In addition, a small case overflow comparison group was used to strengthen the basic study design. Case information was collected at the following points in time (with the number of families providing data at each point reported in parentheses):

1. Intake—the beginning of IFPS (453)
2. Termination of IFPS (453)
3. Twelve months after IFPS intake (263)
4. If and when "service failure" occurred (136)

Between September 1985 and June 1987, pre- and post-treatment data on 453 families that received intensive family preservation services were collected. Data regarding family functioning and child placement were collected 12 months after IFPS intake from 263 families that had entered treatment sufficiently early in the course of the study to be eligible for inclusion in a one-year follow-up.[4]

Data were collected at two IFPS program sites in Utah and four sites in Washington. The two states were selected because they represented two different organizational auspices for the delivery of a similar model of family preservation services, the Homebuilders model. Utah's services were provided directly by public child welfare employees of the Department of Social Services; while in Washington, the Department of Social and Health Services contracted with the Behavioral Sciences Institute (BSI)—a private agency—for the provision of family preservation services.

At the Homebuilders program in Washington, a total of four program sites were used (Pierce, King, Spokane, and Snohomish counties). These program sites were chosen because they were the most well established and served a variety of urban, suburban, and rural clients (however, the Snohomish site served more rural families). Families accepted by the program were seen within one day of referral. Therapists carried caseloads of two families at a time because services are intensive and limited to 30 days' duration.

In contrast, the Utah IFPS therapists carried caseloads of four to six families, but served them over a 60-day period. One of the Utah sites (Kearns) served mostly urban clients; while the Ogden site served both urban and rural clients. These programs were begun in 1982 and 1984, respectively, and were the two major IFPS sites in the state at the time. With the exception of caseload and length of treatment, the casework methods employed by both programs were similar, as most of the Utah therapists had received more than 30 hours of training in the Homebuilders model. In addition to formal training and individual supervision, therapists in each IFPS program met weekly in teams to review cases.

Child placement episodes were monitored through computerized information systems that tracked placement payments in both states. In addition, placements were identified by maintaining contacts with referring and IFPS workers and by conducting interviews with primary caretakers at service termination and at the end of the 12-month follow-up period. If, at any time during the monitoring period of the study, a child from a participating family ran away or was placed for two weeks or more, service was considered to have failed. At that point, primary and secondary caretakers, the IFPS therapist, and his or her supervisor were interviewed to identify the attributed causes of placement.

Intake Criteria

In both states, families were eligible for service if, and only if, one or more of their children were deemed "at risk of imminent placement." To meet this criterion, referring workers must have been planning to place a child within one week if family preservation services were not provided. In Utah, about 40% of the cases came directly from a Juvenile Court judge or a screening committee, which had determined that the child was to be placed immediately if family preservation services were not offered. In the remaining cases (60%), protective services workers determined that placement was imminent and made a referral to family preservation services.

In Washington, referrals came from two different units within the State Division of Child and Family Services. Workers from Children's Protective Services (CPS) (serving children in danger of abuse or neglect) and Family

Reconciliation Services (FRS) (serving ungovernable children and families in conflict) referred families to Homebuilders. According to agency standards, referrals could be made only when children were in danger of imminent out-of-home placement. CPS referrals accounted for 45.5% of all Washington referrals, and the remainder came from Family Reconciliation Services.

In both states, cases were accepted when a child's safety could be maintained with service and at least one parent was willing to schedule an initial meeting with the IFPS worker. According to the criteria outlined above, all referrals were screened for appropriateness by an IFPS supervisor, intake coordinator, or a local placement screening committee. In both states, less than 20% of the referrals were not accepted for service. The reasons for nonacceptance included the following: children ran away, children were not in danger of imminent placement, the client refused the service, or the worker was unable to locate the family.

Case Overflow Comparison Group

To estimate failure rates in the absence of family preservation services, a small "case overflow" comparison group comprised of 26 Utah families that were referred, but not served, by the IFPS program was formed (Bickman, 1990). These families were referred for family preservation services during the project period, met the criteria for admission, but could not be served because the IFPS therapists had full caseloads. The families received traditional child welfare and/or mental health services (e.g., protective supervision, counseling on an outpatient basis, youth services) and were tracked for 12 months or until the children at risk were placed, whichever occurred first.[5] Child and family demographic data and information about the placement location(s) of the children during the follow-up period were gathered for each family (see the Findings section).

Definition of Service Success and Failure

Service failure was defined as: "The placement of a child outside the home for 2 weeks or more in a non-relative setting during the provision of family preservation services or within 12 months following IFPS intake." (Runaway behavior for two weeks or more was also included in this failure category.) Conversely, *service success* was defined as family preservation during the service and the follow-up period. The definition of success is one of the more conservative possible; and because data were collected on all possible non-relative out-of-home conditions, a variety of sub-analyses by treatment outcome (e.g., in-home, runaway, foster care) could be performed.

It is recognized that the measure of success utilized in this study may elevate "failure" or "placement rates" by the inclusion of children who run away from home or who go to live with neighbors or friends. Comparisons with other studies may also be difficult because some programs rely only on worker reports and others on case records at case termination for placement information (thereby not detecting some runaway episodes or private placements). In addition, a few research studies (e.g., Nelson et al., 1988) have not counted any substitute child care episodes during the treatment period as "official placements" if the child returned home before case termination. We regard the lack of a uniform outcome measure as a serious problem in the field, and readers are cautioned that the definitions of "placement" and treatment "success" may make placement rates observed in different IFPS or family-centered studies incommensurable.

The service failure outcomes reported below do not differentiate between short-term versus long-term placements, as long as they met the study criteria. For example, any out-of-home episodes for two weeks' duration involving any form of substitute care, including shelter care, inpatient psychiatric treatment, and juvenile correction facilities, were counted as service failures. Some of the children in the study returned to their families three to six weeks after removal; and by including shorter term out-of-home episodes, failure rates in this study may be inflated.

Measures of Child, Parent, and Family Functioning

Family functioning and case outcomes were assessed through the application of a number of different instruments, which drew information from self-reports from child caretakers, IFPS therapists, and the children served. The CWLA Family Risk Scales were used to measure changes in various aspects of child, parent, and family functioning. These scales were developed by the Child Welfare League of America as part of a study of child placement preventive services in New York state. Scale items are fully anchored by three to five sentence descriptions, and focus on parenting capacity, individual (both parent and child) functioning, and environmental conditions that have shown to be associated with out-of-home placement and have the potential to be altered through treatment (Magura & Moses, 1986; Magura, Moses, & Jones, 1987). Changes in family adaptation and cohesion were measured using the Family Adaptation and Cohesion Scale (FACES III) (Olson, Portner, & Lavee, 1985). In addition, changes in family and nonfamily social support were assessed using a social support inventory developed by Robert Milardo (1983).

Data were also collected on a variety of case and service characteristics; including the type and amount of clinical and concrete services provided, as well as the amount of in-person and phone contacts with clients. In this chapter these data, along with data describing specific changes in child and family functioning, consumer satisfaction, and placement causes, will not be described because of the chapter's focus upon differential child placement rates (see Fraser, Pecora, & Haapala, in press).

Results

Demographic Characteristics of the Families and Children

Child Caretakers

Parenting functions in the families participating in the study were carried out by birth parents, stepparents, and relatives. In a few families, adults who were unrelated to the children identified as being at-risk of placement fulfilled caretaking roles. Approximately 41% of the homes were headed by single parents (single parents by divorce or separation and single, never-married parents), while 19% of the homes were headed by both birth parents. The proportion of single-parent households was higher in Washington (43%) than in Utah (38%). On average, Utah families were slightly larger than Washington families (4.7 versus 4.3 members), and they were less mobile, having changed addresses significantly fewer times than Washington families (see Table 1.1).

The child caretakers in Utah and Washington were qualitatively different in a number of areas. In Washington, more than 93% of the primary caretakers were women; whereas in Utah, 86% were women. Primary caretakers in Washington were significantly younger and better educated. Compared to their Utah counterparts, they were more likely to be renting their homes. There were no differences in age or education of the secondary child caretakers between the states; however, 9.2% of the secondary caretakers were female in the Utah sample, while 3.5% were female in the Washington sample. Although not statistically significant, caretaker ethnicity in the two states differed with a higher percentage of ethnic minority clients served in Washington (18.3%) compared to Utah (13.5%).

Table 1.1 Caretaker and Family Characteristics at Intake by State

General characteristics		UT	WA	Total
Primary caretaker				
Age (Years)	M	38.2	35.0[a]	36.0
	SD	7.5	6.8	7.1
Female (%)		86.5	93.2[a]	91.1
Education (Years)	M	11.9	12.4[a]	12.3
	SD	1.8	2.1	2.0
Secondary caretaker				
Age (Years)	M	39.4	37.5	38.1
	SD	9.0	10.0	9.7
Female (%)		9.2	3.5[a]	5.3
Education (Years)	M	12.6	13.0	12.9
	SD	2.3	2.3	2.3
Household size	M	4.7	4.3[a]	4.5
	SD	1.9	1.6	1.7
Non-caucasians served (%)		13.5	18.3	16.8
Family structure (%)				
Birthparent together		22.0	17.7[b]	19.0
Single parent, divorce or separation		36.9	36.7	36.7
Birthparent with stepparent		27.7	19.3	21.9
Birthparent living with other adult		8.5	12.5	11.3
Single, never married		1.4	5.8	4.4
Other		3.5	8.0	6.6
Case referral source (%)				
Child Protective Services		59.0	45.5[b]	49.3
Family Reconciliation Services		0.0	54.5	39.1
Youth Services		15.6	0.0	4.4
Juvenile Court		24.6	0.0	6.9
Self-referred		0.8	0.0	0.2
Religious affiliation (%)				
Catholic		9.4	14.1[b]	12.6
LDS (Mormon)		62.6	4.6	22.7
Protestant		2.9	36.6	26.1
None		15.8	31.7	26.7
Other		9.4	13.1	11.9

continues

Table 1.1 continued

Degree of religious involvement[c]	M	3.84	3.90	3.88
	SD	1.3	1.4	1.4
Number of address changes in last five years	M	1.8	2.4[a]	2.2
	SD	2.1	2.3	2.2
Renting home (%)		43.0	61.2[b]	55.8
Caretaker structure (%)				
Living together, married		51.1	39.9[b]	43.4
Living together, unmarried		8.5	11.6	10.6
Not living together		15.6	11.6	12.8
Single caretaker		23.4	35.7	31.9
Other		1.4	1.3	1.3
Family gross income (%)[d]				
$5,000 and under		8.8	10.1[b]	9.7
5,001 – 10,000		23.5	33.2	30.2
10,001 – 15,000		19.9	16.9	17.8
15,001 – 20,000		12.5	15.0	14.2
20,001 – 25,000		16.9	6.8	9.9
25,001 – 30,000		10.3	6.5	7.7
Over 30,000		8.1	11.4	10.4
Primary caretaker				
Major source of family income (%)				
Job		73.0	62.8	66.0
Social Security		5.0	3.2	3.8
Income assistance (e.g., GA, AFDC)		16.3	29.1	25.1
Retirement		.7	.0	.2
Unemployment		1.4	1.3	1.3
None		0.0	.3	.2
Other		3.5	3.2	3.3

[a]Indicates that the two states differ significantly at the $p \leq .05$ level using ANOVA F-test.

[b]Indicates that the two states differ significantly at the $p \leq .05$ level using X^a test.

[c]Degree of religious involvement rated on a five-point scale, ranging from "none" to "great".

[d]Cost of living statistics for the major data collection sites indicate that cost of living in the Utah sites (Salt Lake City and Ogden = 95.6) was lower than for most of the Washington sites (Spokane = 91.6; Tacoma = 102.5; and Seattle = 108.5). These scores are the percentage of the average score for all metropolitan areas participating in the national Chamber of Commerce survey, anchored at a "mid-management" style of living and including the following cost categories: grocery items, housing, utilities, transportation, health care, and miscellaneous goods and services (American Chamber of Commerce Research Association, 1989).

Family Characteristics

Reflecting state economic and cultural differences, the families in Utah and Washington differed on measures of income, participation in public assistance programs, child caretaking responsibility, home ownership, and religious affiliation. In Utah, 32.3% of the families reported incomes of less than $10,000; while in Washington, 43.3% had incomes less than $10,000. Similarly, more than 35% of the Utah families reported gross incomes that exceeded $20,000; whereas less than 25% of the Washington families had incomes above that level. Roughly 30% of the Washington sample reported receiving some form of public assistance; whereas in Utah, 17% of the sample reported receiving general assistance (usually AFDC as an income source). Close to two thirds of the families in Utah were Mormon, compared to less than 5% in Washington. But in degree of religious involvement, the states did not differ.

Characteristics of Children at Risk

Most of the families in the study had only one child at risk of placement. But 101 families had two or more children at risk. The average age of oldest children with the potential of removal (PR) was 12.5 years. Many of the first, second, and third oldest children had been placed out of the home previously, with a substantial proportion attending school half the time or less. Few of the cases (less than 13%) were reunification cases where children were being returned to their families from substitute care. Most of the children not at home at intake were in the process of returning home from a short-term shelter care facility before the family preservation service period began.

The children at risk of placement served by the six IFPS sites differed significantly regarding their age and a few other variables. The Utah children were, on average, older than the children served by the Washington sites. The mean age of the oldest children at risk of placement in Utah was 14.0 years, compared to 11.9 years for the Washington children. The Utah children also had experienced more previous placements (see Table 1.2).

Demographic Characteristics of
the Utah Case Overflow Comparison Group

In all but one of the 26 comparison group families, one child was designated as being at risk. In one family, two children were at risk. The families averaged 4.2 members, and all but two families were Caucasian.

Table 1.2 Characteristics of Children at Risk of Out-of-Home, Non-Relative Placement at Intake by State[a] [b]

General characteristics		UT	WA	Total
Children at risk who were adopted (%)		4.3	3.5	3.8
Age of children at risk				
Oldest Child	M	14.0	11.9[c]	12.5
	SD	2.6	4.3	4.0
Second oldest	M	12.7	9.5[c]	10.6
	SD	3.2	4.9	4.6
Third oldest	M	11.7	7.7[c]	9.0
	SD	3.6	4.5	4.6
Prior placements of children at risk				
Oldest child	M	1.05	.43[c]	.60
	SD	1.4	.8	1.1
Second oldest	M	.97	.38[c]	.58
	SD	1.2	.9	1.1
Third oldest	M	.81	.33[c]	.49
	SD	1.1	.7	.9
Length of time (months) of prior placements (if one) of children at risk				
Oldest child	M	4.1	4.9	4.6
	SD	5.2	6.7	6.2
Second oldest	M	3.5	4.9	4.1
	SD	3.3	5.8	4.6
Third oldest	M	5.8	4.2	5.1
	SD	9.2	4.0	7.1
Oldest child at risk				
Place at time of referral (% not at home)		29.1	18.5	21.4
Place at time of intake (% not at home)		12.6	12.1	12.3
Projected placement (% out of home)		89.4	93.5	92.4
School attendance (% attending half or less of time)[b]		33.8	24.6[d]	27.2
Proportion of children with no drug/alcohol involvement[b]		32.5	69.3[d]	59.6
Major handicapping conditions:				
Learning problems,		20.5	10.8	13.4
Psychiatric problems		10.8	0.4	3.2
Previous outpatient counseling services (% involved)[b]		74.7	68.8[d]	70.4
Previous inpatient counseling services (% involved)[b]		33.3	10.0[d]	16.1
Second child at risk				

continues

Table 1.2 continued

General Characteristics	UT	WA	Total
Place at time of referral			
(% not at home)	30.9	10.0[d]	17.2
Place at time of intake (% not at home)	20.9	7.7[b]	12.2
Projected placement (% out of home)	85.3	93.8	90.9
School attendance (% attending			
half or less of the time)[b]	29.0	17.2[d]	21.6
Proportion of children with no			
drug/alcohol involvements[b]	79.5	97.3[d]	92.4
Major handicapping conditions:			
Learning problems,	15.4	8.5	10.8
Psychiatric problems	9.2	0.0	3.1
Previous outpatient counseling			
services (% involved)[b]	81.0	56.7[d]	64.7
Previous inpatient counseling			
services (% involved)[b]	41.3	9.4[d]	19.9
Third Child At Risk			
Place at time of referral			
(% not at home)	29.2	10.4[d]	16.7
Place at time of intake (% not at home)	16.7	6.4	9.9
Projected placement (% out of home)	83.3	87.8	86.3
School attendance (% attending			
half or less of the time	30.4	21.3	25.5
Proportion of children with no			
drug/alcohol involvement	81.0	93.8	89.9
Major handicapping conditions:			
Learning problems,	23.1	8.3	13.5
Psychiatric problems	7.7	0.0	2.7
Previous outpatient counseling			
services (% involved)[b]	75.0	51.0[d]	58.9
Previous inpatient counseling			
services (% involved)[b]	28.0	8.2[d]	14.9

[a]Including runaway, detention, living with neighbor/friend, or other out-of-home living arrangement of two weeks' duration or more.

[b]The client intake coordinator in Washington recorded much of the client demographic data at intake; while in Utah, these data were recorded by the FPS therapists. So, the differences between the two states should be viewed with caution.

[c]Indicates that the two states differ significantly at the $p \leq .05$ level using ANOVA F-test.

[d]Indicates that the two states differ significantly at the $p \leq .05$ level using X^2 test.

Family structure varied with 12 (46%) of the families characterized as single-parent homes (divorced or separated), and six families (23%) had both birth parents married and living together. Five (19%) of the families were composed of a birth parent and a stepparent.

At the time of referral to family preservation services, 10 of the children (37%) were suspected of drug and/or alcohol use; while 12 additional children (44%) had substantiated drug and/or alcohol usage. Five children (18%) had no drug or alcohol involvement. The majority of children in the comparison group were having school attendance problems. More specifically, 14 (52%) were rated as attending school about half the time or less at the point of referral to family preservation services. Six (22%) were not attending at all, had been expelled, or had dropped out.

Most (15, or 56%) of the comparison group children had some kind of physically, mentally, or emotionally handicapping condition at the time of referral to family preservation services. The most commonly identified condition was an "officially diagnosed psychiatric condition" identified for six (22%) of the children. Four (15%) of the children had some type of learning disability. Fewer than one-half (11, or 41%) of the children had received any inpatient psychiatric or residential treatment services prior to their referral to family preservation services. With the exception of substance abuse and school attendance, the comparison group children did not differ significantly from the experimental group children, at least with respect to the variables measured in the study.

Treatment Success as Indicated by Placement Prevention Rates

Placement Prevention Rates for the Total Study Sample

Intensive home-based family preservation services appear to be useful in preserving families, even when an extremely conservative definition of treatment success is used. One of the more accurate ways of measuring treatment success involves focusing on only the children in each family who were identified as being at risk of placement, because some families had both children at risk and children not at risk in the home.

Placement rates at IFPS case termination for the two states and the total sample are presented in Table 1.3. In addition, the proportions of children who did not experience service failure during the study period have been computed and are listed as "placement prevention rates." This term, while

Table 1.3 Family-Based Intensive Treatment Outcomes by State
(August 14,1985 – August 31, 1987)

Children as the unit of analysis[a]	UT	WA	Total
Number of children identified as being at risk of placement	172	409	581
Number of children experiencing at least one out-of-home placement at case termination[b]	16	25	41
Placement prevention rate at case termination (%)	90.7	93.9	92.9

[a]Includes only the three oldest children, 17 and under, living at home, which represents 94.7% of the children identified as potential removals (PRs) in the study.

[b]Placement is defined here as child placement with a non-relative or continuous runaway behavior for two weeks or more. Case termination occurred, on average, 30.2 days after intake in Washington and 62.8 days after intake in Utah. These placement statistics reflect the actual number of child placements that occurred before or at the time of case termination.

indicating the relative success of the two IFPS programs, must be viewed with caution, as a number of control group studies (ours among them) have found that not all children designated "at risk of placement" are actually placed if family preservation services are not offered.

Across all 581 children from 446 eligible families, the placement prevention rate at case termination was 92.9%. For Utah ($n = 172$), the rate was 90.7%, and for Washington ($n = 409$), it was 93.9%. That is, on average, 93% of the at-risk children receiving family preservation services remained with their families or relatives.[6] However, some recent studies have included placements with relatives as "treatment failure." We believe that caring for children using extended family members is a positive outcome for many children and is a successful tradition adhered to by many ethnic groups. In spite of the informal use of family members, a considerable number of relative placements are being partially supported through state funds. To allow comparisons between this study and other studies, a special analysis was conducted, and a treatment success rate that includes placements with relatives as case failures was calculated.

Only four children were placed with relatives at or before case termination (two children were placed in Utah, and two in Washington). For the total sample of children ($N = 581$), the treatment success rate at case termination, adjusted by including relative placements, was 92.3%. For the Utah cases, it was 89.5%; for Washington cases, it was 93.4%.

Placement Prevention Rates
for the 12-Month Follow-Up Sample

The monitoring of some families over a 12-month period of time after IFPS intake allowed project staff to assess service success over a standardized period of time. There is some concern in the field regarding holding a short-term intervention such as this one responsible for long-term success, especially when the IFPS therapists do not have control over the quality of follow-up services or the case decisions that are made after family preservation services have been completed.

As expected, treatment success rates declined over time: 67% of the 342 children who were able to be followed for 12 months remained with their families or relatives for all 12 months after the start of family preservation services. By state, the Homebuilders staff in Washington achieved a 70.2% child-based success rate ($n = 245$) and the Utah Family Preservation Services staff had a 58.8% success rate ($n = 97$).

Placement Locations of the Children
in the 12-Month Follow-Up Group

The most restrictive placement locations of the 113 children who experienced treatment failure at any time during IFPS treatment or the follow-up period were identified (approximately 30 children had more than one placement). Most of the children in the "failure" category were placed in foster care (47, or 41.6%), with the next largest group running away for two weeks or more (16, or 14.2%). A number of the children were placed in group homes (16, or 14.2%), inpatient psychiatric facilities (10, or 8.9%), residential treatment (9, or 8%), or shelter care (9, or 8%). Smaller numbers of children left home to live with friends (5, or 4.4%) or were adjudicated delinquent and placed in a juvenile corrections facility (1, or 1%).

Placement Prevention Rates
Using "Official" Placements

A number of IFPS studies have monitored the incidence of only "official" child placements (foster care, group care, residential treatment, or psychiatric hospitalization) known to workers at case termination, or identified through management information system reports in order to calculate success rates. For comparison purposes with these studies, the placement prevention rates using these categories were calculated. The placement prevention rates will be slightly lower compared to other studies because interviews with primary caretakers were also used to gather the placement data, and privately arranged placements were included as failure cases. Nevertheless, the placement prevention rate for the total sample of cases 12 months after IFPS intake was 75.7%, with 78% of the children served by the Homebuilders program and 70.1% of the Utah children avoiding placement in these types of substitute care facilities.

Case Overflow Comparison Group and Outcomes

In comparison to the treatment group, 23 (85.2%) of the 27 children (from the 26 families) in the Utah case overflow comparison group were placed during or after receiving more traditional child welfare or mental health services. Thus the child-based placement prevention rate for the comparison group was 14.8%, compared to 58.8% for the Utah experimental group.

A more rigorous analysis of the comparison group and experimental group cases was conducted by matching comparison group and experimental group cases on the following case characteristics: child race, child gender, previous child placement for inpatient treatment, child suspected or substantiated substance abuse, child degree of school attendance, family income, child handicap status, family structure, and household size. For each comparison group case, cases from the Utah follow-up sample that could be matched on as many of these characteristics as possible were identified. Then one case was randomly selected for use as a matched comparison case (see Table 1.4). The placement rate for the subset of matched IFPS treatment cases was 44.4%, which was significantly lower than the placement rate for the comparison group cases (85.2%). The results of this analysis provide another indication of the differential effectiveness of family preservation services compared to traditional services.

Study Limitations

The following study limitations need to be taken into account in reviewing the findings:

Reactivity and Limitations
in Caretaker Recall

Although interviewers were carefully trained and confidentiality was guaranteed, it is possible that child caretakers and workers responded in socially desirable ways to questions regarding child placement. In addition, during the 12-month follow-up interviews, caretakers were asked to recall "informal" placements of their children with neighbors, friends, relatives, and others who may have helped families after the termination of family preservation services. Respondents' recall with regard to such events may have poor reliability.

Differential Family Participation
in the Research Study

In Utah, virtually all eligible families elected to participate in the study; but in Washington, 46% of the families served by Homebuilders during the study period participated in the research project. Of the families that did not participate, half (51%) were not asked to participate by their workers. About one-fourth (24%) refused to participate, and 20% were not afforded the opportunity to participate because of research administration problems (e.g., research staff unavailable, new workers not oriented to research project). Finally, 5% of the families were in such crisis that they were excluded from the study for treatment reasons.

It is possible, therefore, that the research sample from Washington did not represent the true Homebuilders client population regarding problem severity, because the treatment success rates reported for the Homebuilders program as a whole have been 8% to 10% higher than those reported for the study sample (indicating that a slightly more troubled set of families were included in the study).[7] However, a comparison of client demographics and other characteristics between Homebuilders families who did and did not participate found no significant differences.

Limitations of the Comparison Group
Design and Sample

The comparison group employed for this study was based on tracking 26 of the 38 families (68%) that were referred but not served by the Utah IFPS units (the other 12 families were early referrals who could not be traced by the IFPS supervisors after the case overflow procedures were developed). It is possible that the 12 families not tracked successfully avoided child place-

Table 1.4 A Comparison of Treatment Success of the Utah Comparison Group Cases and a Matched Set of Cases that Received Intensive Family Preservation Services (N=27)

Comparison group case ID number	Race[a]	Gender	Previous child inpatient treatment[b]	Child substance abuse[c]	Degree of school attendance[d]	Family income[e]	Child handicap status[f]	Family structure[g]	Household size[h]	Comparison group	Treatment group	(Number of matching cases)[i]
										Cases where treatment failure (F) occurred within 12 months after intake		
1	X	X	X	X	X	M[j]	X	X		F		(1)
2	X	X	X	X	X	M	X	X	X		F	(1)
3	X	X	X	X	X	X	X			F		(2)
4	X	X	X	X	X	X	X			F		(1)
5	X	X	X	X	X	M				F		(2)
6	X	X	X	X	X					F		(3)
7	X	X	X	X	X	X	X			F	F	(2)
8	X	X	X	X	X	X				F	F	(1)
9	X	X	X	X	X	X	X			F	F	(1)
10	X	X	X	X	X					F	F	(1)
11	X	X	X	X	X	X				F		(2)
12	X	X	X	X	X	X	X	X	X	F	F	(1)
20	X	X	X	X	X	X			X	F	F	(2)
21	X	X	X	X	X	X	X	X	X	F	F	(1)
22	X	X	X	X	X	X			X	F		(0)

continues

22

Table 1.4 continued

Case	a	b	c	d	e	f	g	h	i
23	X	X	X	X	X	X		F	(10)
24	X	X	X	X	X	X	X	F F	(2)
25	X	X	X	X	X	X X	X	F F	(1)
26	X	X	X	X	X				(8)
27	X	X	X	X	X				(8)
28	X	X	X	X	X	X	X	F F	(5)
29	X	X	X	X	X	X	M	F F	(2)
30	X	X	X	X	X	X			(2)
31	X	X	X	X	X	X	X	F	(3)
32	X	X	X	X	X	X		F F	(5)
33	X	X	X	X	X			F	(7)
34	X	X	X	X	X			F	(1)

[a] Race for each child was coded either Caucasian or Ethnic Minority.

[b] This variable measured whether or not the child was placed previous to IFPS treatment. Some form of inpatient treatment facility such as residential treatment center, alcohol or drug abuse inpatient treatment, state or private psychiatric hospital was noted.

[c] Drug or alcohol usage was coded as either (1) none; (2) suspected; or (3) substantiated.

[d] Degree of school attendance was coded as either (1) attending all or the majority of the time; (2) attending less than half of the time; (3) not attending or formally "dropped out"; or (4) not attending because of summer vacation during the time of treatment or too young for school.

[e] Family income was coded as (1) $10,000 or less; or (2) $10,001 and over.

[f] Child handicap status included (1) none; (2) any physical or intellectual handicap; or (3) officially diagnosed psychiatric problem.

[g] Family structure was coded as (1) two-parent family (including parent living with another adult); (2) single-parent (including never-married parents, single parent divorced or separated, and grandmother caring for children alone); or (3) other family structure.

[h] Household size was coded as (1) 1-4 persons; or (2) 5 or more persons.

[i] This column contains the total number of treatment group cases that had the same characteristics as the comparison group cases. If more than one treatment case was located, the matching case from the treatment group was randomly selected and its placement status noted on the table.

[j] M=Data was missing for a particular comparison group case.

ment with the assistance of conventional services. Thus, the observed place-ment rate for the comparison group may have been lower had all the comparison group cases been tracked successfully. Counterbalancing this potential bias is the fact that only the referring workers, and not the compar-ison group families, were interviewed for the comparison condition follow-up. Some privately arranged placements or runaway episodes, therefore, may not have been identified. On balance then, comparison group place-ment rates should be interpreted with caution, for the sample size is small, the follow-up interview method differed from that of the treatment condi-tion, and the findings describe only the public agency (Utah) sites.

Discussion

Evidence for Service Effectiveness

Because of the careful client tracking and follow-up methods used, the findings from this project contribute to the growing confidence and opti-mism characterizing intensive home-based family preservation programs. Even when placements with relatives and privately arranged placements were defined as treatment failures, the treatment success rates of the Homebuilders program model matched or exceeded those of most other IFPS or family-centered treatment programs using comparable intake cri-teria.

As indicated by the 12-month follow-up data, treatment success rates declined over time. It may be that some families may need periodic bursts of home-based service or "tune-ups" to stay together after the initial family preservation services have been completed (B. Lantz, personal communica-tion, June 1, 1988). Conversely, it may take time to arrange a placement, or community follow-up services may be unavailable or inadequate.

The placement rates for the case overflow comparison group indicate that, at least in Utah, most of the children referred for family preservation services in this study were indeed at risk of out-of-home placement. Al-though a number of placements were not prevented by the IFPS therapists, the success rates were significantly higher for families that received family preservation services than for families in the case overflow condition. Re-ported elsewhere, other outcome measures in the study supported the ob-served findings as positive changes in child, parent, and family functioning and were highly correlated with treatment success.[8]

Public Agencies Can Effectively Deliver
Family Preservation Services

Despite the more successful family preservation rates demonstrated by the private agency (Washington state program), the data indicate that public child welfare IFPS programs can provide an effective service. There are, however, a variety of challenges associated with delivering IFPS through a public agency. These include staff recruitment, organizational environment, workload management, program stability, and worker turnover (Pecora, Kinney, Mitchell, & Tolley, 1990). Additional studies using control group designs and qualitative measures are necessary to more fully identify the differential effectiveness of family preservation services delivered under each auspice.

Implications for the Design
of Family Preservation Services

One of the critical questions that must be addressed is: What service components and treatment techniques are responsible for helping children and their parents to remain together? At present, the merits of in-home versus office-based provision of family-centered services are being debated along with the effectiveness of different treatment models with certain clients. While experimental studies are needed, the findings of this study have important service delivery implications.

Client Advocacy and Service Intensity

Although data analyses are still being conducted to more fully identify the correlates of treatment success, the Homebuilders philosophy of client advocacy, provision of concrete services, and focus on skill-building appears to be important elements of service. These factors have been reported as correlates of service success in other studies of placement prevention services (see Horejsi, 1981; Jones, 1985; and Jones, Magura, & Shyne, 1981). Immediate client contact by caseworkers and provision of intensive services to families may be important factors as well. Most families were contacted by workers within two days of referral to the program, and they received an average of eight hours of face-to-face and one hour of phone contacts in the first week of service. Over the total service period (four to eight weeks—depending upon the state), workers provided, on average, a total of 37 hours of client contact (Lewis, 1990).

Clinical Services in the Home

Another important component of family preservation services appears to be the amount of time that workers spend in clients' homes or neighborhoods. The preponderance of client contact time was spent in families' homes, and primary caretakers rated the in-home provision of the services as one of the most helpful program components. A variety of clinical services—including crisis intervention, individual counseling, and family therapy—were provided in the home setting. These clinical services were accompanied by in vivo teaching of practical skills, such as anger management, parenting, and conflict-resolution techniques. Many parenting skills are more easily demonstrated and generalized when they are taught in the home at the time that an actual child-parent incident arises (e.g., setting limits around use of toys or the television, managing child behavior at bedtime, handling children who are fighting). An in-home locus of services is therefore important for both family assessment and treatment.

Intake Criteria

Because of resource limitations, the risks to workers who enter homes during family disturbances, and other reasons, screening criteria to help ensure that programs serve clients who are most able to benefit from this service are needed. Although this study and a number of others (see also Nelson et al., 1988; Yuan, McDonald, Alderson, & Struckman-Johnson, 1990) have begun to identify factors associated with treatment success and failure (e.g., child substance abuse, delinquency, and parental attitudes toward placement), it is too early to set definitive program parameters because treatment programs vary and because even families with many "high risk" characteristics succeed in many cases. Nevertheless, a beginning set of intake criteria must be developed if we are to target scarce program funds. And for families with higher failure rates, specialized services to augment the basic IFPS model may be useful to develop and test.

Critical Questions Facing the Field

As implied by the discussion above, there are a number of critical research and program design questions that remain to be addressed in this area. For example, one of the most important questions focuses on what types of outcome criteria should be emphasized in this field. If one adheres to the belief that changes in child and family functioning are important to monitor, which measures of improvement in child or family functioning should be promoted for use in family preservation services? We found that third party observations or assessments would have been helpful to validate worker and parent ratings, but many challenges are encountered in implementing valid procedures for accomplishing this in the field, not the least of which is funding.

Second, in terms of examining placement prevention, how do we differentiate between desirable child placements and those that should have been prevented by this service or some other combination of services? From interviews with IFPS therapists, supervisors, and parents, we learned that many of the child placements were viewed as the best possible case outcome, given the child or family situation (Fraser et al., in press). However, despite the collection of data regarding primary caretakers' views of the appropriateness of child placement, the social desirability of placements was not formally assessed. Consequently, it was not possible to distinguish between those placements that should have been prevented and those that may have been in the best interest of the child and his or her family. How should this issue be addressed in gauging program effectiveness? From another perspective, what will interviews with the *children* served by this program tell us about how to measure treatment success?

Third, and related to the above question, how can the quality and stability of a child's living arrangement best be determined? Although multiple outcome measures were used to assess the effects of family preservation services on family members, our study did not extensively examine the quality and stability of the child's living situation after services ended. For example, the project was unable to track the movement(s) of a child among different relatives (if it occurred), and did not interview children after treatment termination regarding their perceptions of the adequacy of their living arrangements. Both the quality and the stability of a child's living arrangement are important outcome variables, as discussed by Fanshel and others (see, for example, Fanshel, Finch, & Grundy, 1989; Wald, Carlsmith, & Leiderman, 1988).

Fourth, what is an acceptable level of success for this program with particular groups of people, especially when control group designs are employed? Findings must be weighed in relation to accurate cost-effectiveness data, because a 30% success rate may indeed be cost-effective if early cost analyses in this area are sustained by more rigorous research.

Fifth, for children and families with different constellations of problems, what IFPS program models and service strategies are most helpful? There are a large number of questions related to this area that must be addressed:

1. How important is the provision of services in the home (versus services provided primarily in an office)? The primary caretakers and the workers in the FIT study felt it was very important to deliver services in the home and neighborhood settings.

2. How intensive must the service be to achieve treatment success? For example, should the level of client contact for certain types of cases be four, six, or 10 hours per week?

3. How long should family preservation services be delivered before clients are terminated or referred to a less intensive "maintenance" type of service?

4. What theoretical frameworks for clinical practice are most helpful for particular types of families? Unified theoretical frameworks that describe one or more of the competing models of IFPS intervention have yet to be articulated.

5. How important is it to deliver both clinical and concrete services to families? Are both necessary for particular types of families? Is it more cost-effective for the primary therapist to provide both types of services? The FIT study found that concrete services were correlated with goal attainment in a number of areas (Lewis, 1990), and the number of hours of "enabling" concrete services is emerging as a significant variable in some of the multivariate analyses of treatment success as well. (See Fraser, Pecora, & Haapala, in press.)

6. What worker skills and attitudes are essential for successful treatment? Few studies have examined the effects of variations in these variables, yet worker education and training are thought to be important influences on therapist style and effectiveness.

7. What agency structures and supervisory supports promote the successful delivery of this service? Successful family preservation services programs will likely decrease in service effectiveness if these program components are not maintained.

Conclusion

Family Preservation and other forms of Family-Centered Services are not a panacea. These services represent just one part of a continuum of child and family services, which includes such programs as mental health counseling, day treatment, special education, foster family-based treatment, residential group care, and adoption. In our view, there will always be a need for substitute care and other types of services for particular types of families.

Clearly, both further analyses of the data and additional studies using control groups are necessary to address the questions listed above and to more fully identify the place of family preservation services in the continuum of social services. The data from the entire FIT study, however, indicate that combining the Homebuilders philosophy, emphasizing client respect and advocacy, with in-home interventions, clinical services, concrete services, and the teaching of skills empowers parents with both the skills and the resources necessary to create a safer, more enriching home environment for their children. This bodes well for advocates of intensive home-based family preservation services and, more important, for the families that they serve.

Notes

1. See, for example, Bryce and Lloyd (1981); Callister, Mitchell, and Tolley (1986); Compher (1983); and Maybanks and Bryce (1979).

2. For critical reviews of selected evaluation studies of family-centered or family preservation services, see Frankel (1988), Jones (1985), Magura (1981), and Stein (1985).

3. For studies of program effectiveness of family-centered services see, for example, AuClaire and Schwartz (1986); Jones (1985); Jones, Newman, and Shyne (1976); Nelson, Emlen, Landsman, and Hutchinson (1988); and Szykula and Fleischman (1985). For studies of IFPS program effectiveness, see Haapala and Kinney (1988); Haapala, McDade, and Johnston (1988); Hinckley and Ellis (1985); Kinney, Haapala, Booth and Leavitt (in press); Kinney and Haapala (1984); and Kinney, Madsen, Fleming, and Haapala (1979).

4. Pre- and post-treatment data were collected for all 453 families, with treatment failure regarding child placement monitored for 446 families whose first, second, or third oldest children in the home were potential removals. In addition, 26 families were studied as part of a Utah case overflow comparison group. Families that entered treatment in the second year of the project were ineligible for follow-up because 12 months' time had not elapsed between the date of entry into treatment and the termination of the project's data collection activities. Thus the follow-up sample consisted only of families that received family preservation services between September 1985 and August 1986. However, even though project timelines limited the size of the 12-month follow-up sample, all families, regardless of date of intake, were tracked through August 13, 1987. The length of follow-up for families that entered treatment after August 1986 varied from one to almost 12 months. Data from those families are analyzed in other project reports.

5. All cases categorized as successes were tracked for the full 12-month follow-up period.

6. Placement prevention rates at case termination can also be calculated through survival analysis by identifying the number of families intact at the mean case termination date for each program. But these statistics are usually slightly higher because some cases that are served longer than the average may experience placement but are not included (see Pecora et al., 1990, p. 302).

7. In addition, differences in placement rates between the FIT study and program statistics published by the Behavioral Sciences Institute stem from the definition used for "case failure." Many IFPS agencies (including the Behavioral Sciences Institute) normally count only placements in state-funded forms of substitute care (e.g., foster family care, group care, residential treatment, inpatient psychiatric care) occurring within a specific time after IFPS treatment. Placements with friends or relatives are not counted as case failures. As mentioned earlier, comparisons of "treatment success" among various IFPS or family-centered programs must

use similar measures, such as intake criteria, follow-up periods, and definitions of treatment failure, to be valid.

8. For more information, see Fraser, Pecora, and Haapala (in press, Chapters 8, 10, & 11).

References

American Chamber of Commerce Researchers Association. (1986). *Cost of living index—second quarter of 1989, 22*(2), Louisville, KY: American Chamber of Commerce.

AuClaire, P., & Schwartz, I. M. (1986). *An evaluation of the effectiveness of intensive home-based services as an alternative to placement for children and their families.* Minneapolis: Hennepin County Human Service Department & the University of Minnesota, Hubert H. Humphrey Institute of Public Affairs.

Bickman, L. (1990). Study design. In Y. Y. Yuan & M. Rivest (Eds.), *Evaluation resources for family preservation services.* Newbury Park, CA: Sage.

Bryce, M., & Lloyd, J. C. (Eds.). (1981). *Treating families in the home: An alternative to placement.* Springfield, IL: Charles C. Thomas.

Callister, J. P., Mitchell, L., & Tolley, G. (1986). Profiling family preservation efforts in Utah. *Children Today, 15,* 23-25, 36-37.

Child Welfare League of America. (1989). *Standards for service to strengthen and preserve families with children.* Washington, DC: Author.

Compher, J. V. (1983). Home services to families to prevent child placement. *Social Work, 28,* 360-364.

Cook, T. D., & Campbell, D. T. (1979). *Quasi-experimentation: Design and analysis issues for field settings.* Chicago: Rand McNally.

Edna McConnell Clark Foundation. (1985). *Keeping families together: A case for family preservation.* New York: Edna McConnell Clark Foundation.

Emlen, A., Lahti, J., Downs, G., McKay, A., & Downs, S. (1978). *Overcoming barriers to planning for children in foster care* (DHEW Publication No. [OHDS] 78-30138). Washington, DC: U.S. Department of Health and Human Services, U.S. Children's Bureau.

Fanshel, D., Finch, S. J., & Grundy, J. F. (1989). Modes of exit from foster family care and adjustment of time of departures of children with unstable life histories. *Child Welfare, 68*(4), 391-402.

Fanshel, D., & Shinn, E. (1977). *Children in foster care: A longitudinal investigation.* New York: Columbia University Press.

Frankel, H. (1988). Family-centered, home-based services in child protection: A review of the research. *Social Service Review, 62,* 137-157.

Fraser, M. W., Pecora, P. J., Haapala, D. A., & Associates. (in press). *Families in crisis: The impact of intensive family preservation services.* Hawthorne, NY: Aldine.

Geismar, L., & Ayers, B. (1958). *Families in trouble.* St. Paul: Family-Centered Project.

Haapala, D. A., & Kinney, J. M. (1988). Avoiding out-of-home placement of high-risk status offenders through the use of intensive home-based family preservation services. *Criminal Justice and Behavior, 15*(3), 334-348.

Haapala, D. A., McDade, K., & Johnston, B. (1988). *Preventing the dissolution of special needs adoptive families with children in imminent risk of out-of-home placement through the provision of intensive family preservation services: The Homebuilders model.* Federal Way, WA: Behavioral Sciences Institute.

Hinckley, E. C., & Ellis, W. F. (1985). An effective alternative to residential placement: Home-based services. *Journal of Clinical Child Psychology, 14*(3), 209-213.

Horejsi, C. R. (1981). The St. Paul family-centered project revisited: Exploring an old gold mine. In M. Bryce & J. C. Lloyd (Eds.), *Treating families in the home: An alternative to placement.* Springfield, IL: Charles C. Thomas.

Jones, M. A. (1985). *A second chance for families: Five years later.* New York: Child Welfare League of America.

Jones, M. A., Magura, S., & Shyne, A. W. (1981). Effective practice with families in protective and preventive services: What works? *Child Welfare, 60*(2), 67-80.

Jones, M. A., Newman, R., & Shyne, A. W. (1976). *A second chance for families: Evaluation of a program to reduce foster care.* Washington, DC: Child Welfare League of America.

Kinney, J. M., & Haapala, D. A. (1984). *First year Homebuilders mental health project report.* Federal Way, WA: Behavioral Sciences Institute.

Kinney, J. M., Haapala, D. A., Booth, C., & Leavitt, S. (1990). The Homebuilders model. In J. K. Whittaker, J. Kinney, E. Tracy, & C. Booth (Eds.), *Reaching high-risk families: Intensive Family Preservation Human Services.* Hawthorne, NY: Aldine.

Kinney, J. M., Haapala, D. A. & Booth, C. (in press). *Homebuilders: Keeping families together* (preliminary title). Hawthorne, NY: Aldine.

Kinney, J. M., Madsen, B., Fleming, T., & Haapala, D. (1979). Homebuilders: Keeping families together. *Journal of Consulting and Clinical Psychology, 45,* 667-673.

Lewis, R. (1990). *Service-related correlates of treatment success in intensive family preservation services for child welfare.* Unpublished doctoral dissertation, University of Utah, Graduate School of Social Work.

Lloyd, J. C., Bryce, M. E., & Schulze, L. (1980). *Placement prevention and family reunification: A practitioner's handbook for the home-based family-centered program.* Iowa City: University of Iowa, School of Social Work, National Resource Center on Family-Based Services.

Magura, S. (1981). Are services to prevent foster care really effective? *Children and Youth Services Review, 3,* 193-212.

Magura, S., & Moses, B. S. (1986). *Outcome measures for child welfare services.* Washington, DC: Child Welfare League of America.

Magura, S., Moses, B. S., & Jones, M. A. (1987). *Assessing risk and measuring change in families: The family risk scales.* Washington, DC: Child Welfare League of America.

Maybanks, S., & Bryce, M. (Eds.). (1979). *Home-based services for children and families: Policy, practice, and research.* Springfield, IL: Charles C Thomas.

Milardo, R. M. (1983). Social networks and pair relationships: A review of substantive and measurement issues. *Sociology and Social Research, 68,* 1-18.

Nelson, K., Emlen, A., Landsman, M., & Hutchinson, J. (1988). *Family-based services: Factors contributing to success and failure in family-based child welfare services* (Final report). Iowa City: The University of Iowa, School of Social Work, National Resource Center on Family-Based Services.

Olson, D. H., Portner, J., & Lavee, Y. (1985). *FACES III.* St. Paul: University of Minnesota, Department of Family Social Sciences.

Pecora, P. J., Kinney, J. M., Mitchell, L., & Tolley, G. (1990). Agency auspice and the provision of family preservation services. *Social Service Review, 64*(2), 288-307.

Pine, B. A. (1986). Child welfare reform and the political process. *Social Service Review, 60,* 339-359.

Rossi, P. H., & Freeman, H. E. (1989). *Evaluation—A systematic approach*. Newbury Park, CA: Sage.

Rzepnicki, T. L. (1987). Recidivism of foster children returned to their own homes: A review and new directions for research. *Social Service Review, 61,* 56-70.

Stein, T. J. (1985). Projects to prevent out-of-home placement. *Children and Youth Services Review, 7,* 109-122.

Szykula, S. A., & Fleischman, M. J. (1985). Reducing out-of-home placements of abused children: Two controlled field studies. *Child Abuse and Neglect, 9*(2), 277-283.

Wald, M. S., Carlsmith, J. M., & Leiderman, P. H. (1988). *Protecting abused and neglected children*. Stanford: Stanford University Press.

Yuan, Y. Y., McDonald, W. R., Alderson, J., & Struckman-Johnson, D. (1990). *Evaluation of AB 1562 in-home care demonstration projects: Final report*. Sacramento, CA: Department of Social Services, Office of Child Abuse Prevention.

2

Family Preservation Services as an Alternative to the Out-of-Home Placement of Adolescents:

The Hennepin County Experience

IRA M. SCHWARTZ
PHILIP AuCLAIRE
LINDA J. HARRIS

Intensive home-based services have emerged as an innovative strategy for strengthening families, for preventing out-of-home placement of children, and for reuniting children with their families. This chapter presents the results of a study of the effectiveness and impact of family-centered, home-based services implemented within the Child Welfare Division of the Hennepin County (Minnesota) Community Services Department.

Intensive home-based services were developed by the Child Welfare Division largely in response to the high numbers of children in out-of-home care, particularly residential treatment, and the associated high costs of such treatment. The first intensive home-based treatment unit was created in August 1985. The unit consisted of eight specially trained social workers, who worked exclusively with families with a seriously emotionally disturbed adolescent who had been approved for placement. The activities of this unit are the focus of this evaluation.

AUTHORS' NOTE: The authors wish to thank Charles Gershenson for reviewing and critiquing an earlier draft of this paper. This paper was made possible in part by support from the First Bank of St. Paul Foundation and the Hennepin Department of Community Services.

Study Questions

This study was designed to answer the following two questions:

1. To what extent is the new intensive home-based service unit successful in serving as an alternative to out-of-home placement?
2. Are there particular kinds of cases that the unit is more effective with than others?

In other words, Hennepin County child welfare officials, county board members, and the researchers were interested in whether the service provided by this unit would prove to be an effective alternative to placement. They were also interested in the potential for this experiment to generate policy and program data that might contribute to a more efficient and effective allocation of resources.

Study Method and Procedures

To the greatest extent possible and feasible, the study has been designed to avoid the major methodological problems often encountered in the evaluation of the impact of home-based crisis intervention and intensive service programs for children and families.[1] Specifically, the study design:

1. Unambiguously defines the population eligible for services;
2. Identifies equivalent treatment and non-treatment groups; and
3. Includes long-term follow-up for treatment and non-treatment group clients.

Study cases were selected during the period of August through December 1985 and were tracked through December 31, 1986. This means that cases assigned in December 1985 were followed for 12 months. Cases assigned in August 1985 were followed for 16 months.

The sampling procedures developed for implementation by the Child Welfare Division were designed to fit as closely as possible with normal Division operating practices and procedures. In addition, as a matter of policy, Hennepin County (and the Child Welfare Division) does not deny or delay service to eligible clients, particularly in crisis situations often associated with an out-of-home placement issue. The case sampling plan was developed within the constraints imposed by these two factors. The last factor precluded the possibility of assigning clients to either of the two study conditions by a simple random selection procedure from a large pool of cases awaiting service. However, the procedures developed and described below are, in the opinion of the authors, methodologically sound and unencumbered by some of the problems often encountered in studies of this type.

Throughout the sampling period, a log of all Child Welfare Division clients for whom out-of-home placements had been requested was maintained. Cases were listed in the order in which the placement request was received by the Division; thus, at any given time, the last case entry in the log was the most recent case for which a request was reviewed and either approved or disapproved. Hennepin County policy and procedures require that all requests for placement be reviewed at two levels. The requests are first reviewed by the appropriate Child Welfare Division unit supervisor; the requests are then referred to and reviewed by the appropriate Division manager. In the case of requests for residential treatment center (RTC) placements, an additional review stage is required and involves a consideration of the placement request by a multidisciplinary screening committee. This review process was in effect during the sample selection period. A client was eligible for participation in the study if he or she:

1. Was approved for out-of-home placement;
2. Was an adolescent (12-17 years of age);
3. Was not a ward of the state; and
4. Was not under court order into placement.

Clients meeting each of the criterion constituted the pool of the study-eligible cases. During the sampling period, cases were assigned to treatment services from the eligible pool of cases in an unsystematic manner in accordance with the following procedure:

1. The occurrence of an opening in the home-based treatment unit resulted in a request for a case referral from the unit.
2. Upon receipt of a request for a case from the unit, a case aide consulted the log and referred to the unit the most recently listed case eligible for study participation. If a case was unavailable at that time (when, for example, eligible and available cases had already been referred for placement services), the case aide referred the *next* eligible and available case to the unit.
3. In instances where the home-based treatment unit had more than one opening at a given time, the same procedure was followed. If, for example, the unit had two openings, the two most recently listed cases were referred; if two cases

were not available at the time of the request, then the next two available cases were referred to the unit.
4. In the absence of a request from the home-based unit, cases were referred for placement services in accordance with usual Division procedures.

This assignment procedure was monitored throughout the study period and identified two groups of cases: those unsystematically assigned to the home-based treatment unit, and those study-eligible, but not assigned to the unit. From this latter group, a number of cases equal to the number of treatment cases were randomly selected at intervals throughout the sampling period to serve as a comparison group.

Subjects

By the end of the sampling period, 58 cases had been unsystematically assigned to the home-based service unit (treatment group) and 58 cases had been randomly selected to serve as the comparison group. The assignment procedure resulted in a two-group experimental design with unsystematic assignment to the treatment group and random assignment to the comparison group.

The cases assigned to the treatment group received the services described in a section of this chapter, titled "The Home-Based Treatment Program." The cases assigned to the comparison group were placed in foster homes, hospitals, group homes, and residential treatment centers.

The analysis of the impact of the home-based service program is limited to 55 clients. Three clients assigned to the home-based service unit were in placement at the time of referral and remained in placement throughout the study period. For comparison group clients, out-of-home data presented include the first post-assignment placement episode. For home-based service clients, all placement episodes experienced by a client, from the date of assignment to the group through December 1986, are included. Furthermore, as used in this report, a placement episode refers to one discrete and continuous stay in a placement of a particular type, regardless of the length of that stay.

Initially, the plans for the study called for a sample of 250 to 300 cases. Unfortunately, because of economic and other related factors, the Child Welfare Division adopted a policy to implement intensive home-based services agency-wide while the study was in progress. This decision eliminated the possibility for including more than 116 cases in the study sample. One adverse consequence of this decision was that it ruled out the possibility for addressing in a meaningful way the second research question outlined above. However, what can be evaluated is the extent to which families involved in intensive home-based services, who are engaged in treatment, are more likely to succeed in the treatment than are those who are uninvolved in treatment.

Data Collection

An extensive array of information has been collected as part of the evaluation effort. The categories of information include:

1. Client Characteristics. A wide range of client characteristics data (e.g., age, sex, race, type of problem(s), child and parental attitude to placement, and so forth) have been collected for treatment and comparison group cases.
2. Out-of-Home Placement History. A comprehensive out-of-home placement history (by type of placement, date entering and exiting placement, length of stay, and outcome) also has been collected for each treatment and comparison case. The history includes all placement episodes prior to the date that a case was approved for placement during the sampling period.
3. Post-Service Placement Tracking. Out-of-home placement activity (by type of placement, date entering and exiting, length of stay, and outcome) is monitored monthly (for a period of at least 12 months) for each treatment and comparison case.
4. Client Treatment Record. An extensive service history is available for each home-based service case. Service history information includes (but is not limited to): length of participation in intensive home-based service; distribution of service time (by time with family, child, collaterals, and so forth); specification of presenting problem(s); goal setting and achievement; use of additional hard and soft services; and termination circumstances.
5. Social Worker Perceptions. Unit social workers participated in a series of interviews focusing on their perceptions and experiences with the service model as implemented within the Child Welfare Division. In addition to structured interviews, workers responded to a questionnaire focusing on characterizing clients served during the study period, intervention techniques employed, types of goals set, problems of client engagement, and so forth.

With the exception of unit social worker interviews, all information has been extracted from existing Community Services Department/Child Welfare Division data files. Also, all data for analysis have had client identifiers removed to assure confidentiality. All major events and case history information, including all out-of-home placements, are recorded in the data files.

Because of this, we are relatively confident that the follow-up data accurately reflect all post-assignment placement episodes.

The Home-Based Treatment Program

The family preservation or home-based service model implemented within the Child Welfare Division of the Hennepin County Department of Community Services contains a variety of features and key characteristics in common with other family-centered, home-based programs. Among these elements are:

1. Time-limited treatment (the goal was to try to limit services to four weeks);
2. Service in the client's home;
3. Low worker caseloads (two families per worker);
4. Intensive worker involvement with all family members, significant others, and collaterals (including contact beyond normal working hours and on weekends);
5. Case teaming;
6. Utilization of a structural family therapy approach; and
7. An explicit focus on providing and exploring alternatives to out-of-home placement.

Results

Sample Characteristics

Home-based and comparison group clients were compared on 12 study-relevant variables. There were no significant differences in 10 of the 12 comparisons. Demographic findings for the combined 116 home-based and comparison group subjects in the study show that there are slightly more male subjects than female (54% versus 46%); more than two-thirds of the subjects are white; and less than half the children in the study were 14 years or younger (45%), whereas more than half the subjects (55%) were 15 years or older. Almost half (49%) of all study subjects lived in two-parent families, with 45% living with only one parent, and the remaining 6% living in other arrangements. Almost half (45%) of all study subjects had two or more siblings, more than one-third (35%) had one sibling, with the remaining one-fifth (20%) of the study subjects having no siblings. Negative attitudes toward placement were held by more than one-fourth (28%) of all the children in the study, but by only 6% of the parents. Of those study subjects having a sibling, more than one-fourth (28%) of all study subjects had a sibling who had been previously placed. Concerning past involvement with the justice system, less than one-fifth of all study subjects had experienced a previous status offense (17%) or non-status offense (19%).

There were statistically significant differences between the home-based and comparison groups on two variables. The first concerns area of residence. There were significantly more members of the home-based service group who resided in the city of Minneapolis (62%) than comparison group members (35%). The second between-group difference concerns past placement episodes. More than half (52%) of the comparison group clients had experienced one or more past placement episodes, compared to less than half (43%) of home-based service clients who had one or more past placement episodes. It is important to note, however, that the difference between the two groups in terms of total days in previous placement is *not* statistically significant.

Treatment and comparison group clients were identified as having serious and, in most instances, multiple problems at the time placement was recommended. Clients in both groups were reported to have had significant behavioral, family, school, health, and substance abuse problems. A significant number in each of the groups had a history of abuse or neglect, and many had been known by juvenile justice authorities.

As stated earlier, all of the youth in the study sample had been approved for out-of-home placement. Table 2.1 below indicates the preferred placements and the expected lengths of stay for various youth in each of the groups.

As can be seen, residential treatment centers and treatment group homes were identified more often than any other placement resource as the preferred placements for youth in both the home-based service and the comparison groups. In fact, residential treatment centers and treatment group homes were considered to be the preferred placements for more than two-thirds of the youth in the home-based service group and for slightly more than half of the youth in the comparison group. With respect to the expected length of time in placement, nearly 50% of the requested placements were expected to be for a period of 6 to 11 months; approximately 20% were anticipated to last one year or longer.

Question 1: To what extent are the new intensive home-based services serving as an alternative to out-of-home placement?

Table 2.1 Placement Plans at Time of Sample Selection and Expected
Length of Stay by Sample

| | Sample | | | |
| | Home-based | | Comparison | |
Placement plans	n	%	n	%
Foster home	9	15.5	12	20.7
Treatment foster home	3	5.2	2	3.4
Agency group home	1	1.7	5	8.6
Treatment group home	19	32.8	15	25.9
RTC[a]	20	34.5	16	27.6
RTC-MR[a]	1	1.7	1	1.7
Primary treatment	1	0.7	4	6.9
Outpatient treatment	0	0.0	1	1.7
Extended rehabilitation	1	1.7	1	1.7
Group home	2	3.4	0	0.0
N/A	1	1.7	1	1.7
Total	58	100.0	58	100.0

Expected length of stay				
5 months or less	14	24.1	13	22.4
6 – 11 months	26	44.8	30	51.7
12 months	5	8.6	6	10.3
13 or more months	5	8.6	7	12.1
Unknown	8	13.8	2	3.4
Total	58	100.0	58	100.0

[a]RTC = residential treatment center; RTC-MR = residential treatment center for mentally retarded clients.

Of the 55 cases referred to the home-based services group, 24 (43.6%) remained in their own homes throughout the entire study period. Thirty-one, or 56.4%, experienced some type of placement. Of the 31 who were placed, 14 (45%) were placed once, and 17 (55%) experienced multiple placements. Five of the 17 (29%) who experienced multiple placements were placed twice, and 12 (71%) were placed three or more times. Five comparison group clients did not enter their scheduled placements. Of the 53 comparison cases, 34 (64%) experienced multiple placements. Seventeen, or 50% of those placed, were placed twice, and another 17 (50%) were placed three or more times.

Table 2.2 Total Episodes by Placement Type and Sample Type

	Sample[a]			
	Home-Based		Comparison	
		% of all		% of all
Placement type	n	episodes	n	episodes
Shelter	43	56.6	48	35.8
Chemical dependency treatment	2	2.6	8	6.0
Group foster home	2	2.6	2	1.5
Treatment foster home	0	0	3	2.2
Group home	10	13.2	21	15.7
RTC[b]	15	19.7	36	26.9
Correctional placement	0	0	1	0.7
Psychiatric hospital	0	0	2	1.5
Mental retardation	0	0	1	0.7
Foster home	3	3.9	11	8.2
Family placement	1	1.3	1	0.7
Total episodes	76	100.0	134	100.0

NOTE: Twenty-four home-based service clients were not placed out of their homes during the study period. Therefore, only 31 of the home-based service clients accounted for the 76 placement episodes experienced by the group. Five comparison group clients did not enter their scheduled placements; 53 comparison group clients accounted for 134 placement episodes. The number of subjects in each group refers to the number of subjects who were placed.

[a]Thirty-one clients comprised the service group sample and 58 the comparison sample.

[b]RTC = residential treatment center.

The data in Table 2.2 indicates that comparison group clients experienced almost twice as many placements as did clients in the home-based service group who were placed. However, the average number of placements experienced by clients in each group was approximately the same (2.45 in the home-based service group, and 2.3 in the comparison group).

Comparison group clients experienced 7,260 more days in placement than did their home-based service group counterparts (12,037 days versus 4,777 days).

The data available allowed the computation of the expected number of placement days for each group. The data in Table 2.3 shows the number of expected placement days for each group and the actual number and proportion utilized. The home-based service group utilized only 21% of its expected placement days compared to 46% for the comparison group. Even if one excludes the amount of time the comparison group spent in its initial placement upon assignment, the home-based service group still utilized a

Table 2.3 Expected Placement Days, Placement Days Actually Utilized, and Percent of Potential Days Utilized, by Sample

	Sample	
	Home-based group	Comparison group
Expected placement days	22,740	25,980
Placement days utilized		
All	4,777	12,037
Excluding shelter	3,313	10,584
Shelter only	1,464	1,453
Percent of potential days utilized		
All	21.0	46.3
Excluding shelter	14.6	40.7
Shelter only	6.4	5.6

smaller percentage of expected placement days (21% compared to 32%). The data also indicates that both groups utilized approximately the same number and percentage of placement days of shelter care. There was, however, a large difference between the groups with respect to the number and percentage of days utilized in other placements (e.g., foster homes, treatment foster homes, group homes, and residential treatment facilities).

Relationship Between Involvement in Treatment and Placement Outcomes

Goal-setting and, to a lesser extent, the degree of progress in achieving goals are treated as proxy measures of the extent to which family members are willing to invest and actively engage in the treatment process. The willingness of family members and the ability of a treatment team to cooperatively establish a problem-relevant set of treatment goals are central to the home-based service model implemented within the Child Welfare Division. Implicit within the service model is the assumption that families who are engaged in the treatment process, to the extent that they are willing to set goals and actively work toward goal achievement, are more likely to have a positive outcome than are families less willing (or able) to actively participate in the treatment process.

Table 2.4 Percent of Expected Placement Days Utilized by Number of
Goals Set: Home-Based Service Group

	Percent of placement days utilized		
Number of family goals set	All placement types	Shelter only	Excluding shelter
None set (*n*=22)	26.3	4.3	22.2
At least one goal set (*n*=33)	17.4	7.4	10.2

Based on the results presented in Tables 2.4 and 2.5, this assumption
appears to be well founded. From Table 2.4, it may be seen that the proportion of available time in placement utilized by families who set treatment
goals (or a goal) is lower than the percentage of available time utilized by
families who did not set goals. Considering placements of all types, children
in families not setting goals utilized 26% of available placement time. By
way of contrast, children in families who did set treatment goals utilized
17% of the time in placement available to them. Furthermore, the difference
between the two sub-groups is even larger if shelter placements are excluded from this calculation.

While goal-setting appears to be related to the percentage of available
placement time utilized, the relationship between level of goal progress
achieved and the latter outcome measure is more ambiguous. From Table
2.5, for example, it may be seen that the degree of goal progress achieved by
children is not consistently related to the percentage of available time in
placement utilized. The level of goal progress achieved by a child's par-
ent(s), however, does seem to be related to the percentage of available time
utilized. Children in families where parents are judged by a treatment team
as having achieved significant goal progress utilized only about 5% of
placement days available. By way of contrast, children whose parents ex-
hibited minimal goal progress utilized 25% of available placement days.
These data appear to support the view that a family's degree of active
involvement with a home-based service team and, in particular, parental
involvement in problem solving and goal achievement are strongly related
to a child's likelihood of out-of-home placement.

Service intensity is measured by two variables: the total number of days
that a family was active with a home-based treatment team, and total hours
of direct and indirect service provided. While higher total service hours are
associated with smaller proportions of available time in placement utilized,

Table 2.5 Percent of Expected Placement Days Utilized by Level of Child and Parent Goal Achievement: Home-Based Service Group

| | | Percent of placement days utilized | | |
Level of goal-achievement	n	All place-ment types	Shelter only	Excluding shelter
Child				
Minimal	16	12.4	4.9	7.5
Moderate – high	13	18.1	11.5	6.6
Parent				
Minimal	16	25.2	11.0	14.2
Moderate – high	15	4.9	4.0	0.9

the relationship is fairly weak (see Table 2.6). In addition, the possibility that the relationship is non-linear is evident in Table 2.7.

Discussion

This study examined the impact of intensive home-based services as an alternative to the out-of-home placement of seriously emotionally disturbed adolescents in the Child Welfare Division of the Hennepin County Department of Community Services. The results indicate that the model of intensive home-based services implemented in the county can be an effective method for preventing placements and keeping families together. This is the case even for youth approved for placement in such costly and restrictive settings as residential treatment centers, group homes, and hospitals. The findings also suggest that the ability to cooperatively engage families in treatment goal-setting and to actively involve parents in achieving treatment goals may be important factors in preventing placements.

While the proponents of intensive home-based services will welcome these findings, there are a number of issues raised by the study that need to be addressed. For example, while 24 of the intensive home-based service clients were never placed, 31 had to be removed from their homes. Moreover, many were removed more than once, and some were placed for long periods of time. This raises the possibility that the model of intensive home-based services implemented in Hennepin County was inappropriate

Table 2.6 Correlations Between Service Intensity Measures and Percent of Expected Placement Days Utilized: Home-Based Service Group

Service intensity measure	All place-ment types	Shelter only	Excluding shelter
Days	+.01	+.03	−.01
Total hours	−.10	+.05	−.15

for a large proportion of the cases. It also raises the possibility and, in our judgment, the reality that some seriously emotionally disturbed adolescents will not be amenable to home-based interventions and must be placed outside of their homes.

This indicates that researchers and practitioners should test various models of family preservation and intensive home-based services to try to determine which models are effective with particular kinds of cases. Also, future research should be directed toward identifying those cases that are unlikely to be responsive to home-based interventions and would benefit from services provided outside of the home.

Table 2.7 Percent of Expected Placement Days Utilized by Level of Service Intensity: Home-Based Service Group

Service intensity measures	All place-ment types	Shelter only	Excluding shelter
Treatment days			
Low[a]	20.6	4.3	16.3
Medium	26.8	10.4	16.4
High	16.7	4.2	12.5
Total treatment hours			
Low[b]	20.6	1.5	19.1
Medium	28.4	11.4	17.0
High	14.4	5.3	9.1

[a]Low refers to 28 treatment days or less, medium to 29 to 45 treatment days, and high to 46 to 114 treatment days.

[b]Low refers to 11 total treatment hours or less, medium to 12 to 20 total treatment hours, and high to 21 to 50 total treatment hours.

In addition, it is generally accepted that one of the critical components of intensive home-based services is the necessity to provide services that are, in fact, intensive. The findings of this study did not suggest that service intensity was related to preventing placements. This issue needs to be explored further in greater depth in future studies.

Note

1. For an overview and review of methodological issues, see: Magura, S. 1981. Are services to prevent foster care effective? *Children and Youth Services Review, 3,* 193-212; and Stein, T. J. 1985. Projects to prevent out-of-home placement. *Children and Youth Services Review, 7,* 109-121.

3

Evaluating the Impact
of Intensive Family Preservation
Services in New Jersey

LEONARD H. FELDMAN

Ever-growing numbers of single-parent families, families living below the poverty line, teen births, child abuse and neglect reports, and substance abusers, in combination with declining informal and extended family supports, have led to a nationwide crisis in child welfare services. Traditional public child welfare services appear unable to provide enough support and services to fragile families to enable them to function adequately and fulfill societal expectations. Increased caseloads, greater numbers of children entering foster or institutional care, and higher rates of repeat abuse are telling indicators of the need to develop new strategies that can respond to worsening conditions in our nation's high-risk communities.

One strategy to address these conditions is in-home services. These services have been adopted by New Jersey's Division of Youth and Family Services (DYFS), the state's public child welfare agency.

DYFS began a pilot Family Preservation Services (FPS) program in four of its 21 counties during August 1987. A competitive bidding process was used to select the private agencies that would receive contracts to deliver FPS services under the supervision and guidance of DYFS.

The FPS program was modeled after Homebuilders, a crisis-intervention-oriented prevention program that originated in Tacoma, Washington, in 1974. Target families were those in which placement of a child (children) outside the home into foster, group, or institutional care appeared imminent unless changes in family coping strategies and behavior patterns occurred.

Families were referred to the FPS program by a variety of community agencies.

Study Focus and Prior Research

The evaluation of the New Jersey initiative began in September 1987 and was designed to address the state's interest in the effectiveness of these services as well as to contribute to existing literature. The study was designed to address one of the gaps in this research literature to date—the minimal use of control groups to determine the net effect of the Homebuilders' intervention. Thus, the major distinction between this and past studies was the use of an experimental design.

Prior Research

Evaluations and follow-up studies of Homebuilders programs have been conducted on programs in Washington State (Akamine, O'Neill, & Haymond, 1980; Haapala, 1983; Haygeman, 1982; Kinney, Madsen, Fleming & Haapala, 1977); Utah (Pecora, Fraser, Bartlome, McDade, Haapala, & Lewis, 1986); and Minnesota (AuClaire & Schwartz, 1986). More recent studies have been completed in New York City (Mitchell, Tovar, & Knitzer, 1988); California (Yuan & McDonald, 1988); and Iowa (Fuqua, 1988).

The only study that has included a comparison group was that of AuClaire and Schwartz (1986), although Yuan and McDonald (1988) have planned an experimental design for the third year of their study. AuClaire and Schwartz studied the impact of crisis intervention and intensive home-based services on the prevention of placement of 116 adolescents, 58 receiving intensive services for a maximum of four weeks, and 58 control subjects receiving traditional services. Preliminary findings reflect no differences in the number of placement episodes; however, the intensive services group had placements that were shorter in duration and utilized a smaller proportion of available placement days. Clients who completed the treatment program spent significantly less time in placement than those who did not actively engage in treatment.

While most of these studies reported positive findings for the families receiving family-based services, it would be misleading to draw more than tentative conclusions about the effectiveness of the Homebuilders' type intervention program. As Jones (1985, p. 37) notes, the lack of a control group can "exaggerate the success of existing preventive service programs, foster a belief that we have the answers on how to prevent placement and that substantial savings will accrue as a result."

Barth and Berry (1987, p. 86) also warn that "current evidence on the efficacy of these increasingly popular programs stops far short of showing their benefits for abused and neglected children or the lasting stability of family units where placement was averted."

Study Questions

This evaluation was undertaken to redress a gap in the literature through the implementation of an experimental design. By comparing and contrasting the experiences of clients receiving intensive services with a similar group of clients receiving traditional preventive services, the study attempted to answer the following specific questions:

1. Was the Homebuilders model actually employed by the FPS staff?
2. Was the FPS program more successful than traditional programs in maintaining children at risk of placement in their own homes, and were these gains maintained over time?
3. Were FPS families functioning on a higher level at case closure relative to both their baseline scores and to families receiving traditional services?
4. Were differential outcomes for the FPS families related to client characteristics and problems or ecological variables, such as level of stress, social support, and the community risk variable?

Method

Research Design

The New Jersey study was planned as a true experiment. This involved random assignment of eligible families to an intensive treatment (FPS) or to a traditional community service. The functioning of both the intensive service group (the experimental group) and the traditional service group (the control group) was assessed before and after treatment.

This design improves upon past Homebuilders program evaluations by effectively controlling for most threats to the internal validity (Campbell & Stanley, 1966). The experimental design is considered the best technique to link changes in intervention with specific outcomes in a "cause-and-effect manner" (Conner, 1980, p. 63; Jones et al., 1976).

Assignment to FPS Services

Prior to assignment to one of the four New Jersey FPS treatment sites in Cape May, Cumberland, Essex, and Hudson counties, all referrals were reviewed by a designated screening body in each county, which attempted to assess the appropriateness of the referral the same day it was received. If the family met the profile of the "risk of placement protocol," and a treatment slot was available, the DYFS research office was contacted to randomly assign the family to either the experimental or the control group. The FPS protocol was developed using placement decision standards contained in the New Jersey Division of Youth and Family Services' Manual of Policy and Procedures (1979, p. 6-7) in conjunction with material from a study conducted by Meddin (1984). According to the FPS protocol, families had to meet the following conditions to be eligible for participation in the program:

1. Children were age birth to 18 years.
2. The child(ren) was at risk of a first-time out-of-home placement (actually could be 30 days or fewer of placement).
3. All other viable and less intensive community services had been utilized by the family and had not been successful, or it was anticipated would not be successful in stabilizing the family and averting placement.
4. Referred families must have at least one parent or significant adult who would let the FPS worker in the house or would be willing to meet at a neutral location.
5. Families with a primary problem of imminent or actual homelessness would not be considered eligible for referral to FPS.
6. Families with substance abuse problems would be assessed on a case-by-case basis.[1]

No waiting lists were maintained. If a treatment slot was not available, a client could be re-referred at a future date if appropriate; for example, the family situation met the selection criteria.

Subjects

The number of FPS families selected to participate in the research from each treatment site was to be proportional to that site's minimum contractual level of service so as to not unduly interfere with the referral and treatment process, especially in the two smaller, rural counties. It was expected then

Table 3.1 Number of Study Families by Site and Sample Status

	Sample status			
Site	FPS	Control	Turnbacks	Total
Cape May	18	12	8	38
Cumberland	26	24	4	54
Essex	31	29	4	64
Hudson	21	22	6	49
Total	96	87	22	205

that 34 cases would be drawn from Cape May, 48 from Cumberland, 66 from Essex, and 52 from Hudson for a total of 200 families. The actual number of cases drawn from these four offices is displayed in Table 3.1.

The pressure to end the random selection of clients and the slower-than-anticipated rate of referral necessitated both a premature end to the research intake in the original four counties and the addition of a fifth site, Mercer County.

Random assignment and tracking of cases began in September 1987.[2] At present, 237 families are in some stage of being tracked by research staff. The 32 Mercer County families are excluded from this analysis because not enough time had elapsed to track them over the course of 12 months. Thus the sample of 183 families reported on in this paper consists of 96 families receiving FPS services and 87 control group families receiving traditional community services. An additional 22 families were referred to the FPS sites, but were "turnbacks." These cases were rejected within three days of referral because they did not meet program selection criteria, or the caretaker refused to participate in the program, or the children were deemed at imminent risk of harm and had to be removed.

Intervention Description

The four FPS treatment sites in Cape May, Cumberland, Essex, and Hudson counties received referrals during normal working hours from three sources: local Division of Youth and Family Services field offices, the County Family Court/Crisis Intervention Units, and regional community mental health crisis centers.

Families with children at risk of placement that were randomly assigned to the FPS program received the full range of services that FPS was designed to provide. These included: a family assessment consisting of identifying the problem areas, prioritizing areas of intervention, identifying the frequency, intensity and duration of problem behaviors, examining environmental conditions, considering all family members' interactions in the problems and in the solutions; identifying the contingencies influencing the problem; and setting achievable and measurable goals. The treatment orientation is primarily behavioral but includes therapeutic techniques from other orientations, such as Client Centered and Rational Emotive Therapy. The repertoire of treatment services included, but was not limited to: crisis intervention; diffusion of violence; life skills; home management and maintenance; budget training; advocacy with schools, legal services, and medical services; child management training; employment services; assertiveness and communications skills training; and help in finding food, shelter, transportation, and other resources (Behavioral Sciences Institute, n.d.).

If the family was randomly assigned to the control group, the responsibility for determining the appropriate treatment and follow-up was left to the referring agency. This most typically involved offering existing, traditional community services; for example, less intensive counseling interventions by the referral source, referral to other community resources such as mental health agencies, youth advocacy programs, DYFS monitoring, or Family Court intervention. In some cases, placement was initiated. It is important to note that after termination from FPS, experimental group families also utilized these same community services.

Measures

Study data depended on the instruments and data elements listed in Figure 3.1. The study variables in Figure 3.1 are listed in temporal order of collection with their related scales and instruments. Based on reliability and validity scores reported below, it is believed that all of the instruments have adequate psychometric properties.

The Family Environment Scale (FES)

The FES is one of nine Social Climate Scales developed by Moos and Moos (1981). It measures a family member's perception of the social-environmental characteristics of his or her nuclear family. The 90 true-false statements are factored into 10 subscales that assess three main dimensions: relationships, personal growth, and system maintenance. Cronbach's alpha was "in an acceptable range" for all 10 FES subscales. Test-retest reliabilities of each scale were found to range between .68 and .86 after an eight-week interval (Moos & Moos, 1981).

Figure 3.1 Study Variables.

1. Antecedents to Service Delivery
   a. Family Functioning
      Family Environment Scale (Moos & Moos, 1981)
      Child Well-Being Scales (Magura & Moses, 1986)
   b. Level of Stress
      Life Stress Scale (Egeland et al., 1980)
   c. Perceived Level of Social Support
      Interpersonal Support Evaluation List (ISEL) (Cohen & Hoberman, 1983)
   d. Community Level "Risk" Variable
      District Factor Group (DFG) (Cooperman, 1984)
   e. Reason for Referral to FPS
      Child(ren)'s presenting problem
      Parental dysfunction
      Family characteristics: ethnicity, size, family structure

2. Measures of Agency Interventions and Degree of Therapist Participation
   with the Homebuilders' Model:
   a. Intensity of Contact
      Number of visits
      Hours of contact
   b. Type of Service Provision
      Client Clinical Services Checklist
      Concrete Services Rating Sheet
   c. Duration of Service Provision
   d. Goal Setting
      Goal Attainment Scaling (GAS) (Kiresuk & Sherman, 1968)

3. Case Outcomes:
   a. Out-of-Home Placement
      Type
      Number
      Duration
   b. Changes in Level of Family Functioning
      FES score changes
      Child Well-Being Scales score changes
   c. Changes in Perceived Level of Social Support
      ISEL score changes
   d. Goal Achievement and Client Participation
      Changes in GAS score

The Child Well-Being Scales (CWBS)

The CWBS measures a family's or child's position on up to 43—child welfare related—anchored rating scales. "Each scale measures a concept that is related to one or more physical, psychological, or social needs that all children have: the degree to which this set of needs is met defines a child's state of overall well-being" (Magura & Moses, 1986, p. 83). The scales are scored in terms of adequacy or inadequacy and cover four dimensions: parenting role performance, familial capacities, child role performance, and child capacities.

Change scores can be calculated for an overall composite index and for three factors derived through a factor analysis (Magura & Moses, 1986, p. 172). The three factors are Household Adequacy, Parental Disposition, and Child Performance. Household Adequacy refers to meeting the most basic needs of daily life. This factor may be strongly affected by the financial state of the family. Parental Disposition refers to the emotional willingness and capacity of the parent(s) to care for the children. The third factor, Child Performance, measures educational performance and misconduct.

Test-retest reliability was found to be satisfactory with a mean value of kappa = .65. Inter-rater reliability was also found to be "moderately high." Cronbach's alpha was .89 for the composite Child Well-Being Scales (Magura & Moses, 1986, p. 180-182).

The Life Event Scale (LES)

The LES was developed by Egeland and Deinard. This 39-item scale measures recent life stresses experienced by a lower-class population. Each item on the LES is scored on a four-point scale to account for the degree of disruption involved and readjustment required after an event occurs. Cochrane and Robertson (1973, p. 135), who developed the precursor to the LES, found that their "instrument is reasonably reliable . . . and has been used in studies of antecedents of illness." Egeland, Breitenbucher, and Rosenberg (1980) do not report any studies of reliability or validity.

The Interpersonal Support Evaluation List (ISEL)

The ISEL contains 40 statements concerning the perceived availability of four types of social support: Appraisal support—the availability of someone to talk to about one's problems; Self-esteem support—the availability of a positive comparison when comparing oneself with others; Belonging support—the availability of people one can do things with; and Tangible support—instrumental aid (Cohen, Mermelstein, Kamarck, & Hoberman, 1985, p. 74). Each statement allows the reader to select one of four choices—from definitely true to definitely false.

Cohen and Hoberman (1983, p. 104) demonstrate that the ISEL "is a reliable measure of social support and that its subscales evidence reasonable independence from one another." The ISEL was also found to be moderately correlated (.46) with other measures of social support (Cohen & Hoberman, 1983).

Socioeconomic Status of a Community

The socioeconomic status of a community can serve as one method to distinguish high-risk neighborhoods from more supportive ones. The New Jersey Department of Education has prepared a ranking of the socioeconomic status of all New Jersey school districts. *The District Factor Group (DFG)* was derived from 1980 census data. Each district is ranked from 1 to 10, with 1 being the lowest socioeconomic status. Each of seven factors— Education of residents 25 years and older; Occupation; Housing density; Urbanization; Family income; Percentage of unemployment; and Percentage of families below the poverty level—was combined, using a principal component analysis to create the single ranking (Cooperman, 1984).

Goal Attainment Scaling (GAS)

The GAS attempts to measure the attainment of time limited expected service outcomes. Information is collected about the person for whom goals are to be scaled. A few major areas (goals) for change are specified, and outcome levels, ranging from much less likely than thought to much more likely than thought, for each area are developed to enable the scoring of outcomes. Numerical weights can be added to each area's scale, but are not necessary (Kiresuk & Sherman, 1968).

Woodward, Santa-Barbara, Levin, and Epstein (1978) found the GAS to be reliable and valid. Inter-rater reliability was measured at $r = .84$. They also reported that GAS scores "correlate significantly with every other outcome measure at a low to moderate level ($rs = .12$ to $.39$; $p < .05$)." The GAS was found to be most highly correlated with how the family felt about its presenting problems six months post-termination from treatment (Woodward et al., 1978, p. 472).

Measures of Agency Intervention

Data was collected in terms of the intensity of contact (hours and visits), the duration of the service interval, the types of services provided, and goal content and achievement.

Family Information

Data collected included the reason for referral (primary and contributing factors) to FPS, family characteristics such as structure, number of family members, and standard demographics.

Outcome Data

The primary outcome measure was recording all occurrences, type, and duration of out-of-home placement for a family's target child(ren). For purposes of this study, placement was defined in its most conservative sense as any out-of-home placement of a target child of any duration.

Procedures

Data collection began as soon as possible after a random assignment was made, but no later than the end of the first week of service. Data used in this evaluation was collected in two ways: (a) as part of the normal data collection activities of the treatment agency and therapist; and (b) as part of face-to-face interviews with the primary caretaker in each family unit, conducted by the research staff. The persons responsible for collecting the data and the schedule of data collection are listed in Figure 3.2. For control group cases, termination was considered to be six weeks after they would have been referred to FPS or actual termination of community services, whichever came first.

Results

Sample Characteristics

The characteristics of the experimental and control groups did not differ to a significant degree in terms of the number of target children, age of the target child, family size, family structure, race, DYFS status, referral source, previous placement, primary problem at referral, or socioeconomic status.

All study families had on average 1.1 target children (SD = .43). The control group families had one target child 90.8% of the time, two target children 6.9% of the time. Similarly, the FPS families had one identified target child 88.5% of the time, two target children 9.4% of the time.

FPS families had an average of 2.7 children (SD = 1.4) in total (including non-targeted children). The control group had an average total of 2.4 chil-

Measure	Responsible party	Schedule[a]
Goal Attainment Scaling	FPS therapist	Week 1 termination
Family Environment Scale	FPS therapist/research staff for control group	Week 1 termination 3 months post
Child Well-Being Scales	FPS therapist/referral worker for control group	Week 1 termination
Life Events Scale	Research staff	Week 1
ISEL	Research staff	Week 1 termination 3 months
Measures of Agency Effort	Research staff	Week 1 thru termination
Placement Data	Research staff	Week 1 thru 1 year post
Socioeconomic Status of Community	Research staff	Week 1

Figure 3.2 Data Collection Schedule

[a]Certain control group cases did not receive Week 1 measures to control for a possible threat to external validity due to intrusion of the data collection.

dren (SD = 1.4). The mean age of the target children was 12.97 years (SD = 3.64). The median age was 13.89. Target children ranged in age from 2 months to almost 18 years.

The bulk of the households (57.9%) were single-parent in structure. Another 32.8% were some combination of two parents, biological or stepparent. The balance (9.3%) were families with the parent sharing the household with a nonrelated person. There was little variation in family structure between the groups.

Although not statistically significant, the FPS group had a higher proportion of white families (51%) than the control group (34.5%). The FPS and control groups were 33.3% and 37.9% black and 14.6% and 26.4% Hispanic, respectively. One family in each group was interracial.

One indicator of "at-risk" status is being a client of the state's child welfare agency, The Division of Youth and Family Services. More than 88% of all the families in the study were known to DYFS. This included 90.6% of the FPS families and 86.2% of the control group families. Although most of the families were known to DYFS, only 66.1% of the referrals to the FPS program came from DYFS workers. Another 27.6% of the referrals were from the county family-juvenile crisis units, 5.7% were from crisis mental health units, and 3.6% were from other sources. There was little variation in referral sources between treatment groups.

Another indicator of at-risk status, placement prior to referral, was not different for the two groups. Only 17% of the FPS families and 22.1% of the control families had experienced a prior placement. Thus, overall, 17.4% of the study families had a target child in placement prior to referral to FPS.

The most frequently cited primary problem at referral was out-of-control behavior (59.3%). This category consists of runaway behavior, general out-of-control behavior (i.e., coming and going at will, staying out all night, and so forth), poor parent child relationships, violence toward family members, and juvenile delinquency. The next largest primary referral category was due to abuse, neglect, or risk of abuse or neglect (23.2%). Another 14.7% of the referrals were initiated due to emotional disturbance or a substance abuse problem on the part of the target child(ren). School problems were cited in 1.7% of referrals. Parent emotional problems and/or substance abuse were the primary reason for referral in 1.1% of all referrals. There was little difference in referral problems of the experimental and control groups.

A multiple response tabulation of presenting and secondary problems is displayed in Table 3.2. Counting responses, out-of-control behavior was chosen 53% of the time as a referral problem, with child emotional distur-

Table 3.2 Number and Percentage of Study Families by Referring Problem Category and Sample Status

Referring problem category	Sample status					
	FPS		Control		Total	
	n	%	n	%	n	%
Out-of-control behavior	120	46.9	149	58	269	53.4
Child emotionally disturbed/drugs	49	19.1	40	15.6	89	17.3
Abuse/neglect	39	15.2	27	10.5	66	12.9
School problem	33	12.9	26	10.1	59	11.5
Parent emotionally disturbed/drugs	15	5.9	15	5.8	30	5.8
Total	256	100	257	100	513	100

bance or drug involvement cited in 17% of the responses. When looking across all referral problems, school problems (attendance, behavior, and grades) were identified as 12% of all problems.

The socioeconomic status of a community can serve as one method to distinguish high-risk neighborhoods from more supportive ones. Almost 90% of all cases referred to FPS were in DFG group 1 and 2, the lowest end of the socioeconomic ladder, and more than two-thirds were in group 1. The mean DFG for FPS families was 1.54, with a standard deviation of 1.2 and a range of 1 to 9. The mean DFG for control families was 1.6, with a standard deviation of 1.1 and a range of 1 to 7.

Study Questions

Question 1: Was the Homebuilders model actually employed by the FPS staff?

Based on the short-term involvement (M = 5.35 weeks), the level of intensity of the service provision (M = 54.85 hours per case, and M = 3.26 hours per contact), the goals selected and the types of interventions utilized, it appears that the New Jersey FPS programs followed the Homebuilders model of service delivery.

Service Duration

The mean number of weeks of service for FPS families was 5.35 (SD = 2.26). The median number of weeks of service was six. The service interval ranged from less than one week to nine weeks.

Hours of Intervention

The mean number of face-to-face hours of contact for FPS families was 36.81 (SD = 29.71). The median number of hours was 30.5 with a range of 0 to 226.75 hours. The mean number of total hours (face-to-face, telephone, collateral contacts, and transportation) staff spent working with the FPS families was 54.85 (SD = 40.44). The median was 47.75 hours with a range of 0 to 281 hours. The average total hours of intervention during week one was 12.74 (SD = 10.43). This decreased by week six to a mean of 8.39 hours (SD = 8.2). Over the course of service, the mean of the average number of total hours of intervention per week was 10.09 (SD = 4.93). Of these hours, 6.65 were spent, on average, in face-to-face contact. An average of 3.26 hours was spent per service contact during the service interval. An average of 2.1 hours was spent per face-to-face contact during service provision.

Number of Contacts

The mean number of face-to-face contacts between FPS families and staff was 18.7 (SD = 8.03) over the course of the service interval. The median number of contacts was 17, with a range of 4 to 43 contacts. The mean of the average contacts per week over the life of the case was 3.34 (SD = 1.51).

Goal Achievement

FPS workers, using Goal Attainment Scaling techniques, designated up to six goals for each family. Five different goals were selected by the workers for at least 10% of all study families. The goal selected most often, for more than half the families, related to improving communication skills. These goals reflect the problems of the population serviced and include:

1. Communication Skills 56.8%
2. Parenting Skills 41.5%
3. Compliance with Rules 36.8%
4. Behavior Management Skills 33.7%
5. Engagement 11.6%

Types of Intervention

Intervention services were measured by the use of a Client Clinical Services Checklist and Concrete Services Rating Sheet (Behavioral Sciences Institute, n.d.). Workers checked off all services used during the course of the intervention. Services were divided into the following seven major categories:

1. Child management (use of reinforcement, time out, "I" statements, active listening, and so forth);
2. Emotional management (anger management, depression management, impulse management, rational emotive therapy, and so forth);
3. Interpersonal skills (problem solving, giving and accepting feedback, improving compliance, and so forth);
4. Other clinical (listening to clients, building hope, relationship building, clarifying behaviors, defusing crises, reframing, role playing, and so forth);
5. Advocacy (referral to other services, consultation with other providers, advocating with the schools, utility companies, and so forth);
6. Other services (money management, time management, developing informal support systems, and so forth); and

Table 3.3 Percentage of FPS Families Receiving Categories of Services

Service category	Percent of families
Child management	54.2
Other clinical	53.5
Emotion management	48.8
Advocacy	45.4
Interpersonal skills	36.1
Other services	21.1
Concrete services	8.8

7. Concrete services (help obtain or provide transportation, food, clothing housing, and so forth).

Table 3.3 displays the percentage of FPS families who received specific interventions from each service cluster. The low number of families receiving concrete services was surprising.

Question 2: Was the FPS program more successful than traditional programs in maintaining children at risk of placement in their own homes, and were these gains maintained over time?

Overall, FPS families had proportionally fewer children enter placement, and they entered placement at a slower rate than control group families from intervention through one year post-termination. The net difference in placement rates, however, was statistically significant only from case termination through nine months post-termination. After nine months, the net effect of the FPS intervention appears to dissipate.

Since the family is the unit of analysis in this study, the first placement of a target child within a family was recorded as the placement event for this analysis. Placement rates for the FPS families and the control group families are displayed in Table 3.4. Differences in placement rates were tested with a chi-square test for goodness of fit. As a review of this table indicates, at termination, 7.3% ($N = 7$) FPS families had a child enter placement. This compares favorably with 14.9% ($N = 13$) control families having a child enter placement, yet the difference is not statistically significant. However, from case termination up to nine months' post-termination, the FPS families fared better than the families receiving traditional services. Significantly fewer FPS families had a child enter placement for the first time at one month, two months, three months, six months, and nine months' post-termi-

Table 3.4 Placement Data by Months Since Termination and Study Sample

	Study Sample		
Months since termination	FPS	Control	
0	7.3[a]	14.9[a]	$\chi^2(2, N{=}183){=}2.01$[b]
1	12.5	26.4	$\chi^2(2, N{=}183){=}6.60^*$
2	15.6	29.9	$\chi^2(2, N{=}183){=}4.55^*$
3	21.9	36.8	$\chi^2(2, N{=}183){=}4.23^*$
6	29.2	49.4	$\chi^2(2, N{=}183){=}8.19^*$
9	37.5	55.2	$\chi^2(2, N{=}183){=}5.05^{**}$
12	45.8	57.7	$\chi^2(2, N{=}183){=}2.03^*$

[a]Numbers are percentages that reflect percentage of total FPS or total control sample entering placement at each time period.

[b]Equations are data for chi-square test of goodness of fit to assess differences in distributions of FPS and control samples in placement at each time period.

$^*p \leq .05$.

$^{**}p \leq .01$.

nation than did the families receiving traditional services (see Table 3.4). Figure 3.3 displays initial placements as a function of elapsed time from intervention.

By the end of the first year, post-termination, 45.8% ($N = 44$) of the 96 FPS families had at least one of their children, who was a target of the FPS intervention, enter placement. In the control group, 57.5% ($N = 50$) of the 87 families receiving traditional services had a child enter placement. While the FPS families did considerably better with more than 54% of the families not experiencing a placement of a target child, the difference between the FPS and the control group was not statistically significant at 12 months. Thus, between nine months and one year post-termination, any net intervention effect dissipates.

FPS families have a child enter placement at a slower rate than the families receiving traditional services. The FPS families had their first placement event after 4.3 months on average. The control group families had their first placement event after 2.4 months on average $t(82.9) = 2.60$, $p < .05$.

However, there were no statistically significant differences in the level of restrictiveness of the placement, type of placement, total number of placement events, or total time in placement during the first year. (These conclusions depend on data taken on the first target child to enter placement during

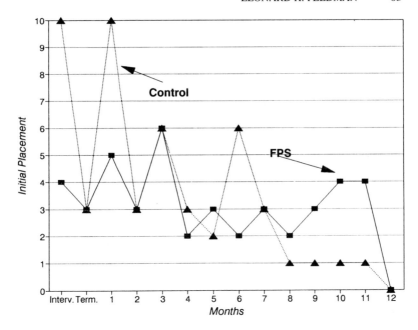

Figure 3.3 Placement as a function of elapsed time from intervention.

the study period). For example, there were 2.8 placements for the control group and 2.6 for the FPS families. The range was between one and 12 placements. Cumulative time in placement averaged 8.96 months for children in the control families and 7.9 months for the FPS children.

Question 3: Were the FPS families functioning at a higher level at case closure relative to their own baseline and to families receiving traditional services?

To some extent, FPS families functioned at a higher level at case closure. On 10 of 18 scales assessing support, family functioning, and child well-being, the FPS families scored higher at Time 3 than Time 1 at the $p < .01$ level. These data are displayed in Table 3.5.

However, FPS families did not generally improve to a greater degree than did control families. Differences between FPS families' scores between T^1 and T^3 and control families' scores between T^1 and T^3 were tested. On only two of the same 18 scales noted above were there statistically significant differences between the FPS and control samples at the $p < .01$ level. FPS

Table 3.5 Functioning Data by Measure and Time Period for FPS Families

Measure	Time 1[a]	Time 3[a]	
ISEL			
Appraisal support	2.86	3.12	$t(72) = 3.68^{**}$[b]
Tangible support	2.99	3.16	$t(72) = 2.55^*$
Self-esteem support	3.05	3.20	$t(72) = 2.10^*$
Belonging support	2.95	3.24	$t(72) = 4.27^{**}$
Family Environment Scale			
Cohesion	4.48	5.73	$t(79) = 4.12^{**}$
Expressiveness	4.38	5.03	$t(79) = 2.64^{**}$
Conflict	4.69	3.75	$t(79) = 3.75^{**}$
Independence	5.25	6.28	$t(79) = 4.46^{**}$
Achievement orientation	5.53	5.93	$t(79) = 2.06^*$
Intellectual—cultural	4.34	5.44	$t(79) = 3.40^*$
Active—recreational	3.99	3.99	$t(79) = 0.00$
Moral—religious	5.66	5.80	$t(79) = 0.63$
Organization	4.95	5.71	$t(79) = 2.91^{**}$
Control	5.23	5.35	$t(79) = 0.56$
Child Well-Being Scales	Time 1	Time 2	
CWBS composite	84.26	87.46	$t(93) = 5.41^{**}$
Household adequacy	93.36	94.01	$t(93) = 1.20$
Parental disposition	76.81	81.82	$t(93) = 5.25^{**}$
Child performance	81.72	86.71	$t(91) = 3.58^{**}$

[a]Mean scale scores for the FPS sample at Time 1 or Time 3.
[b]Statistics for 1-tailed t-tests for dependent means of difference between Time 1 and Time 3 scale scores.
  *$p \leq .05$.
**$p \leq .01$.

families were functioning at a higher level than control families on those scales. These data are displayed in Table 3.6.

Question 4: Were differential outcomes for the FPS families related to family characteristics and problems or ecological variables such as stress, social support, and the community risk variable?

A number of bivariate analyses were conducted to determine the relationship between key variables and entry into placement. The following family and ecological variables were examined: family size, the number of target children, family structure, race, prior placements, the District Factor Group,

Table 3.6 Functioning Data by Measure and Time Period[a] for FPS and Control Samples

Measure	FPS	Control	
ISEL			
Appraisal support	0.26	0.29	$t(46.22) = 0.20$[b]
Tangible support	0.18	0.38	$t(48.85) = 1.37$
Self-esteem support	0.14	0.83	$t(54.78) = 0.49$
Belonging support	0.28	0.64	$t(42.00) = 1.33$
Family Environment Scale			
Cohesion	1.25	0.14	$t(54.70) = 2.08^*$
Expressiveness	0.65	0.57	$t(53.81) = 0.18$
Conflict	−0.94	−0.57	$t(45.29) = 0.72$
Independence	1.03	0.00	$t(48.40) = 2.32^*$
Achievement orientation	0.40	0.25	$t(42.77) = 0.36$
Intellectual—cultural	0.90	−0.11	$t(85.48) = 2.77^{**}$
Active—recreational	0.00	0.54	$t(70.48) = 1.19$
Moral—religious	0.14	0.46	$t(52.20) = 0.82$
Organization	0.76	0.04	$t(54.03) = 1.57$
Control	0.13	0.14	$t(71.97) = 0.80$
Child Well-Being Scales			
CWBS composite	3.20	0.57	$t(96.41) = 2.40^*$
Household adequacy	0.64	0.78	$t(109.52) = 0.17$
Parental disposition	5.05	0.45	$t(109.02) = 2.85^{**}$
Child performance	4.99	1.16	$t(111.13) = 1.71$

[a]Mean scale scores for the FPS and control samples between T^1 and T^3.

[b]Statistics for 1-tailed t-tests for independent means to test difference between FPS and control samples on each scale between T^1 and T^3.

$^*p \le .05$.

$^{**}p \le .01$.

the treatment site, scores on the Child Well-Being Scales, Family Environment Scales, Level of Stress Scale, and the ISEL Scales.

Statistically, family characteristics were not significantly related to entry of a child into placement. Some of the differences between families where placement occurred and those where placement did not occur, even though not statistically significant, are of interest. FPS families that did experience a placement were: more likely to be minority (55.3%) than white (36.7%); more likely to enter placement after referral by the county crisis intervention units (61.1%) than families referred by DYFS (44.6%); more likely to have a primary referral problem related to poor parenting and behavior or emotional problems on the part of the child (56.6%) than abuse or neglect (37.5%); and more likely to be living with their father or a relative (73.3%) than their mother or with both parents (36.7%).

Only the composite score (M = 89.32, SD = 7.67 vs. M = 85.25, SD = 8.89), and two of the three subscales on the Child Well-Being Scales, the parental disposition (M = 84.47, SD = 12.76 vs. M = 78.67, SD = 12.76) and child performance (M = 89.55, SD = 12.66 vs. M =83.48, SD = 15.07) subscales at case termination were significantly higher for the families that did not experience a placement event than for the families that did have a child enter placement [$t(83.61)$ = 2.35, $p < .05$, $t(84.36)$ = 2.32, $p < .05$, $t(82.45)$ = 2.08, $p < .05$, respectively).

Discussion

The New Jersey Family Preservation Services Program, a Homebuilders model of family-based services, was effective in preventing and delaying placement of children at-risk of placement, when compared to a group of families receiving traditional community services.

By termination of the FPS service, seven of 96 (7.3%) families had experienced a placement. This compares favorably to 13 of 87 (14.9%) of the control group families, although the difference was not statistically significant. One year later, 44 of 96 (45.8%) of the FPS service families had experienced a placement. Fifty of 87 control group families (57.5%) had at least one target child enter placement. The net effect of the intervention was greatest for the FPS families between one month and nine months' post-termination. The effect seems to dissipate after nine months.

One explanation, then, for the first finding might be that families experiencing a placement prior to termination of service were somehow different, with more difficult problems, or were more dysfunctional than the families that managed to avoid or postpone placement. However, this was not borne out in comparisons of demographics, family structure, presenting problems, community risk variables, or family functioning measures.

In the case of families that had a placement event after nine months' post-termination, the effect of the intervention might have dissipated. Such a dissipation might not be unreasonable to expect. However, there is evidence in the literature that demonstrates the long-term effectiveness of parent training programs to handle children who are problematic (Webster-Stratton, Hollinsworth, & Kolpacoff, 1989).

Fisher (1984) followed up a cohort of families one year after they had received time-limited treatment in a child guidance center. Based on questionnaires completed by the parents, he found no evidence of deterioration in case outcomes. However, almost 38% of the respondents in the follow-up sample received additional professional treatment in the one-year period after termination. A return for additional services does not have to be construed as a treatment failure. In fact, given the potential for problems and crises to recur, within the context in which the families referred to FPS live, it is not implausible to believe that periodic follow-up is a necessity to retain any gains achieved during the initial intervention.

It is conceivable that some of the control group families participated in services that provided effective tools for handling child-related problems. It is a weakness in the current study, due to limitations in resources, that services received by the control group families were not tracked and compared to the FPS families. We do know, however, that the level of in-home service intensity and availability was much higher for the FPS group than for the control group families who received traditional community services.

One interesting question, raised by the finding of a drop-off in the net gain between the two groups after nine months, would be to determine whether the gain in net impact could be sustained if FPS initiated follow-up visits of their families at periodic intervals during the first year post-termination. The purpose of the follow-up would be to reinforce what was taught, ensure that necessary community resources were engaged by the family, and provide additional social support.

The importance of using a control group was made evident by the placement status of the families receiving traditional services. While the children referred to FPS were screened to be at imminent risk of placement, less than three-fifths of the families receiving traditional community services had a child enter placement during the first year post-termination. In earlier research, Leeds (1966) followed a sample of at-risk DYFS families for nine months and found that only one-fifth of the families experienced a placement. Two explanations might be plausible: (a) predicting the likelihood of placement is a difficult task for most workers (Segal & Schwartz, 1985; Stein and Rzepnicki, 1984); and (b) a situational crisis, precipitating the need for placement, may often resolve itself so that the original impetus for the placement is either no longer present or as pressing. This argument is buttressed by the fact that FPS is organized as a short-term, intensive, crisis intervention program. Even though there was little gain measured on either the Family Environment Scale—a measure of perceived family functioning and climate—or the ISEL—a measure of perceived social support relative to the control group—the majority of FPS families and more than 40% of the control families avoided placement of their target children, despite reporting high life events scores (stress scores) and living in high-risk neighborhoods. In fact, only 19.4% of these families had experienced the placement of a target child prior to their FPS referral.

While the FPS families improved on seven of the 10 subscales and composites of the Family Environment Scale, and on the overall composite and two of three subscales of the Child Well-Being Scale, the study variables did not differentiate placement outcomes very successfully. Therefore, it was not possible to develop a model, using these variables, that would predict placement outcome with a high degree of probability. A number of reasons may contribute to this failure.

First, family functioning has been demonstrated to be moderately stable. Functioning at referral is correlated with family functioning at termination (Kowal et al., 1989). Thus, there may not have been enough variability in the functioning scores used in this study to aid in differentiating placement cases from non-placement cases.

Second, it is also possible that many placement decisions, which in the case of the families under study could be initiated by the caretaker, a child, or the referral agency, are haphazard and not highly related to average family functioning. For example, from the perspective of the agency worker, there may be a reluctance to place either because the worker is opposed to the use of placement as a service or because placement resources are limited.

Another limitation of the present study may have been in not collecting and tracking case level data sensitive to the issues that precipitate a crisis leading to placement. Gutstein, Rudd, Graham, and Rayha (1988) found that the "sense" of crisis experienced by a caretaker can be fleeting. The need for placement may be very situational and fleeting as well. They noted, "Although the majority of parental ratings described the adolescent's presenting problems as 'severe' or 'catastrophic' at the outset of treatment, only a small minority were rated as such following treatment" (p. 205). This is not to discount the very real problems that the families who are referred to FPS face everyday, just the fluid nature of the perceptions of families as they move in and out of states of chaos.

Reid, Kagan, and Schlosberg (1988) point to other variables that could differentiate children who enter placement from those who do not. For placement cases, children were found to have "more problems and more serious problems; families had fewer resources, used services less, made less progress and were less satisfied with the agency's efforts" (p. 33).

The key issue for a program such as Family Preservation is to intervene during a crisis, not only to resolve the current issue, but also to help families develop coping resources to get through the next crisis without the need for placement of a child. Given the variation in the net effect of the intervention, it was not clear from the measures used in this analysis that a *net increase in coping ability* occurred.

Of course, this argument ignores an important issue regarding placement: Not all placements are either inappropriate or harmful to children or their families (Wald, 1988). In fact, it is possible that the intensive nature of the FPS intervention, in allowing for a complete assessment of the family, may verify that placement, even if short-term, is an appropriate service at that time. To examine this hypothesis, further analysis will be completed on the cohort of FPS families who experienced a placement during treatment.

In summary, this study has demonstrated the feasibility and necessity of conducting controlled studies to determine the net effect of family preservation type programs. While demonstrating unequivocally a positive short-term effect for the intervention in terms of placement, the study has raised new questions about the correlates and the predictability of placement. Further study is required to put in context the reduced net effect of the FPS service during the service delivery period and for the long term.

Notes

1. As FPS therapists became more experienced during the first year of operation, the screening criteria were gradually broadened to accept children with previous placements of 90 days, six months, and, ultimately, unlimited duration. Since the variability in the placement criteria affected both the FPS group and the control group at the same time, there is little reason to believe this was a study limitation.

2. All FPS staff had an opportunity to work with several families prior to the beginning of data collection. This enabled them to gain experience utilizing the Homebuilders model.

References

Akamine, T., O'Neill, B. A., & Haymond, C. J. (1980). *Effectiveness of Homebuilders' family counseling intervention.* Pullman: Department of Education, Washington State University.

AuClaire, P., & Schwartz, I. (1986). *An evaluation of the effectiveness of intensive home-based services as an alternative to placement for adolescents and their families.* Minneapolis: Hennepin County Community Services Department and The Hubert H. Humphrey Institute of Public Affairs, University of Minnesota.

Barth, R., & Berry, M. (1987). Outcomes of child welfare services under permanency planning. *Social Service Review, 61,* 71-90.

Behavioral Sciences Institute. (n.d.) *Overview of Homebuilders Program.* Tacoma: Behavioral Sciences Institute.

Campbell, D., & Stanley, J. C. (1966). *Experimental and quasi-experimental design for research.* Chicago: Rand McNally.

Cochran, M. M., & Brassard, J. A. (1979). Child development and personal social networks. *Child Development, 50,* 601-616.

Cochrane, R., & Robertson, A. (1973). The life events inventory: A measure of the relative severity of psycho-social stressors. *Journal of Psychosomatic Research, 17,* 135-139.

Cohen, S. (n.d.). [Revised version of Interpersonal Support Evaluation List (ISEL)]. (Available from S. Cohen, Department of Psychology, Carnegie-Mellon University).

Cohen, S., & Hoberman, H. M. (1983). Positive events and social supports as buffers of life change stress. *Journal of Applied Social Psychology, 13,* 99-125.

Cohen, S., Mermelstein, R. Kamarck, T., & Hoberman, H. M. (1985). Measuring the functional components of social support. In I. G. Sarason & B. R. Sarason (Eds.), *Social support: Theory, research and applications* (pp. 73-94). Boston: Dordrecht.

Conner, R. F. (1980). Ethical issues in the use of control groups. In R. Perloff & E. Perloff (Eds.), *Values, ethics and standards in evaluation.* San Francisco: Jossey-Bass.

Cooperman, S. (1984). [Memo to chief school administrators]. Trenton: State of New Jersey, Department of Education.

Egeland, B., Breitenbucher, M., & Rosenberg, D. (1980). Prospective study of the significance of life stress in the etiology of child abuse. *Journal of Consulting and Clinical Psychology, 48,* 195-205.

Fisher, S. G. (1984). Time-limited brief therapy with families: A one-year follow-up study. *Family Process, 23,* 101-106.

Fuqua, R. W. (1988). *Iowa family preservation evaluation report.* Ames: Iowa State University, Department of Child Development, Child Welfare Research and Training Project.

Gutstein, S. E., Rudd, M. D., Graham, J. C., & Rayha, L. L. (1988). Systemic crisis intervention as a response to adolescent crises: An outcome study. *Family Process, 27,* 201-211.

Haapala, D. (1983). *Perceived helpfulness, attributed critical incident responsibility, and a discrimination of home-based family therapy treatment outcomes: Homebuilders model.* Federal Way, WA: Behavioral Sciences Institute.

Haygeman, J. A. (1982). *The interpersonal checklist: Its use in identifying client families associated with success or relapse after termination with the Homebuilders program.* Olympia: Washington State Department of Social and Health Services, Juvenile Justice Unit.

Jones, M. A. (1985). *A second chance for families.* Washington, DC: Child Welfare League of America.

Jones, M. A., Newman, R., & Shyne, A. W. (1976). *A second chance for families—Evaluation of a program to reduce foster care.* Washington, DC: Child Welfare League of America.

Kinney, J. M., Madsen, B., Fleming, T., & Haapala, D. A. (1977). Homebuilders: Keeping families together. *Journal of Consulting and Clinical Psychology, 43,* 667-673.

Kiresuk, T. J., & Sherman, R. E. (1968). Goal attainment scaling: A general method of evaluating comprehensive community mental health programs. *Community Mental Health Journal, 4,* 443-453.

Kowal, L. W., Kottmeier, C. P., Ayoub, C. C., Komives, J. A., Robinson, D. S., & Allen, J. P. (1989). Characteristics of families at risk of problems in parenting: Findings from a home-based secondary prevention program. *Child Welfare, 68*, 529-538.

Leeds, S. (1986). *Promoting family stability: Final report of the New Jersey performance contracting study*. Trenton: Bureau of Research, Evaluation and Quality Assurance, New Jersey Division of Youth and Family Services.

Magura, S., & Moses, B. S. (1986). *Outcome measures for child welfare services—Theory and applications*. Washington, DC: Child Welfare League of America.

Meddin, B. J. (1984). Criteria for placement decisions in protective services. *Child Welfare, 63*, 367-373.

Mitchell, C., Tovar, P., & Knitzer, J. (1988). *Evaluating the Bronx Homebuilders program: The first thirty families: An interim report*. New York: Bank Street College of Education, Division of Research, Demonstration and Policy.

Moos, R. H., & Moos, B. S. (1981). *Family environment scale manual*. Palo Alto, CA: Consulting Psychological Press.

New Jersey Division of Youth and Family Services. (1979). *Policy and procedures—Casework policy and procedures*. Trenton: New Jersey Division of Youth and Family Services.

Pecora, P. J., Fraser, M. W., Bartlome, J. A., McDade, K., Haapala, D., & Lewis, R. (1986). *The family based intensive treatment project: Selected research findings from the first year*. Salt Lake City: Social Research Institute, Graduate School of Social Work, University of Utah.

Reid, W. J., Kagan, R. M., & Schlosberg, S. B. (1988). Prevention of placement: Critical factors in program success. *Child Welfare, 67*, 25-36.

Segal, U. A., & Schwartz, S. (1985). Factors affecting placement decision of children following short-term emergency care. *Child Abuse and Neglect, 9*, 543-548.

Stein, T. J., & Rzepnicki, T. E. (1984). *Decision making at child welfare intake: A handbook for practitioners*. Washington, DC: Child Welfare League of America.

Wald, M. S. (1988, Summer). Family preservation: Are we moving too fast? *Public Welfare*, 33-46.

Webster-Stratton, C. W., Hollinsworth, T., & Kolpacoff, M. (1989). The long-term effectiveness and clinical significance of three cost-effective training programs for families with conduct-problem children. *Journal of Consulting and Clinical Psychology, 57*, 550-553.

Woodward, C. A., Santa-Barbara, J., Levin, S., & Epstein, N. B. (1978). The role of goal attainment scaling in evaluating family therapy outcome. *American Journal of Orthopsychiatry, 48*, 464-476.

Yuan, Y. Y., & McDonald, W. R. (1988). *Evaluation of AB 1562 demonstration projects: Year two interim report*. Sacramento: Walter R. McDonald & Associates.

4

Populations and Outcomes in Five Family Preservation Programs

KRISTINE E. NELSON

The expansion of family-based placement prevention services since the enactment of the Adoption Assistance and Child Welfare Act of 1980 (P.L. 96-272) has highlighted the need for more comprehensive information about the structure, practices, and outcomes of family preservation programs. One of the central questions about these programs has concerned the populations served and whether the selection criteria, which may include types of problems, risk of harm to the child, and imminence of placement, predetermine their generally high success rates.

Some critics have argued that the only families who are kept together by preventive services are those with few problems to begin with (Frankel, 1988; Magura, 1981). Magura's study, for example, found that children from families with more severe problems more often ended up in placement. While it is true that studies often find that families with more problems or more severe problems have less positive outcomes (Jones, 1985; Jones & Halper, 1981; Kagan, Reid, Roberts, & Silverman-Pollow, 1987; Rzepnicki, 1987; Szykula & Fleischman, 1985; Turner, 1984), the central concern should be whether family-based programs are serving the families who are most at risk of separation. (Regardless of whether families are more or less at risk, there may be a correlation between number and severity of problems and outcome.) Or, to put it more bluntly, whether family preservation programs, in their selection and eligibility criteria, are "creaming" by treating the less difficult cases in the child welfare system.

To look at these and other unresolved questions about family-based services, the National Resource Center on Family Based Services (FBS), in conjunction with the Regional Research Institute for Human Services at Portland State University, conducted a two-year exploratory study to gather descriptive information and analyze factors contributing to success and failure in 11 family-based child welfare programs across the country (Nelson, Emlen, Landsman, & Hutchinson, 1988).

Although the family-based programs in the study provided a broad array of services and used different service delivery models, they had several characteristics in common. First was their commitment to maintaining children in their own homes whenever possible. Second, sharing a family systems perspective, the programs focused on the whole family rather than the "problem child" and recognized both the interdependence of family members and the crucial connections between the family and its larger environment. Third, services were time-limited and based on goal-oriented treatment plans determined in conjunction with the families themselves. Finally, the programs provided comprehensive services, delivered either directly by the family-based worker or in coordination with other providers.

The main questions addressed in this analysis are: (a) Are success rates (i.e., non-placement) in family-based services due to selection factors? and (b) What factors distinguish placement from non-placement cases? While these questions can be answered definitively only through rigorously controlled experimental studies, we can partially test the hypothesis that high non-placement rates at program outcome are due to the selection of less difficult families for family preservation services by comparing them to a known population, the child protective services and juvenile justice samples studied by Magura and Moses (1986) in developing the Child Well-Being Scales.

Method

The study examined 11 family-based pre-placement programs in six states: Colorado, Iowa, Minnesota, Ohio, Oregon, and Pennsylvania. The programs were well established and were selected to represent a variety of treatment populations and organizational and community contexts. Of the original 11, five of the home-based programs are included in this analysis because they are most similar to the intensive family preservation services under examination in this volume.

Subjects

Subjects were 248 families who had been treated in one of the five programs studied. To be included in the sample, the primary child(ren) of concern could not have been continuously out of their homes for more than 30 days preceding or following referral to the family-based program. Using a table of random numbers, families were selected for inclusion in the sample from lists of families seen during the study period (1982-1985). Using this procedure, approximately 25 cases that remained intact and approximately 25 cases that ended in placement were selected from each of the five programs.

Procedures

Data were extracted from the case records of families by trained case readers. All case readers, who were mostly graduate and undergraduate social work students, received two days of training in data collection procedures from National Resource Center (NRC) or Regional Research Institute staff. Case coding took place in the agencies and averaged 1.5 hours per case. Because data collected included information about reason for closure, type and reason for placement, and restrictiveness of placement, coders were not blind to the outcome of the cases. (For further detail on methodology and research instruments, please refer to Nelson et al. [1988], chapter 2 and appendices.)

Reliability of coded data was assessed in two ways: (a) inter-rater reliability of key variables, and (b) inter-item reliability of additive scales. Three-fourths of the tested variables demonstrated levels of reliability acceptable for outcome research in child welfare (Magura & Moses, 1986, pp. 185, 187). Low reliability reduces the size of relationships and the significance of the variables affected and, therefore, leads to underestimating rather than overestimating effects (Magura & Moses, 1986, pp. 192-193). Since variables with low reliability were unlikely to produce falsely positive results, they were not excluded from the analyses.

Measures

Child Well-Being Scales

Part of the case record review included the completion of the Child Well-Being Scales for each case. The Child Well-Being Scales have many strengths, including behavioral indicators that leave little room for bias, high inter-rater reliability, and desirable psychometric properties. They have been extensively tested for reliability and validity in relevant populations. Response categories, which are normally rated by a social worker, consist of rank-ordered, descriptive paragraphs for each of 43 scales.

Before the Child Well-Being Scales (CWBS) scores of the families in this sample can be compared to those of the child protective services and juvenile justice cases studied by Magura and Moses (1986), the comparability of the scales in terms of content, coding, and reliability must be addressed. Only nine of the 43 CWBSs were identical in content and of sufficient frequency to allow comparisons. Because the current study relied on case records rather than social workers' reports, we ruled out 23 of the 43 CWBSs. In addition, several of the scales for which reliability and norms are reported in Magura and Moses were revised in the final version of the scale and are not the same as those employed in this study. Happily, the nine scales used in this analysis include many of the scales found to be most predictive of placement in studies of family preservation services (Yuan & Struckman-Johnson, in press).

The comparable family/caretaker scales included: Parental Relations, Capacity for Child Care, Acceptance and Affection, Motivation to Solve Problems, and Cooperation with Services. In our data the ratings are scores for the primary caretaker, and in the CWBS data, for the family as a whole, although the scales address caretaker functioning. The comparable child scales included: Disabling Condition, Abusive Physical Discipline, Children's Misconduct, and Children's Family Relations. In both the CWBS and FBS samples all children's scores are averaged, excluding missing data, which is the equivalent of assigning the mean of rated scales to the missing cases, "thus avoiding a forced correlation between the composite scores and the amount of missing data" (Magura & Moses, 1986, p. 170). Since it is deemed "unrealistic" to require that all scales be rated given the variability in families and case situations, Magura and Moses recommend using a cutoff point of 50% missing data. More than half the scores possible for all children in the family were missing in only one of the aggregated child scales, Abusive Physical Discipline. Hence, this scale was excluded from the multivariate analyses. For the other three aggregated scales, from 27% to 35% of all possible scores were missing. (Only the number of cases in which information was missing for all the children in the family is reported for the CWBS sample [see Table 4.3].)

Although the CWBS sample data were coded by social workers, Magura and Moses coded a subset of cases from case records and compared these data with social worker assessments to judge the reliability of this method of data collection. The major difficulty in using case records was insufficient information to rate levels on the scales. If the scales were rated on a "problem/no problem" basis, reliability between case reader and worker was high ($k = .66$ for no problem, $k = .82$ for some problem). Magura and Moses concluded that "Overall, the analysis does seem to support the reliability of the CWBS; problems as stated in the records are generally consistent with those rated on the scales" (p. 182).

In view of these findings, family/caretaker subscales have been analyzed on a problem = 1, no problem = 0 scale, excluding missing data. The reliability of these ratings in the 20 cases assessed by a second coder ranged from .51 to .79 using a *phi coefficient*. These represent acceptable levels of reliability in applied research and meet the standards of reliability employed by Magura and Moses. In order to compare children's scores, the average of their scores was used, since this is what is reported by Magura and Moses (1986). In accordance with their findings, aggregated scales were more reliable than single subscales. Reliability for the children's averaged scales in this subsample ranged from .68 to .78 using Pearson's *r*.

Placement

The primary outcome measure was placement or non-placement of a child at the termination of family-based services. A child was not counted among the placements if he or she was moved from a temporary placement back home before the termination of services. On the other hand, children living with relatives and friends at the time of termination were counted as placements.

Results

The results section will first review the characteristics of programs and samples studied; it will then present data pertaining to major study questions.

Program Characteristics

A brief description of each program will further define both the commonalities and the differences between the programs. (See Table 4.1 for further details on the five programs.) The two programs that served younger families referred for child abuse and neglect will be discussed first, followed by the three programs that primarily served families with older children experiencing problems with juvenile offenses.

Table 4.1 Characteristics of Five In-Home Placement Prevention Programs

Agency	Primary treatment approach	Concrete services provided by	Staff education	Average caseload	Average duration (days)	% Teamed
Franklin County Children's Services (FCCS)	Casework, individual/ family counseling	Family specialist	MSW/BA team	10.0[a]	214.0[b]	100.0
Iowa Children & Family Services (ICFS)	Family support, counseling, advocacy	Family preservation worker	BA/ a few MA	6.6	231.3	0.0
Dakota County Human Services Department, MN	Systemic family therapy	Case manager	MSW/MA/ BSW	4.9[a]	87.1	48.0
Lutheran Social Service of MN (LSS)	Family systems/ therapy	Family preservation worker	MSW/ MA/ BA/ BSW	5.5	149.4	0.0
Intensive Family Services (IFS)	Family systems/ multiple impact therapy	Case manager	MSW/MA/ a few BA	10.7	158.9[b]	41.0

[a]Teamed cases are counted in each worker's caseload.
[b]Mean much higher than median; medians = FCCS (172), IFS (109)

Franklin County Children's Services (FCCS), part of the county-based social service system in Ohio, is responsible for providing child welfare services to a mostly inner-city population in Columbus, Ohio. The Home-Based Family Centered Services program began as a two-year grant-funded pilot in 1983 and received initial training in family systems from the

National Resource Center on Family Based Services. Two teams composed of an MSW-level social worker, a BA/BSW family specialist, and the unit supervisor provide time-limited services (median of six months) to families approved for FCCS-paid placements. The program is regarded as a last resort to prevent placement and also serves families for whom reunification of an already-placed child is the goal. Neglect, physical abuse, family relationship problems, and substance abuse are common reasons for referral. Intervention and assessment are based on a casework model that draws on cognitive and behavioral theory and includes reality therapy and family counseling. The social worker is responsible for developing the case plan, and the family specialist provides concrete services and skill development, including family planning, transportation, homemaker services, and recreational services. Projecting from sample data,[1] one fourth of the families seen during the study period experienced placement[2] at the termination of home-based services, but half of the children were placed with friends or relatives.

Iowa Children and Family Services (ICFS), a statewide private social service agency, offers a number of different programs, including the In-Home Family Counseling Program in Ottumwa, Iowa, initiated in 1980 in response to a Department of Human Services' request for proposals. This program is used as an alternative to institutional, residential, and foster care and as a preventive service to families at risk of abuse, neglect, or family breakdown. It operates cooperatively with the Family Therapy program of the Ottumwa District Office of the Iowa Department of Human Services, which sees families who can benefit from less intensive service in an office setting. Most referrals come from the Department and involve physical abuse or family relationship problems, including marital problems and parent-child conflict. After a one- to two-week assessment period, in-home counselors, working alone to cover a broad geographical area, provide counseling, teaching, role-modeling, and family advocacy, as well as concrete and supportive services for a service period averaging 7.5 months. At termination, placement of one or more children occurred in a projected 19% of the cases during the study period. One third of the placements were with friends or relatives, one-third with foster families, and about one-fourth in group or institutional settings.

The Dakota County Human Services Department, part of Minnesota's state-supervised, county-administered system, started the Intensive Services (IS) program in 1979 as one element of a more general Placement Alternatives Program. Dakota County comprises relatively affluent suburbs south of Minneapolis. The program combines counseling services similar to those offered in a community mental health center, emphasizing the Milan model of family therapy, with a social service approach that includes outreach and work with the family in its environment. Nearly all the cases involve parent-child conflict, and more than half are referred due to status offenses. Intensive therapy is provided to families in one- to two-hour meetings once a week for an average of three months. In addition, IS therapists, often working in teams, provide education and information on parenting, substance abuse, sexuality, and advocacy for concrete services. The referring human services worker maintains case management responsibilities, and a paraprofessional program within the agency provides parenting education and support to low-functioning families. A projected 20.7% of the families seen during the study period experienced placement at the termination of services, 40% in foster families, and 24% in group homes or institutions. No children were placed with friends or relatives.

Lutheran Social Services (LSS) of Minnesota provides an Intensive In-Home Treatment Program to families in a 16-county area in rural western Minnesota. Established in 1981 with funding from two counties, the program provides intensive family therapy, but also emphasizes working with the community and directly providing whatever supportive and concrete services are needed. Workers, based out of their homes in the county they service, work individually and meet once a week for case consultation. Nearly two-thirds of the families in the sample were referred for parent-child conflict, about one-third for delinquency, and one-fourth for physical abuse. In-person contacts averaged six a month over a five-month average service period. By the end of service, a projected 22.7% of the families in the sample experienced placement, 17.6% with friends or relatives, 29.4% in foster homes, and 29.4% in group homes or institutions.

Intensive Family Services (IFS) in Multnomah County, Oregon, was one of four pilot projects begun in 1980 by the Oregon Children's Services Division (CSD), a state-administered public child welfare agency. All IFS programs, whether fielded directly by CSD or purchased from private agencies, must meet the same program standards, including average caseloads of 11, an average service period of 90 days, and a 75% success rate in preventing placement.[3] Operating under a purchase-of-service contract with the state and sharing offices with the CSD branch office, IFS serves the Portland metropolitan area. Cases are referred by county workers who maintain case management responsibilities. Families are most often referred for parent-child conflict, status offenses, substance abuse, and sexual abuse. Nearly 70% of the highest risk children had been placed before, the most of any site in the study. Following an in-depth family assessment, treatment focuses on restructuring the way in which family members respond to the "problem child," often an adolescent, employing structural and strategic family therapy techniques. In 41% of the cases, the families are treated by two or more therapists working as a team. Families were seen an average of twice a month over a median service period of 3.5 months. Only 15.4% of the families had children placed at the end of service, the lowest rate among the five programs in this analysis. More than half were placed in foster homes, 21.7% in group homes or institutions, and only 4.7% with friends or relatives. Due to program guidelines, 28.4% of cases were closed primarily because the 90-day time limit had been reached, resulting in a low level of case goal achievement (47.8%).

In summary, there were similarities and differences among the programs, based on the primary target population they served. The FCCS and ICFS programs served younger families, who most often were referred for neglect and family relationship problems and who received public assistance. Both programs saw families twice a week on average. Treatment focused on neglect and parenting problems, and families received more comprehensive services and more services directly from the family-based workers than in the other sites. In both, one-third to half of the placements were with friends or relatives. In the three home-based programs serving families with older children, families were more often referred for delinquency or status offenses, physical abuse, substance abuse, or parent-child conflict. The programs were less similar than the two serving younger families, even though the Minnesota programs both saw fewer poor families and more intact families with employed adults. (Further details on each program are available in Nelson et al., 1988.)

Sample Characteristics

The majority of families in the sample described in this chapter had incomes below the poverty level (62.5%), although this varied among the programs. On average, the primary caretaker was 34.51 years old (SD = 8.26), and more than 85% were white and female. More than half of the caretakers were married (59.6%). The average number of children in the families was 2.71 (SD = 1.46) with an average age of 10.14 years (SD = 4.83); 88.3% of the highest risk children were the biological children of the primary caretaker; but in families where there was a second adult, only about half were the biological children of the second adult. Nearly three-fourths of the families contained children judged to be at imminent risk of placement at the time of intake.[4] About one-third of the families were known to have received social services for six months or more, and 60.7% of the highest-risk children had at least one prior placement.

Problems reported in more than half the families included child behavior (58.6%), parent-child conflict (55.5%), adult relationships (52.3%), and family relationships (50.9%). Physical abuse (27.0%), neglect (25.9%), status offenses (25.7%), delinquency (24.8%), sexual abuse (19.3%), and substance abuse (17.9%) were each found in fewer cases. Families in this subsample had an average of 3.90 different problems (SD = 2.90).

Question 1: Are success rates (i.e., non-placement) in family-based services due to selection factors?

This question was examined by comparing the CWBS and FBS samples on nine Child Well-Being Scales. Prior to this comparison, the demographic characteristics of the FBS and CWBS samples were examined to assess their comparability. These demographic data are presented in Table 4.2.

The CWBS sample consisted of 240 cases from accepted intakes in three sites: 85 from Texas, 53 from Minnesota, and 102 from Florida. Data from the first two states comprised child protective services cases, with sexual abuse cases oversampled in Texas. The cases in Florida included both CPS and juvenile justice cases. As Table 4.2 demonstrates, the FBS and CWBS samples were reasonably comparable in percentage of single parents, mother's age, and average age of children. Minorities are seriously under-

Table 4.2 Comparison of Sample Demographics: CWBS and FBS Samples[a]

Demographics		CWBS (n=240)	FBS (n=254)
Single parent (%)		56.0	50.9
White (%)		59.0	91.8
Two or more adults (%)		59.0	73.1
Number of children	M	2.4	2.7
	SD	na	1.5
Mother's age	M	33.7	34.5[b]
	SD	na	8.3
Children's age	M	9.4	10.1
	SD	na	4.8

[a]CWBS = Child Well-Being Sample, FBS = Family-Based Service Sample
[b]Average age of primary caretaker (85.9% female)

represented in the FBS sample, and FBS families had both more adults and more children in the household. No breakdown is given of the proportion of juvenile justice cases included in the CWBS sample, so the exact proportion of juvenile justice and child abuse and neglect cases cannot be determined; however, since one of the major differentiating factors between these two populations is age, the similarity in average age of the children in the two sample groups is evidence of a comparable mix of child abuse and neglect and juvenile justice cases in each.

As Table 4.3 demonstrates, despite the difference in data collection methods, seven of the nine Child Well Being Scales examined are comparable in the proportion of missing data, being within 10% of each other, and all subscales had less than the 50% missing data considered acceptable by Magura and Moses (1986, p. 170).[5] In two scales, family/caretaker Acceptance and Affection for the children and Abusive Physical Discipline, there was a much higher incidence of missing data in the case records. These scales, therefore, were excluded from multivariate analyses.

Disregarding missing data, families in the FBS sample had more problems on all of the comparable subscales than the families that Magura and Moses studied in developing the CWBS (Table 4.3). The differences approached or exceeded 20% in six of the nine subscales. Families receiving family-based services had nearly three times more problems with Children's Misconduct and Children's Family Relations, and twice as many problems with Children's Disabling Conditions and Motivation to Solve Problems as the CWBS sample. In addition they had 50% more problems in Parental Relations and Acceptance/Affection for children, although the large amount of missing data in the latter scales may exaggerate the incidence of this problem in the FBS sample.

Child Abuse and Neglect and Juvenile Justice Subpopulations

Although the percentage of single parents, caretakers' average age, and children's average age were comparable between the CWBS and FBS samples, there were significant differences between the child protective services cases (referred primarily for physical abuse, sexual abuse, or neglect) and the juvenile justice cases (referred primarily for status offenses or delinquency) within the FBS sample. As might be expected, children in the juvenile justice subsample were older by an average of 5.4 years (CPS $M =$ 7.82, SD = 4.91; JJ $M =$ 13.25, SD =2.95; $t(177) = -9.33$, $p <.00$) and the

Table 4.3 Comparison of Scale Scores: CWBS and FBS Samples[a]

| | Percent missing | | Percent with a problem[b] | | | |
| | | | | | FBS | |
Scale	CWBS	FBS	CWBS	CPS	JJ	Total
Family/caretaker scales						
Parental relations	35	41	54	80	73	77
Capacity for child care	5	6	39	60	34	47
Acceptance and affection	10	49	41	60	97	67
Motivation to solve problems	5	4	46	81	82	80
Cooperation with services	12	2	40	41	48	45
Average of child scales						
Disabling condition	13	18	20	53	16	39
Abusive physical discipline	16	47	58	78	40	63
Children's misconduct	14	12	29	70	100	83
Children's family relations	14	12	30	80	96	86

[a]CWBS = Child Well-Being Sample, FBS = Family-Based Service Sample
[b]Excluding cases with missing data

child abuse and neglect subsample contained more single parents (CPS = 64.3 %; JJ = 45.2 %; $\chi^2(1, n = 178) = 5.70, p < .05$).

There were also significant differences on some of the CWBSs between these two groups (Table 4.3). The child abuse and neglect subsample had significantly more problems with caretaker's Capacity for Child Care, children's Disabling Conditions, and Abusive Physical Discipline, whereas the juvenile justice subsample had more problems with Children's Misconduct, Children's Family Relations, and Acceptance/Affection by caretakers. All differed to a statistically significant degree at the .01 probability level, except for children's Disabling Conditions, which was significant at the .05 level (the degrees of freedom varied from 88 to 170 due to missing data; the obtained t values ranged from -2.5 to 7.5). Despite these differences, problems in the two FBS subsamples were similar to, or more frequent than, those in the CWBS sample in all areas except children's Disabling Conditions, which was found less often in the juvenile justice subsample.

There were also significant differences between the child abuse and neglect subgroups in outcomes. The lowest placement rates were found in sexual abuse cases (13.1%), followed by physical abuse (17.6%), neglect (20.0%), and status offenses (20.1%). By far the highest placement rate was in delinquency cases (45.9%) $\chi^2(5, n = 241) = 14.32, p < .01$. In addition, the highest-risk children who ended up in placement were more likely to be placed informally with friends or relatives in child abuse and neglect cases (49.7%), but in foster homes (47.4%) or group homes and institutions (33.3%) in juvenile justice cases.

Question 2: What factors distinguish placement from non-placement cases?

This question was examined through the use of discriminant analysis. In this procedure, 27 variables that have been found in prior research to be related to placement, or that were hypothesized to be of importance, were included. These variables included family history and demographic variables, family and child problem variables, and service variables. It is important to note here that this analysis is limited by the presence of missing data and an insufficient sample size to permit testing of the obtained models on independent samples.

Because the differences between child abuse and neglect cases and juvenile justice cases resulted in a great deal of variability on specific measures, different discriminant models were developed for each subpopulation. (While it would be even more desirable to analyze the physical abuse, sexual abuse, neglect, status offense, and delinquency cases separately, as has been done in analyses of the larger data set [Nelson, 1990], the smaller number of cases in this analysis prohibited this approach.)

For child abuse and neglect cases (Table 4.4), the most powerful predictors of placement were substance abuse and concurrent community mental health services. More than half of the placement cases had substance abuse problems (56.3%) or received community mental health services (54.3%), compared to less than one-fourth of the non-placement cases. Slightly more than one-third of the cases involving substance abuse or community mental health services resulted in placement. All but one of the substance abuse cases involved abuse by adults. The third-most powerful predictor in the discriminant analysis was the primary caretaker's cooperation with services. Only one-third of the caretakers in placement cases cooperated fully with services, compared to two-thirds in non-placement cases. More than one-fourth of the cases with less than fully cooperative caretakers terminated in placement.

The last predictor that was also significant at the bivariate level was the number of children at high risk of placement. Forty percent of placement cases had two or more children either in temporary placements or at imminent risk of placement at intake, compared to one-fourth of non-placement cases. More than one-third of the non-placement cases had no children

Table 4.4 Discriminant Analysis of Placement/Non-Placement: Child Abuse and Neglect Cases[a]

Variable	Standardized discriminant coefficient	Within-group correlation	Univariate F
Substance abuse	.55	.57	12.29***
Community mental health services	.54	.51	9.57**
Primary caretaker's lack of cooperation with services	.24	.42	6.74**
Number of children at high risk of placement	.31	.38	5.45*
Child at highest risk attended most or all sessions	−.37	−.27	2.70
Role modeling intervention	.24	.23	2.01
Age of child at highest risk	.47	.06	.16
Canonical correlation	.54		
Chi square	30.23	df = 7	p ≤ .000
% Correctly classified	66.43		
Placement cases	25.50		
Non-placement cases	97.20		
Missing data	2		

[a]$N=96$.
*$p≤.05$.
**$p≤.01$.
***$p≤.001$.

assessed at imminent risk of placement. A high incidence of cases with no child at imminent risk of placement was found in families referred for sexual abuse (50.4%), presumably because the perpetrator was out of the home, and in ICFS (51.2%), which targeted families at risk of abuse and neglect as well as those at risk of placement.

Although not significant at the bivariate level, three additional variables contributed to the discriminant function: session attendance, role modeling, and age of child at risk. Only one-third of the highest-risk children in placement cases attended most or all the intervention sessions, compared to more than half in non-placement cases. About one-third of the placement cases received role modeling as an intervention, compared to less than one-fourth of the non-placement cases; and finally, the child at highest risk was, on average, half a year older in placement cases (placement $M = 9.37$,

SD = 5.44; non-placement M = 8.93, SD = 5.09). Role modeling was especially associated with placement in neglect cases. Only families in which physical abuse was a problem seemed to benefit from role modeling. Altogether the discriminant model for child abuse and neglect cases accounted for 29% of the variance and correctly classified 97.2% of the non-placement cases, but only 25.5% of the placement cases.

Since most of the child abuse and neglect cases were from FCCS and ICFS, it is not surprising that the predictors in this analysis overlapped considerably with those found for the individual programs (Nelson et al., 1988). Variables that were predictive in discriminant analysis for both programs included concurrent mental health services, number of children at high risk of placement, and the age of the child at highest risk. These models, however, accounted for a larger percentage of the variance (FCCS, 70.6% and ICFS, 53.3%) since the samples were more homogeneous than the child abuse and neglect subsample tested here.

The most powerful predictors of placement or non-placement in the juvenile justice sample were variables that described the highest-risk child (Table 4.5). In placement cases, 59.7% had experienced a prior placement, 54% were in a regular class in school, and only one-fourth attended most or all the intervention sessions. In non-placement cases, 28.7% had been in placement before, 79.9% were in a regular class in school, and 53.7% attended most or all of the intervention sessions. Forty percent or more of the highest-risk children who had been in placement before (44.8%), who were in special classes or had dropped out of school (41.2%), or who did not attend most or all the sessions (39.5%) ended up in placement.

Two service characteristics were also significant in bivariate and multivariate analyses. Teaching of new skills occurred in 39.3% of the non-placement cases, and 62% were served by two or more workers. In contrast, only 18.9% of placement cases were taught new skills and only 37.5% were teamed. Two variables describing the severity of the children's problems with family relationships and misconduct also contributed to the discriminant model, although they were not significant at the bivariate level. Children with better family relations and more severe misconduct were more likely to stay with their families. Altogether the variables in the discriminant model accounted for 27% of the variance and correctly classified 88.4% of the non-placement cases and 49% of the placement cases.

The same variables previously appeared in a discriminant analysis of placement and non-placement of status offenders, which accounted for 53.3% of the variance in that sample. Two of the variables concerning the highest-risk child also entered into the model for delinquency cases: regular

Table 4.5 Discriminant Analysis of Placement/Non-Placement: Juvenile Justice Cases[a]

Variable	Standardized discriminant coefficient	Within-group correlation	Univariate F
Child at highest risk of placement			
Prior placement	−.43	−.53	8.41**
In regular class at school	.35	.52	8.14**
Attended most or all sessions	.41	.51	7.70**
Teaching intervention	.32	.37	4.14*
Teamed by 2 or more workers	.27	.36	3.82*
Average score for children's family relations	.47	.22	1.51
Average score for children's misconduct	−.66	−.09	.25
Canonical correlation	.52		
Chi square	24.44	$df = 7$	$p \leq .001$
% Correctly classified	64.10		
Placement cases	49.00		
Non-placement cases	88.40		
Missing data	5		

[a]$N=82$.
*$p \leq .05$.
**$p \leq .01$.

class at school and attendance at sessions. This model accounted for 41% of the variance (Nelson, 1990).

Discussion

The generally consistent pattern of more problems in the FBS sample than in the CWBS sample on all comparable measures, with a greatly increased incidence of problems in specific areas, does not support the hypothesis that the success of family-based services is due to excluding the most difficult cases in the child welfare system. A comparison of the family-based services population in this study to the child protective services and juvenile justice populations studied by Magura and Moses (1986) reveals substantial similarity in demographics and problems. It would appear safe to conclude that the family-based services' client population is no less difficult than the general child welfare population. In scales with similar levels of missing data, it would also seem safe to conclude that the FBS population may have substantially more problems with caretakers' motivation, relationships between parents, children's misconduct, and family relations.

To the extent that there are major differences among the samples examined, they are between families seen for child abuse or neglect and those seen for juvenile justice problems. The child abuse and neglect group has younger children and caretakers and more single parents. The juvenile justice population is older, has more two-parent families, more child behavior and family relationship problems, and, particularly for those referred for delinquency, worse outcomes.

Although prediction of success in keeping families together is less useful from a practice point of view than the ability to predict failure, since programs that screened families to include only those with the highest potential for success would be immediately charged with creaming, it is useful for administrators, evaluators, and policymakers to know that programs that serve a population with fewer substance abuse and mental health problems, more cooperative caretakers, fewer children at imminent risk of placement, and younger children will, in all likelihood, have lower placement rates than programs that serve a more difficult population. It is also important to note that even after these population differences have been accounted for, involving children in the treatment process makes a positive contribution toward preventing placement.

These findings corroborate evidence from other studies that families at greater risk of placement are those families that are receiving concurrent mental health services (Landsman, Leung, & Hutchinson, 1987), have uncooperative caretakers (AuClaire & Schwartz, 1986; DeWitt, 1980; Jones & Halper, 1981; Kinney, Madsen, Fleming, & Haapala, 1977), and have older children (Fraser, Pecora, & Haapala, 1989; Jones, 1985; Rzepnicki, 1987).

Although placement rates are higher, predictability of both success and failure is also much higher for both status offenders and juvenile delinquents than for physical and sexual abuse cases (Nelson, 1990). Especially in status offense cases, children without prior placements, who are in a regular class in school and involved in a treatment process that includes skill-building and teamed interventions, stand a much better chance of remaining at home. Only after all these factors are taken into account does the severity of behavioral and family relationship problems explain placement. These findings support other studies that have identified children with prior placements as being at greater risk of placement (Fraser et al., 1989; Heying, 1985; Jones, 1985; Rzepnicki, 1987).

Future research should more systematically examine the characteristics of client populations and effects of various eligibility requirements on outcomes in family preservation services. In addition, the factors that have been identified in this and other research as contributing to success and failure in family-based services should be tested in experimental and quasi-experimental designs to establish their effects more conclusively. While family history and characteristics seem to be the most consistent determinants of outcome, it is encouraging that some service characteristics, notably teaching skills and teaming in juvenile justice cases and involving the children at risk in services in both child abuse and neglect cases and juvenile justice cases, seem to contribute to family preservation.

Notes

1. Two weighting systems were used in analyzing the data. Since Franklin County and Lutheran Social Services both had fewer than 25 codable placement cases, both placement and non-placement cases were weighted to represent the equivalent of 25 each in analyses that involved placement as the dependent variable. When frequencies are reported or programs are compared to each other, the case data are weighted by the estimated incidence of placement in each agency, so as to present a more accurate picture of family and service characteristics than is provided by equal numbers of placement and non-placement cases, since, in reality, the latter are much more frequent. Application of these weighting systems at times inflated the number of subjects in the analysis.

2. Placements included emergency shelter, supervised independent living, foster family homes, group homes and halfway houses, institutions for mentally retarded/developmentally disabled, residential treatment or psychiatric hospitalization, incarceration, adoptive homes, and formal or informal placement with a friend or relative if it was in response to the family's problem and not a routine visit (e.g., during a holiday or with a noncustodial parent). To be classified as a placement case, at least one child in the family had to be in placement or to have placement planned or imminent at termination of the case from family-based services. A temporary placement from which a child was transferred or returned home before the termination of services was not counted as an outcome of placement.

3. The five counties that provided Intensive Family Services directly were also included in the larger study and proved to be very similar in their operation and results to the Multnomah County program, but have been excluded from this analysis at the request of the editors because the majority of their contacts with families were in the office and thus do not meet the definitional criteria for intensive family preservation services used in this volume.

4. Case readers assessed risk of placement using four categories: (a) low risk: no indication of possible placement in the case record; (b) moderate risk: discussion of possible placement, but not imminent; (c) high risk: placement imminent without family-based services, or just returned from placement; and, (d) temporary placement: child to be returned to family within

30 days of intake into family-based services. To assess imminent risk, some action must have been taken and recorded toward making a placement.

5. Differences between cases with large amounts of missing data on certain Child Well-Being Scales were examined by comparing the means of cases with missing data on the item to those with a score. As might be expected, cases with missing data on Parental Relations had one fewer person in the family and were lower-income; variables consistent with single-parent family status. For both Acceptance and Affection and Abusive Physical Discipline, cases with missing data were those with fewer contacts and services; in short, those about whom less was known and, therefore, recorded. Although they also had significantly older children than cases with complete data, they also were under less stress and had fewer problems, suggesting that scores on these two variables might overestimate the incidence of problems. All the other CWBS items had minimal missing data or percentages of missing data that were comparable to the CWBS sample.

References

AuClaire, P., & Schwartz, I. (1986). *An evaluation of the effetiveness of intensive home-based services as an alternative to placement for adolescents and their families*. Minneapolis: Hennepin County Community Services Department and the Hubert H. Humphrey Institute of Public Affairs, University of Minnesota.

DeWitt, K. N. (1980). The effectiveness of family therapy: A review of outcome research. *Advances in Family Psychiatry, 2*, 437-465.

Frankel, H. (1988). Family-centered, home-based services in child protection: A review of the research. *Social Service Review, 62*, 137-157.

Fraser, M. W., Pecora, P. J., & Haapala, D. A. (1989). *Families in crisis: Findings from the family-based intensive treatment project*. Federal Way, WA: Behavioral Sciences Institute; Salt Lake City: Social Research Institute, University of Utah.

Heying, K. (1985). Family based in-home services for the severely emotionally disturbed child. *Child Welfare, 64*(5), 519-527.

Jones, M. A. (1985). *A second chance for families: Five years later*. New York: Child Welfare League of America.

Jones, M. A., & Halper, G. (1981). *Serving families at risk of dissolution: Public preventive servies in New York City, executive summary*. New York: Child Welfare League of America.

Kagan, R. M., Reid, W. J., Roberts, S. E., & Silverman-Pollow, J. (1987). Engaging families of court-mandated youths in an alternative to institutional placement. *Child Welfare, 66*(4), 365-376.

Kinney, J. M., Madsen, B., Fleming, T., & Haapala, D. A. (1977). Homebuilders: Keeping families together. *Journal of Consulting and Clinical Psychology, 45*, 667-673.

Landsman, M. J., Leung, P., & Hutchinson, J. (1987). *Preventive services to families in four states: Subcontractor's final report for the New Jersey performance contracting study*. Iowa City: The National Resource Center on Family Based Services, The University of Iowa School of Social Work.

Magura, S. (1981). Are services to prevent foster care effective? *Children and Youth Services Review, 3*, 193-212.

Magura, S., & Moses, B. S. (1986). *Outcomes measures for child welfare services*. Washington, DC: The Child Welfare League of America.

Nelson, K. (1990). Family-based services for juvenile offenders. *Children and Youth Services Review, 12,* 193-212.

Nelson, K., Emlen, A., Landsman, M. J., & Hutchinson, J. (1988). *Factors contributing to success and failure in family-based child welfare services.* Iowa City: The National Resource Center on Family Based Service, The University of Iowa School of Social Work.

Rzepnicki, T. L. (1987) Recidivism of foster children returned to their own homes: A review and new directions for research. *Social Service Review, 61*(1), 56-70.

Szykula, S., & Fleischman, M. (1985). Reducing out-of-home placements of abused children: Two controlled field studies. *Child Abuse and Neglect, 9,* 277-283.

Turner, J. (1984). Reuniting children in foster care with their biological parents. *Social Work, 29*(6), 501-505.

Yuan, Y., & Struckman-Johnson, D. (In press). Intensive home-based treatment: Client outcomes and issues for program design. *Family preservation services: Research and evaluation.* Newbury Park, CA: Sage.

5

Placement Outcomes for Neglected Children with Prior Placements in Family Preservation Programs

YING-YING T. YUAN
DAVID L. STRUCKMAN-JOHNSON

Two major concerns regarding child welfare services are the number of children who experience multiple placements and the large percentage of neglect cases in the substitute care population. The multiple placements experienced by children in substitute care has been a long-standing concern (National Commission on Children in Need of Parents, 1979). Indeed, foster care drift was one of the major issues that the Adoption Assistance and Child Welfare Act of 1980 (P.L. 96-272) sought to address.

The high level of attention is due to the impact on children and the magnitude of the problem. Children who experience multiple placements are less likely to benefit from services due to the stresses associated with changes in home environment. Children who stay in placement for longer periods of time have more placements, and their chances of being reunited with their parents decrease (California Department of Social Services, 1987).

AUTHORS' NOTE: This chapter is based on research conducted for the Office of Child Abuse Prevention, California Department of Social Services, under contract KED6012. We are grateful to the Office of Child Abuse Prevention Services, the county child welfare departments, the project agencies, the therapists, and the families who participated in the study. The views expressed in this chapter are solely those of the authors and do not represent the California Department of Social Services; Walter R. McDonald & Associates, Inc.; or the University of South Dakota.

National data for 1985 showed that nearly half of the children in care in 19 states had been previously placed (American Public Welfare Association [APWA], 1988). Data from particular states tend to replicate this finding.

There has been less agreement on the criticalness of neglect as compared to other types of maltreatment. Definitions of neglect often reflect a community standard regarding supervision, cleanliness, medical care, and so forth; and public attention often focuses on physical and sexual abuse while neglect is "forgotten" (Daro, 1989). Neglect is commonly defined more broadly than physical abuse; a general definition would be that neglect is the deprivation of necessities, or the failure to provide needed, age-appropriate care (Walter R. McDonald & Associates, Inc. [WRMA], 1990). In a study of lack of supervision cases, which are often included under the category of neglect, Jones (1988) found that if a stringent definition was used, the allegation usually was viewed as having potentially serious consequences; if a less stringent definition was used, the allegation was considered to have unknown consequences.

There is, however, consensus on the magnitude of the problem. Neglect accounts for the largest percentage of cases of reported child maltreatment. In an analysis of 1986 data from 14 states, constituting 41% of the U.S. child population, the American Association for the Protection of Children found that 54.9% of more than 323,000 children had been reported for allegations of deprivation of necessities. The report estimated that 429,000 children were maltreated by neglectful parents (for a rate of 67.78 per ten thousand), again the largest for any category of maltreatment (American Humane Association [AHA], 1988). It was found that neglect cases differed from "all maltreatment" cases in that there was a higher frequency of single female head of households (51% for neglect cases, compared to 36% for all maltreatment cases), and that employment and economic difficulties were reported at higher rates. Age, sex, and ethnic characteristics of both perpetrators and victims were similar, with the exception that there was a higher percentage of female perpetrators (70%). On 81% of all neglect reports, protective services cases were opened (AHA, 1988).

Besharov (1988) has argued that social deprivation and neglect are more likely to be reasons for placement than physical abuse. The APWA analysis of substitute care data from 1985 reported that, when all reasons for children being in substitute care are considered, 59% of children entering care were placed as a result of parental neglect or physical or sexual abuse. Approximately two-thirds of these children had been placed in substitute care for reasons of neglect. Another 16% were cases caused by parental conditions such as mental illness, homelessness, or substance abuse (APWA, 1988). If the number of children in the parental conditions category is combined with the neglect category, approximately 55% of the children in substitute care are the victims of child neglect. With the increased attention to parental drug addiction and its effects on young children, neglect could increase as a cause of child protection reporting and case opening.

Preplacement Prevention Services

These and other factors have led child welfare advocates and practitioners to attach great importance to the objective of providing services to children and their families in their own homes, as an alternative to substitute care, and to develop preplacement prevention services as required by P.L. 96-272.

One of the most highly regarded types of preplacement prevention services is family preservation, or intensive in-home services. Intensive in-home services are a subset of the category of family-based services that are provided to families whose children are at risk of placement. They are distinctive in that they are usually very short term (4-12 weeks), utilize small caseloads of two or three families per worker, and combine both counseling and concrete services. The overall philosophy of service has been influenced by Homebuilders of Tacoma, Washington (Haapala & Kinney, 1979). Briefly stated, this model of service provides intensive services in their own homes for families whose children would otherwise be removed from the home and placed in substitute care. Services include family therapy, skills building, parenting training, and help in obtaining basic services such as food, housing, and transportation. Components of social learning theory, ecological systems theory, and family systems theory are often used (Barth, 1988). As with other preplacement prevention services, the goal is to prevent placement, focusing on children who are at risk of imminent placement.

Although these trends in child welfare have been identified, relatively little attention has been given to the question: "Are preplacement prevention programs more successful with some types of families than others?" Based on a comprehensive study on child abuse and prevention, Daro (1989) argued that service components must be combined for specific types of families and that, in particular, it was most difficult to find effective services for neglect cases:

> The most cost effective treatment plan in instances of child sexual abuse involving family members seems to be a combination of family and group counseling for the

victim, the victim's siblings, the perpetrator, and the perpetrator's spouse. In cases of child neglect, the most efficient interventions will combine family counseling with parent education and basic care services such as babysitting, medical care, clothing, and housing assistance. (p. 197)

Until recently, family preservation services have not fully examined whether the outcomes of such programs vary for different types of families. This is due in part to the fact that in the early stages of implementation, in-home services were provided by agencies on a relatively small scale, and evaluations studied small populations (Frankel, 1988; Hinckley & Ellis, 1985; Leeds, 1984). Thus, evaluations were able to describe the populations served and, to a certain extent, the outcomes of these populations, but were more limited in their ability to assess the impact of such programs on different types of clients. Moreover, the success rate of such programs was often reported as high as 95%; and the study group therefore resulted in few families who did not succeed in being prevented from placement. Recently two studies have evaluated programs with more clients, namely, the evaluation of the Homebuilders projects in Utah and Washington (Fraser, Pecora, & Haapala, 1988); and the evaluation of 11 family-based programs conducted by the National Resource Center on Family Based Services (NAFBS) (1988). Both studies have discussed the characteristics of families who are more likely to be placed than other families. Papers based on these studies are included in this volume. As the interest in family preservation services has resulted in several statewide implementations, there is now the potential for more focused research on specific questions of high concern to child welfare services providers and administrators.

Study Questions

The following research questions concerning the placement outcomes of children who receive intensive in-home care services are addressed in this chapter:

1. Are previously placed children more likely to be placed after intensive family preservation treatment than never-placed children?
2. Are children identified as being at risk of imminent placement due to neglect more likely to be placed after intensive family preservation treatment than children who are at risk for other reasons?

3. Are previously placed and neglected children more likely to be placed after intensive family preservation treatment than previously placed children who were not neglected?

4. What factors are associated with placement after intensive family preservation treatment?

Method

In order to examine these questions, data were collected from a three-year evaluation of eight demonstration projects in California. These projects were located in the following agencies: Eastfield Ming Quong; Families First; Hillsides Home for Children; Home Start Inc.; Sacramento Children's Home; San Mateo County Mental Health Department; Turning Point of Central California, Inc.; and Victor Valley Child Abuse Task Force. All of the major components usually found in family preservation programs are found in the California demonstration programs. The only characteristic that is not commonly a part of the intensive in-home services model is that services were provided by licensed clinical social workers or licensed marriage, family, and child counselors. The evaluation resulted in the collection of common data on more than 700 families and more than 1,500 children (Yuan, McDonald, Wheeler, Struckman-Johnson, & Rivest, 1990).

Study Participants

Families were included in the evaluation if they were determined to be at risk of placement, were referred to the project by a local child welfare agency, and had received intensive in-home services. The study included 1,740 children in 709 families.

Measures and Instruments

Characteristics of Families and Children

Characteristics of families and children were defined in terms of demographic characteristics, dependency status, disabilities, and family functioning.

Family functioning was assessed by the Child Well-Being Scales (Magura & Moses, 1986). The Child Well-Being Scales is a well documented instrument with acceptable validity and reliability scores; it is fully grounded with detailed descriptions of each ranking; it covers a great deal of family information which is usually collected during assessment; and it is well accepted by practitioners of various treatment philosophies. Following Seaberg (1988), each of the CWBS indices was used as a separate measure.

Information relating to demographic characteristics, dependency status, and disabilities was obtained from each family's therapist at intake. CWBS data were obtained at intake and termination from service from each family's therapist. Training regarding how to complete the CWBS was provided to therapists at each project. Therapists were asked to leave blank those CWBS items they did not have sufficient information to score.

Reason for Risk

Reason for risk of imminent placement was defined in terms of nine categories: potential physical abuse, past/current physical abuse, potential physical neglect, past/current physical neglect, potential emotional maltreatment, past/current emotional maltreatment, potential sexual abuse, past/current sexual abuse, and failure to thrive. Reason for risk of placement was determined by the referral source. In this chapter, neglect cases consisting of both the potential cases and past/current cases of maltreatment were compared with all other types of maltreatment. (California State law defines neglect as the negligent treatment or maltreatment of a child by a parent or caretaker under circumstances indicating harm or threatened harm to the child's health or welfare [Office of the Attorney General, 1985].)

Placement

Placement was defined as any out-of-home placement known to the Department of Social Services, including emergency shelter, relative's home, foster family care, group home care, residential treatment care, and juvenile detention. Recognized relative placements and planned substitute care arrangements were included as foster care, whereas placements with relatives that were not under the supervision of the department were not included. Runaways and placements known only to the Department of Mental Health were not included, given the young age of most of the children in the study and the difficulty of obtaining this information.

Placement data were drawn from children's case records and provided by personnel working for the county in which the child's project was located. Data on the number of placements prior to receiving intensive services were collected at referral to services, and data on placements during an eight-month period after referral were collected by surveying the county offices.

A prior placement was defined as any placement initiated before a child was referred for services. A placement outcome was defined as any placement that took place during the eight months subsequent to the referral date. Placements that began before the referral to the program and ended before the termination of intensive in-home services were considered as reunification cases. Such placements were counted as prior placements and not as placement outcomes. Children who were placed prior to referral and remained in placement throughout the provision of services were counted as having had a prior placement and a placement outcome. The maximum number of placement outcome days analyzed was set at 240 days per child. Thus the number of placement outcome days was limited to the eight-month follow-up period.

Procedures

The accuracy of study data was assessed, in ways that were possible, in light of the constraints under which the study was operating. Data pertaining to reasons for risk of imminent placement were reviewed by therapists' supervisors and by the study team's data quality control staff, whose task was to confirm the internal consistency of data.

Placement data were validated through discussions with the local county representatives who provided the data, internal consistency checks, and a random review of case records at each site. Selected items on each case were validated through a comparison of the county case record and project case data.

Results

Sample Characteristics

The average age of the children served was 6.7 years, with 9% less than one year old, 35% preschoolers, 42% of elementary school age, and 14% adolescents. Eighty-seven percent of the children served were considered at the time of referral to be at risk of removal; and 13% were not categorized as being at risk of removal, but were other siblings in the family. Of the children considered to be at risk, 42.9% were at risk due to physical abuse; 33.3% were at risk due to physical neglect; 11.9% were at risk due to sexual abuse; 5.8% were at risk due to emotional neglect; and 6.1% were at risk for other reasons. One-fifth (20.1%) of the children were reported as having one or more disabilities; 19.8% of those attending school were performing below current grade level.

Nearly half of the children had experienced one or more placements prior to being referred for intensive in-home services: 36.8% had one prior placement; 9.9% had two or more prior placements. The largest group of previously placed children had been most recently placed in family foster homes (46.5%); 20.4% had been in emergency shelter care; 18% had been in relative placement; and 15.1% had been in other types of placements. These and other characteristics are described more fully in Table 5.1.

Table 5.1 Characteristics of 1,740 Children Served

Characteristic	n	%
Relationship to primary caretaker		
Biological child	1,632	96
Adopted child	7	0
Stepchild	22	1
Foster child	4	0
Other child relative	42	3
Unknown	33	—
Sex		
Male	885	51
Female	855	49
Age category		
Less than 1	159	9
1–5	615	49
6–12	724	42
13 or older	239	14
Unknown	3	—
Ethnicity		
Black	282	16
Caucasian	835	49
Hispanic	454	27
All other races	137	8
Unknown	32	—
Education		
At grade level	773	79
Below grade level	193	20
Above grade level	9	1
Not applicable or unknown	765	—
Physical location		
Own home	1,500	87
Other relative home	120	7
Foster home	55	3
Group home	5	0

continues

Table 5.1 continued

Characteristic	N	%
Residential treatment center	3	0
Shelter	18	1
Other	31	2
Unknown	8	—
Disabilities		
No impairment	1,200	80
Vision impairment	17	2
Hearing impairment	16	2
Speech/language impairment	39	3
Orthopedic impairment	12	1
Developmental disability	31	2
Learning disability	63	4
Emotional or psychological dysfunction	91	6
Alcohol/drug dependency	12	1
Other serious chronic condition	23	2
Unknown	236	—
Number of previous placements		
None	894	54
One	616	37
Two	126	8
Three	22	1
Four	6	0
Five	5	0
More than five	6	0
Unknown	65	—
Type of most recent previous placement		
Other relative home	139	18
Foster family	360	47
Group home	30	4
Residential treatment center	38	5
Mental health facility	16	2
Juvenile detention	18	2
Emergency shelter	158	20
Respite	7	1
Other	8	1
Not applicable or unknown	966	—
Length of most recent previous placement (weeks)		
Less than 1	212	29
1–4	244	33
5–8	77	10
9–24	69	9

continues

Table 5.1 continued

25–36	25	3
37–95	67	9
96 or more	30	4
Not applicable or unknown	1,007	–
Reason at risk of removal		
Potential physical abuse	289	17
Past/current physical abuse	358	21
Potential physical neglect	153	9
Past/current physical neglect	349	20
Potential emotional maltreatment	45	3
Past/current emotional maltreatment	43	3
Potential sexual abuse	42	2
Past/current sexual abuse	137	8
Failure to thrive	14	1
Other	78	5
Not applicable	219	13
Unknown	13	–
Dependency petition status		
None	654	39
None–program is alternative	341	20
Filed–pending	117	7
Filed–not adjudicated dependent	63	4
Adjudicated dependent	491	29
Other	7	0
Not applicable or unknown	67	–

NOTE: Percentages do not include missing data. Percentages may not add to 100 due to rounding.

The families of these children were young, single-parent households. The average age of the adults was 32 years; 47% of all primary caretakers were under 30 years of age. Forty-nine percent of the households were headed by single parents. Fifty-nine percent of the households were receiving public assistance. More than half of the families (57% of primary caretakers) served were Caucasian; Hispanics were the next-largest group to be served (22% of primary caretakers); and Blacks were the third-largest group served (15% of primary caretakers). Table 5.2 summarizes the characteristics of the 709 families served by the projects.

Table 5.2 Characteristics of 709 Families Served

Characteristic	n	%
Family status		
Birth parents together	167	24
Single parent (divorced)	131	19
Single parent (separated)	108	19
Single parent (never married)	102	15
Single parent (widowed)	13	2
Birth parent (remarried)	94	14
Birth parent (with other adult)	50	7
Other relative household	19	3
Adoptive parents	2	0
Other	9	1
Unknown	14	–
Family income in dollars		
Less than 5,000	64	13
5,000–9,999	191	38
10,000–14,999	119	24
15,000–19,999	41	8
20,000–29,999	40	8
30,000 or more	46	9
Unknown	208	–
Receiving public assistance		
Yes	420	62
No	261	38
Unknown	28	–
Characteristics of Primary Caretakers		
Sex		
Male	81	11
Female	628	89
Age category		
Less than 20	31	5
20–24	93	14
25–29	152	23
30–34	200	30
35–39	123	18
40–44	41	6
45 or older	36	5
Unknown	33	–
Ethnicity		
Black	106	15
Caucasian	396	57

continues

Table 5.2 continued

Hispanic	155	22
All other races	38	6
Unknown	14	–
Education		
Less than high school	207	36
High school diploma	175	30
2 years college	142	24
More than 2 years college	58	10
Unknown	127	–
Employment		
Full-time	165	24
Part-time	54	8
Unemployed (looking)	91	13
Unemployed (not looking)	344	45
Chronic unemployed	28	4
On leave	9	1
Unknown	18	–
Physical location		
Own home	628	90
Other relative home	40	6
Group home	2	0
Shelter	10	1
Separated living elsewhere	2	0
Other	9	3
Unknown	7	–
Disabilities		
No impairment	428	65
Vision impairment	8	1
Hearing impairment	7	1
Speech/language impairment	6	1
Orthopedic impairment	9	1
Developmental disability	9	1
Learning disability	14	2
Emotional or psychological dysfunction	87	13
Alcohol/drug dependency	75	11
Other serious chronic condition	16	2
Unknown	50	–

NOTE: Percentages do not include missing data. Percentages may not add to 100 due to rounding.

Table 5.3 Placement Status of Children by Reason for Risk of Placement and Number of Prior Placements

Reason for risk of placement	Number prior placements	Placed		Not placed		Total
Neglect	0	32	(18.8)[a]	138	(71.2)	170
Other	0	29	(6.1)	450	(93.9)	479
Neglect	1	69	(32.9)	141	(67.1)	210
Other	1	49	(13.5)	313	(76.5)	362
Neglect	2 or more	20	(30.3)	46	(69.7)	66
Other	2 or more	31	(33.3)	62	(66.7)	93
Total		230		1150		1380

NOTE: The 360 study children not included in the table are those not identified at-risk at the time of intake (e.g., siblings of children at-risk), those with missing data for reason at-risk of removal, and those with missing data for placement status (e.g., children from families unavailable for followup).

[a]Numbers in parentheses are percent of row.

Research Questions

Question 1: Are previously placed children more likely to be placed after intensive family preservation services than never-placed children?

Findings show that previously placed children are more likely to be placed after treatment than never-placed children [χ^2 (1, $n = 1380$) = 45.61, $p < .001$]. As a review of Table 5.3 indicates, the placement rates of children with multiple placements increased with the number of prior placements: 9.4% of children with no prior placements were placed; 20.6% of children with one prior placement were placed; and 32.1% of children with two or more prior placements were placed.

Question 2: Are children identified as at risk of placement due to neglect more likely to be placed after intensive family preservation treatment than children who are at risk of placement for other reasons?

Findings show that neglected children were placed more frequently than children placed for other reasons. As a review of Table 5.3 indicates, 27.1% of neglected children had placement outcomes, while 11.7% of children with other maltreatment had placement outcomes. A chi square analysis applied to these data indicated that the distributions were significantly different, [$\chi^2(1, n = 1380)$ = 50.84, $p < .001$].

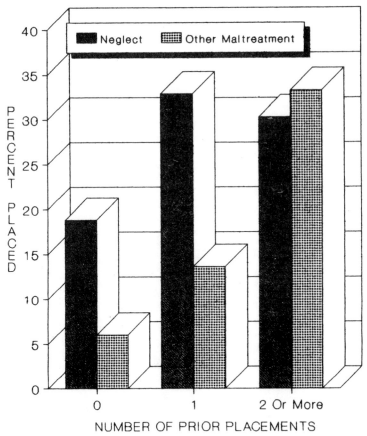

Figure 5.1 Placement Rates of Children by Number of Prior Placements and Reasons at Risk (N=1,380)

Question 3: Are previously placed and neglected children more likely to be placed after intensive family preservation treatment than previously placed children who were not neglected?

There are complex relationships among prior placement history, reason for being at risk of imminent placement, and use of placements after intensive family preservation treatment. As a review of Figure 5.1 indicates, almost one-fifth (18.8%) of the children who had no prior placement history, but who were at risk due to neglect, were placed, while only 6.1% of children who had no prior history, but who were at risk of abuse due to other maltreatment, were placed. Children with one prior placement and a history of neglect were placed at a rate of 32.7%, while children who had one prior but were at risk due to other maltreatment had a placement rate of 13.5%. In both instances, children with neglect risk factors were placed at almost three times the rate as children with other maltreatment factors [$\chi^2(5, n = 1380) = 108.97, p < .001$]. However, placement rates are equivalent for those at risk due to neglect and those at risk due to other maltreatment, once a child has had two or more prior placements.

Question 4: What factors are associated with placement after intensive family preservation treatment?

The preceding analyses showed that prior placements and neglect as a reason for risk of placement are clearly related to the probability of placement. It was also of interest to determine: (a) what additional factors might be related to placement, (b) how these additional factors relate to prior placements and reason for risk of placement, and (c) how well all factors identified as related to placement could predict actual placement outcome. A series of stepwise multiple discriminant analysis was conducted to simultaneously answer these three questions. The stepwise technique was selected because it allows for the selection of a "best set" of predictors from a group of measures potentially related to a classification variable, such as placement outcome, while concurrently describing the relationship between the selected measures. It should be noted that the selection of measures in our case was based on the concept of using all available data, rather than an a priori theory concerning what constituted high risk children and families.

In the first analysis, we focused on child indicators. The set of potential predictors included in the analysis, along with their means, is presented in Table 5.4. Only 1,576 of the 1,740 study children were available for the analysis due to missing data on one or more of the analysis variables. This sample is larger than one described in Table 5.3, however, since we were able to include in the discriminant analysis siblings not identified as at risk. The results of the analysis are summarized in Table 5.5. Eleven predictors were identified as adding to the discrimination between children who were placed and those who were not at a probability level of <.15. The overall multivariate test statistics indicate that, taken together, these 11 predictors can significantly discriminate between children who were placed and those who were not placed ($p < .0001$). The R^2s are an indication of the amount of the variance accounted for by each indicator. They provide an indication of

Table 5.4 Means of Variables Provided to the Child Indicator Based Stepwise Multiple Disriminant Analysis by Placement Status

	Placement status	
Child indicator variable	Placed (n=229)	Not placed (n=1347)
Child Well Being Scales at intake		
Abusive physical discipline	81.5	73.5
Deliberate deprivation of food/water	99.1	98.5
Physical confinement or restriction	95.9	96.7
Threat of abuse	74.6	78.4
Child's family relations	77.1	82.5
Child's misconduct	76.0	80.3
Child Well Being Scales at termination		
Abusive physical discipline	92.5	94.7
Deliberate deprivation of food/water	99.2	99.1
Physical confinement or restriction	96.9	97.7
Threat of abuse	79.2	88.4
Child's family relations	83.6	88.5
Child's misconduct	78.1	86.2
Coping behavior of child	74.9	78.4
Other variables		
Age	6.5	6.8
Sex	1.5	1.5
Ethnic origin (Caucasian/other)	1.5	1.5
Location (at home/not at home)	1.2	1.1
Number of prior placements	1.0	0.5
Reason for risk = abuse (Y/N)	1.8	1.8
Reason for risk = neglect (Y/N)	1.5	1.9
Reason for risk = sexual abuse (Y/N)	1.9	1.9

the absolute ability of an indicator to discriminate between children who were placed and those who were not and an indication of the importance of a particular variable to make that discrimination relative to other variables. (It should be noted that the R^2s reported are partial R^2s. This means that the values listed in the table are adjusted for the other variables included in the equation. That is, the values account for variance given the other variables in the equation. To the extent that variables in the equation share variance, any of the individual predictors could account for more variance alone than

Table 5.5 Stepwise Disriminant Analysis Between Children Who Were Placed and Children Who Were Not Placed

Multivariate test statistics

Statistic and value	F-Value	df	p<
Wilks' Lambda = 0.864	22.367	11, 1564	.0001
Pillai Trace = 0.136	22.367	11, 1564	.0001

Partial R^2 s and Fs when entered

Variable name	Partial R^2	F when entered	p<	Standardized canonical coefficient
Number of prior placements	0.0487	80.491	.0001	0.48
Reason for risk of removal is neglect	0.0350	57.092	.0001	−0.45
Threat of abuse at termination	0.0267	43.089	.0001	−0.44
Abusive physical discipline	0.0084	13.264	.0003	0.27
Child's misconduct at termination	0.0065	10.244	.0014	−0.24
Child's location (home/not at home)	0.0064	10.140	.0015	0.23
Deliberate deprivation of food/water	0.0042	6.599	.0103	0.20
Physical confinement/restriction	0.0027	4.260	.0392	−0.14
Child/family relations	0.0022	3.387	.0659	−0.20
Child's misconduct	0.0017	2.680	.1018	0.16
Reason for risk of removal is abuse	0.0014	2.173	.1406	0.12

NOTE: All measures are at intake unless otherwise noted.

when considered with other variables.) The table also includes standardized canonical coefficients for the selected predictors. These may be viewed as comparable to beta weights in a multiple regression in that they are indicative of the relative importance of each predictor in the discrimination between the groups. Not surprisingly, these coefficients correspond fairly well to the partial R^2s.

Inspection of Table 5.5 suggests that number of prior placements, neglect as a reason for risk of removal, and threat of abuse at termination are most important in the discrimination between children who were placed and those who were not. The issue of overlap in variance between predictors may be addressed by an inspection of the correlations among the predictors that are shown in Table 5.6. Given the large sample size, most of the correlations are statistically different from zero. Few, however, appear to be practically significant. Child's misconduct at intake is related to the same measure at

Table 5.6 Pearson Product-Moment Correlations Among Variables
Selected in the Child Indicator Based Stepwise Multiple
Discriminant Analysis[a]

Variables[b]	A	B	C	D	E	F	G	H	I	J	K
A	1.0	−.13	−.07	−.03	−.21	−.12	−.03	−.03	−.12	−.21	.00
B		1.0	−.07	−.26	−.05	−.14	−.01	−.12	−.12	−.07	−.48
C			1.0	.23	.26	−.04	.12	.10	.29	.17	.17
D				1.0	.16	−.01	.09	.21	.30	.28	.48
E					1.0	−.01	.05	.13	.50	.68	.06
F						1.0	−.03	.02	−.02	−.02	.05
G							1.0	.14	.12	.08	.03
H								1.0	.20	.18	.14
I									1.0	.59	.17
J										1.0	.14
K											1.0

NOTE: All variables were measured at intake unless otherwise noted.
[a]All correlations above 0.06 in absolute value are significant with p values < .01.
[b]A = Number of prior placements; B = Reason for risk of removal is neglect; C = Threat of abuse at termination; D = Abusive physical discipline; E = Child's misconduct at termination; F = Child's location (home/not at home); G = Deliberate deprivation of food/water; H = Physical confinement/restriction; I = Child/family relations; J = Child's misconduct; K = Reason for risk of removal is abuse.

follow-up and to family relations at intake. This appears to have reduced the variance accounted for by child's misconduct in the analysis. Abuse as a reason for risk of removal is related to both neglect as a reason for risk of removal and abusive physical discipline. This probably reduced the variance accounted for by abuse as a reason for risk of removal, but it should be noted that the relationship between abuse as a reason for removal and neglect as a reason for risk of removal is to some degree an artifact due to the coding structure. The majority (although not all) of those not at risk of removal due to neglect were at risk of removal due to abuse.

The final result of the first multiple discriminant analysis is presented in Table 5.7. The classification table shown is the result of computing composite scores for each child, based on the linear combination of the 11 predictors selected by the analysis, and comparing those scores to the means of the placed and not placed groups on the same composite scores. Each child is predicted to belong either to the placed or not placed group, and the correspondence between the predicted and actual state for each child is the tabulation shown. It may be noted that, although the analysis could not account for a large portion of the variance, the linear combination of the 11

Table 5.7 Classification Analysis from the Prediction Equation Developed in the Child Indicator Based Stepwise Multiple Discriminant Analysis

	Predicted status		
Actual status	Not-placed	Placed	Total n
Not-placed	880 (65.33)	467 (34.67)	1347
Placed	61 (26.64)	168 (73.36)	229
Total n	941 (59.71)	635 (40.29)	1576

NOTE: Cell contents are frequency and (percent of row).

variables was able to predict placement status well above the chance level. We were able to predict correctly the placement status of 73.36% of those who were placed and 65.33% of those who were not placed. It may be argued that at least some children who were predicted as placed, but not actually placed, should have been placed. Thus, the 65.33% success rate for predicting unplaced children may be an underestimate of the value of the prediction equation.

Although the linear combination of variables selected by the multiple discriminant analysis was able to successfully predict placement outcome at a level well above chance, the 11 variables together account for only about 15% of the variance in the analysis. Certainly, based on our understanding of the service model, one might posit that such family factors as the parents' willingness to cooperate with the therapists, the amount of service provided, and the resolution of various problem areas would also be among other variables that are important. To determine whether such factors are related to placement after receiving intensive in-home service, a second stepwise multiple discriminant analysis was conducted. In this second case, family-based measures were the focus of the analysis.

Table 5.8 presents the list of family based variables evaluated by the stepwise discriminant analysis. Means for families with one or more children placed and means for families without any children placed are included in the presentation. The results of the analysis are summarized in Table 5.9. A total of 105 of the 709 study families had to be eliminated from the

Table 5.8 Means of Variables Provided to the Family Indicator Based Stepwise Multiple Discriminant Analysis by Placement Status

Family indicator variable	Placed (n=123)	Not placed (n=479)
Intake Child Well Being scores		
Physical health care	86.4	89.9
Nutrition/diet	81.3	87.5
Clothing	91.5	94.5
Personal hygiene	90.2	94.2
Household furnishings	88.1	91.4
Overcrowding	85.6	88.6
Household sanitation	83.6	89.9
Security of residence	94.4	96.3
Availability of utilities	95.3	97.2
Physical safety in home	81.7	88.6
Mental health care	67.0	73.7
Supervision of younger children	79.3	84.9
Arrangements for substitute child care	83.8	88.6
Money management	86.5	90.8
Parental capacity for child care	64.0	73.6
Continuity of parenting	75.7	82.4
Parental recognition of problems	51.3	56.9
Parental motivation to solve problems	67.3	73.3
Parental cooperation with case planning/services	69.5	76.9
Support for principal caretaker	83.0	87.7
Availability/accessibility of services	82.3	84.8
Parental acceptance of/affection for children	67.0	75.0
Parental approval of children	75.3	78.8
Parental expectations of children	72.4	76.1
Parental consistency of discipline	76.6	79.1
Parental teaching/stimulation of children	75.3	82.2
Child Well Being scores at termination		
Physical health care	92.6	95.7
Nutrition/diet	86.2	92.2
Clothing	94.3	96.0
Personal hygiene	93.3	96.0
Household furnishings	90.7	93.5
Overcrowding	88.6	90.3
Household sanitation	87.4	92.7
Security of residence	96.1	97.8
Availability of utilities	97.1	98.5
Physical safety in home	87.3	91.4
Mental health care	79.6	84.7

continues

Table 5.8 continued

Family indicator variable	Placed (n=123)	Not placed (n=479)
Supervision of younger children	86.4	91.2
Arrangements for substitute child care	89.9	94.3
Money management	88.0	94.5
Parental capacity for child care	71.3	80.4
Continuity of parenting	85.8	92.1
Parental recognition of problems	62.0	75.1
Parental motivation to solve problems	74.4	83.4
Parental cooperation with case planning/services	73.2	84.2
Support for principal caretaker	87.7	91.1
Availability/accessibility of services	84.5	87.6
Parental acceptance of/affection for children	74.6	83.8
Parental approval of children	79.3	83.8
Parental expectations of children	77.7	83.8
Parental consistency of discipline	82.2	87.3
Parental teaching/stimulation of children	80.8	87.3
Other variables		
Primary caretaker sex	1.9	1.9
Primary caretaker age	31.5	31.3
Primary caretaker ethnic origin (Caucasian/other)	1.4	1.4
Primary caretaker education	11.5	11.8
Primary caretaker employment status (employed/unemployed)	1.8	1.7
Family status (birth parents together/other)	1.8	1.7
Family income category	4.0	4.7
Receiving public assistance (Y/N)	1.2	1.4
Investigations since referral (Y/N)	1.4	1.8
Number of children in family	2.4	2.5
Number of children in family at risk of placement	2.1	2.1
Number of children not at home	0.4	0.3
Number of children with prior placements	0.7	0.6
Number of children under 5	1.2	1.1
Number of children 6–10	0.7	0.8
Number of children 11–15	0.5	0.5
Number of children over 16	0.1	0.1
Total caseworker travel time for the family	8.7	9.9
Total direct service time for the family	29.5	32.9
Total collateral service for the family	15.8	17.8
Intensity of services (days on which services rendered/days in program)	0.4	0.5

Table 5.9 Stepwise Disriminant Analysis Between Families with One or More Placed Children and Families Without Placed Children

Multivariate test statistics *Statistic and value*	*F-Value*	*df*	*p<*
Wilks' Lambda = 0.749	14.041	14, 587	.0001
Pillai Trace = 0.251	14.041	14, 587	.0001

Partial R^2s and Fs when entered

Variable name	Partial R^2	F when entered	p<	Standardized canonical coefficient
Investigations since referral	0.1351	99.749	.0001	0.70
Parental cooperation with case workers at termination	0.0394	24.552	.0001	0.18
Parental teaching/stimulation of children	0.0169	10.274	.0014	0.15
Number of children 6–10 years	0.0154	9.333	.0024	0.30
Intensity of services	0.0100	6.026	.0144	0.17
Money management at termination	0.0092	5.529	.0190	0.26
Mental health care	0.0080	4.804	.0288	0.19
Continuity of parenting at termination	0.0073	4.366	.0371	−0.15
Total caseworker travel time	0.0073	4.327	.0379	−0.18
Primary caretaker age	0.0072	4.260	.0395	−0.19
Number of children in the family with prior placements	0.0071	4.241	.0399	−0.17
Receiving public assistance	0.0066	3.933	.0478	0.23
Clothing at termination	0.0040	2.352	.1256	−0.14
Recognition of problems at termination	0.0039	2.352	.1277	0.16

NOTE: All measures are at intake unless otherwise noted.

analysis due to missing data. Review of the information presented in the table suggests that whether another investigation of abuse or neglect was conducted after referral to the program is clearly the most important predictor of placement. Although we are unable to determine how many of these investigations are related to neglect issues, recurring investigations are possible indicators of chronic problems that have not been resolved through treatment. A review of the remaining predictors suggests that several factors relating to neglect contribute at least something to the discrimination. For example, teaching and stimulation of the child, money management, mental health care of the child, and continuity of parenting are all facets of care

Table 5.10 Pearson Product-Moment Correlations Among Variables Selected in the Stepwise Multiple Discriminant Analysis of Family Indicators[a]

Variables[b]	A	B	C	D	E	F	G	H	I	J	K	L	M	N
A	1.0	.08	.12	−.08	.04	.19	.07	.15	−.05	.03	−.10	.18	.16	.17
B		1.0	.20	−.02	.08	.38	.06	.16	.06	.04	.00	.14	.22	.50
C			1.0	−.01	.00	.29	.25	.19	.01	.08	−.02	.15	.22	.23
D				1.0	−.08	−.01	−.17	−.05	−.02	.16	−.04	.06	−.10	−.04
E					1.0	−.01	.06	.02	.33	.00	.08	−.07	−.02	.05
F						1.0	.05	.19	−.03	.15	.00	.19	.38	.29
G							1.0	.09	−.06	−.14	−.13	−.02	.11	.11
H								1.0	−.05	.00	−.07	.16	−.12	.16
I									1.0	−.04	.07	−.00	−.12	.04
J										1.0	−.01	.25	.04	.05
K											1.0	−.05	−.01	−.03
L												1.0	.21	.12
M													1.0	.20
N														1.0

NOTE: All measures are at intake unless otherwise noted.

[a]All correlations above 0.10 in absolute value are significant with p values .01.

[b]A = Investigations since referral; B = Parental cooperation with case workers at termination; C = Parental teaching/stimulation of children; D = Number of children 6–10 years; E = Intensity of services; F = Money management at termination; G = Mental health care; H = Continuity of parenting at termination; I = Total caseworker travel time; J = Primary at termination; K = Number of children in the family with prior placements; L = Receiving public assistance; M = Clothing at termination; N = Recognition of problems at termination.

related to neglect. The apparent relevance of the number of children between six and 10 years of age may be related to both a reluctance to place very young children and a reduced need to protect older children who are better able to cope on their own.

The relationship between those variables selected by the multiple discriminant analysis is described by the correlations shown in Table 5.10. As was the case for the correlations between predictors in the child-based analysis, most of the correlations shown are statistically significant due to the large sample size. Only a few are large enough to be of practical concern. One may note that parental cooperation with case workers at termination is related to recognition of problems at termination ($r = .50$) to such an extent that the contribution to the discrimination between the groups of recognition of problems at termination was reduced because of shared variance.

Table 5.11 Classification Analysis from the Prediction Equation Developed in the Family Based Indicator Stepwise Multiple Discriminant Analysis

Actual status	Predicted status		Total
	Not placed	Placed	
Not placed	379 (79.12)	100 (20.88)	479
Placed	29 (23.58)	94 (76.42)	123
Total *n*	408 (67.77)	194 (32.23)	602

NOTE: Cell contents are frequency and (percent of row).

The classification analysis based on the linear combination of the 14 predictors selected in the family indicator-based stepwise multiple discriminant analysis is presented in Table 5.11. Once again, the tabulation represents the comparison of predicted and actual placement status. Despite a relatively small part of total variance accounted for by the discriminant analysis (27%), the results of the classification analysis indicate that placement can be predicted with a reasonable degree of success by the combination of variables selected by the analysis. Placement was predicted correctly for more than 75% of those families placed, and absence of placement was correctly predicted nearly 80% of the time.

Discussion

We have found that, although overall success rates measured in terms of placement prevention may be high, children who are at risk due to neglect have almost 2.5 times the placement rate of children with other types of maltreatment. There is a dramatic difference between children who are at risk due to neglect and those who are at risk for other reasons, regardless of whether they have had prior placements. Placement rates are more equivalent, however, for children who have had two or more placements.

Discriminant analyses conducted using large sets of both child and family-based variables confirm the importance of these factors, but indicate that there are other significant variables related to outcome. Indeed, given the low rates of placement for the total population, and the recognition that there are legal and administrative issues which influence placement decisions, this result is expected. Placement decisions are related to client characteristics and also to such factors as availability of placement resources, statutes and regulations regarding child welfare services, and the judicial process. Nevertheless, the ability to isolate specific concepts that are easily measurable may be very important for policy and program development.

The implications of this analysis are important for both practice and research. Given the high percentage of neglect cases in the child welfare caseload, intensive in-home services must address the service needs of these families. Moreover, the evidence that many of the neglect families have had previous involvement with social services compels practitioners to address how intensive in-home services will meet the needs of such families (Jones, Neuman, & Shyne, 1976; Kaplan, 1986).

The new standards developed by the Child Welfare League of America (1989) redefine family preservation services as "intensive family centered crisis services," and establish the "crisis" as the priority focus of the service.

> The crisis should be viewed by the staff as an opportunity for leverage and for the family members to evaluate their situation and determine how they must change in order to resolve the crisis and remain intact. The crisis should be used to provide the staff with an opportunity for teaching at a time when the family is most amenable to change. . . . After the crisis is resolved the worker should assure the family that arrangements will be made for them to receive follow-up services as needed. (p. 52)

If intensive in-home services are implemented in order to resolve specific crises, chronically neglectful families may require multiple enrollments in intensive in-home programs. Policymakers and administrators will need to assess the impact of this potential. Designing an appropriate array of child welfare and family services, such as day care, family support, respite, and so forth, will be important from both an efficiency and an effectiveness perspective.

We will also need to increase our ability to study the impact of intensive in-home services on different populations. As shown in this paper, neglected children accounted for more than half (52.6%) of the children placed, compared to children at risk due to abuse, emotional maltreatment, sexual abuse, and other forms of maltreatment. However, 72.9% of the children at risk due to neglect were not placed subsequent to receiving services. Therefore, studies that seek to analyze the differentials of lack of success will need to construct the study design carefully. For example, an evaluation of a program with a predicted success rate of 75% would need 500 cases to be able to analyze 125 cases of lack of success. (Retrospective studies are one means of compensating for this problem, but pose other methodological issues. See NAFBS, 1988.) Such studies may help us understand more fully the reasons why some cases of neglect are more difficult to resolve than others. For example, future research may test the hypothesis that the children who did not receive the full benefit of the service were more enmeshed in societal conditions of poverty, such as poor housing, homelessness, and lack of food and clothing, and were more constrained by deeper levels of parental emotional and mental and addictive disabilities than other neglected children.

Although we are increasing our knowledge of the impact of intensive in-home services, new programs will need to look further at the factors that influence placement decisions in order to increase their effectiveness with specific populations, or in order to establish their compatibility with other models of service that also provide alternatives to placement. Future studies will need to examine whether societal factors, family factors, service factors, or regional differences are most influential in contributing to the placement of neglected children who have received intensive in-home services.

References

American Humane Association. (1988). *Highlights of official child neglect and abuse reporting, 1986.* Denver: Author.

American Public Welfare Association. (1988). *Characteristics of children in substitute care and adoption.* Washington, DC: Author.

Barth, R. (1988). Theories guiding home-based intensive family preservation services. In J. Whittaker, J. Kinney, E. Tracey, & C. Booth (Eds.), *Improving practice technology for work with high risk families: Lessons from the "Homebuilders" social work education project* (pp. 91-113). Seattle: Center for Social Welfare Research.

Besharov, D. (1988). How child abuse programs hurt poor children: The misuse of foster care. *Clearinghouse Review, 22*(3).

California Department of Social Services, Family and Children's Services Branch. (1987). *Child welfare services report.* Sacramento: Author.

Child Welfare League of America. (1989). *Standards for services to strengthen and preserve families with children.* Washington, DC: Author.

Daro, D. (1989). *Confronting child abuse: Research for effective program design.* New York: Free Press.

Frankel, H. (1988, March). Family-centered, home-based services in child protection: A review of the research. *Social Service Review,* 137-157.

Fraser, M., Pecora, P., & Haapala, D. (Eds.). (1988). *Families in crisis: Findings from the family-based intensive treatment project.* Salt Lake City: University of Utah, Graduate School of Social Work.

Haapala, D., & Kinney, J. (1979). Homebuilders approach to the training of in-home therapists. In S. Maybanks & M. Bryce (Eds.), *Home based services for children and families.* Springfield, IL: Charles C Thomas.

Hinckley, E., & Ellis, W. F. (1985). An effective alternative to residential placement: Home-based services. *Journal of Clinical Child Psychology, 14*(3), 209-213.

Jones, M. (1987). *Parental lack of supervision.* Washington, DC: Child Welfare League of America.

Jones, M., Neuman, R., & Shyne, A. (1976). *A second chance for families: Evaluation of a program to reduce foster care.* New York: Child Welfare League of America.

Kaplan, L. (1986). *Working with multiproblem families.* Lexington, MA: Lexington Books.

Leeds, S. (1984). *Evaluation of Nebraska's intensive services project: Lincoln and McCook, Nebraska.* Iowa City: National Resource Center on Family Based Services.

Magura, S., & Moses, B. S. (1986). *Outcome measures for child welfare services.* Washington, DC: Child Welfare League of America.

National Commission on Children in Need of Parents. (1979). *Who knows? Who cares? Forgotten children in foster care.* New York: Child Welfare League of America.

National Resource Center on Family Based Services. (1988). *An analysis of factors contributing to failure in family-based child welfare services in eleven family-based agencies: Final report.* Iowa City: Author.

Office of the Attorney General. (1985). *Child abuse prevention handbook.* Sacramento: Author.

Seaberg, J. (1988, Fall). Child Well-Being Scales: A critique. *Social Work Research & Abstracts,* 9-15.

Walter R. McDonald & Associates, Inc. (1990). *Plan for a national child abuse and neglect information system: Final report* (Contract No. 105-88-1731). Washington, DC: National Center on Child Abuse and Neglect.

Yuan, Y., McDonald, W., Wheeler, C., Struckman-Johnson, D., & Rivest, M. (1990). *Evaluation of AB 1562 in-home care demonstration projects: Final report* (Contract No. KED6012). Sacramento: Office of Child Abuse Prevention.

PART II:

Conceptual and Policy Issues

6

Context and the Structure of Practice:

Implications for Research

MARTHA MORRISON DORE

Introduction

From a systems perspective, the context of social services is a constantly evolving, ever-changing environment composed of overlapping and intersecting elements. These elements include, but are not limited to, the immediate sponsoring organization, its interorganizational network, currently existing public policy, and the sociopolitical environment of the era. In the United States, over the past two decades, the sociopolitical environment has embraced a return to family values, a renewed emphasis on the important role played by the family in the nurture and socialization of its members. Emergence of the family as the preferred locus of care began long before the 1980s and the Reagan Administration's conservative perspective on social services. Since the early 1960s, a snowballing shift has occurred in public sentiment and social policy, away from long-term out-of-home care of all types: care for the infirm aged; for adults who are mentally ill or developmentally or physically disabled; and, particularly, for children with a range of special problems and needs. Federal legislation, beginning with the Community Mental Health and Mental Retardation Centers Act in 1963, is a litany of efforts to diminish the use of long-term congregate care for children and adults and to establish family and community as the first-line resource for persons with special needs. Subsequent legislative, administrative, and judicial decision making has reflected a climate of opinion favoring family and community-based care.

Recognition of the need to support families in their efforts to provide such care has been slower in developing, however. Massive changes in the structure and function of the family, a tripling in the number of mother-only households in slightly more than a decade, and a 57% increase in the number of households in which both parents are employed outside the home have occurred simultaneously with the renewed emphasis on family as the preferred locus of care for individuals with special needs of all types (Levitan, Belous, & Gallo, 1988). As a result, the family is less available as a source of nurture and support at the same time as it is being asked to expand these functions.

By the mid-1970s the momentum of the deinstitutionalization movement had highlighted the lack of appropriate and sufficient community-level programs to meet the needs of caregiving families (Dore & Guberman-Kennedy, 1981). Significant growth in the foster care rolls during that period suggested that families were collapsing under the stresses they were experiencing, including the stress of caring for special-needs children without adequate community supports. Efforts to respond to these warning signs forced legislators, administrators, and program planners to look for more satisfactory ways to preserve vulnerable families and help them better care for their children.

Family Preservation as Public Policy in Three Streams of Care

One of the most significant pieces of federal legislation in support of preserving families at risk of family breakdown has been PL 96-272, the Adoption Assistance and Child Welfare Act, passed in 1980. This legislation made family preservation and the prevention of out-of-home placement a formal part of the child-serving mandate, particularly in the child welfare stream. In the decade since its passage, a small revolution has occurred in the conceptualization of child welfare services. Significant shifts have taken place in expectations of service delivery staff, definitions of successful intervention, and the parameters of child welfare decision making (McGowan, 1988).

Supporting families in their caregiving function, in an effort to prevent out-of-home residential or institutional placement, has been the focus of public policy in other child-serving streams as well. The Child and Adolescent Service System Program (CASSP) initiative from the National Institute of Mental Health has actively supported the inclusion of families as partners in the treatment of children with mental or emotional problems. Funded by

NIMH in 1983 in response to the lack of public mental health services for children identified by Jane Knitzer in her book, *Unclaimed Children,* the initial goal of the CASSP initiative was to increase child and adolescent mental health service coordination at the state level (Friedman & Algarin, 1989). However, as the program has evolved, it has increasingly focused on the needs of families in caring for this particular group of special needs children. Although CASSP does not provide funds for direct services, it has influenced service delivery through efforts such as the Families as Allies project at Portland State University, which provides training to parents and professionals across the country. It has strongly supported the development of parent advocacy and support groups such as the Parents Involved Network (PIN), which lobbies on both the state and federal levels for increased mental health services for children and supportive services for their families. CASSP has also funded research on the use of intensive family preservation services with emotionally disturbed children and their families, resulting in the addition of this service type to the continuum of children's mental health services in several states (Stroul, 1988).

In the juvenile justice stream, a consensus had emerged by the early 1970s that community-based alternatives were effective in reducing recidivism among youthful offenders. This sentiment was reflected in the Juvenile Justice and Delinquency Prevention Act of 1974, which has shaped juvenile justice policy since that time (Curran, 1988). This policy calls for the removal of status offenders from secured facilities, including training schools, detention centers, and adult jails, and the diversion of such youngsters from juvenile court processing through preadjudicatory interventions such as family counseling (Galvin & Blake, 1984; Schwartz, Jackson-Beeck, & Anderson, 1984).

While community-based alternatives in the juvenile justice stream have primarily meant smaller, more accessible, and open residential programs located close to home and community, there is some evidence that linkages to the child welfare stream have resulted in growing attention to family as the focus of prevention services (Lerman, 1984). In addition, because the behavior of youthful offenders, particularly status offenders, has often proved amenable to interventions based on social learning theory, interventions which can be taught to parents and other family members, a variety of family-based treatment models has been developed for preventing recidivism and subsequent institutional placement of delinquent youth (Alexander & Parsons, 1973; Gordon, Arbuthnot, Gustafson, & McGreen 1988; Patterson, 1980).

The Programmatic Response
to Family Preservation Policy

One of the manifestations of the renewed valuing of family as a frontline resource is the significant growth of what are often termed intensive family preservation services. Programs offering these services take many names locally and programmatically, but share essential characteristics. They focus services on the family unit rather than on individual family members. They are of short duration and high intensity, meaning that there are many family contacts within a relatively brief period of time. They are crisis-oriented, seeing families on short notice, 24 hours a day and seven days a week. And, finally, clinicians in such programs carry relatively small caseloads and work with families primarily in the family home.

Despite these common elements, however, there is wide variety in how such programs are structured. It is argued here that these structural variations may be viewed as reflecting the contexts in which family preservation programs are embedded, the child-serving streams in which they are located. And, further, that current inadequacies in research on intensive family preservation services may be reflective of the failure of researchers and evaluators to appreciate these contextually based influences on service delivery. Finally, recommendations will be made for identifying these contextual differences and taking them into consideration in evaluating effectiveness of intensive family preservation services.

Family Preservation Services in Context

Although intensive family preservation services are currently most thoroughly developed in the child welfare stream, as previously discussed, such programs are increasingly being employed in the children's mental health and juvenile justice streams as well. Some intensive family preservation service programs serve children from all three systems, and some programs have been implemented that cut across all three systems. Thus there is convergence across systems with respect to both populations and programs. Nevertheless, how these three major child-serving streams have *traditionally viewed* their individual missions with regard to children and their families has important implications for the development of intensive family preservation services. Table 6.1 graphically illustrates potential contextual differences across the three child-serving streams discussed here. In each stream of care there can be fundamental differences in: (a) orientation to problem location; (b) focus of concern; (c) the traditional response to that concern; and, (d) currently held beliefs about out-of-home care of children.

Table 6.1 Contextual Factors in Family Preservation Services

| | Service Stream | | |
	Child Welfare	Mental Health	Juvenile Justice
1) Stream orienta- tion to problem location	parent	child/parent	child
2) Focus of concern	what has been done to child	how child is functioning	what child has done
3) Traditional response to concern	foster care/ in-home monitoring	psychiatric in- patient/residential treatment/ (ind, fam, grp)	incarceration community tmt through MH/CW systems
4) Function of traditional response	rescue child from family	rescue child or family	rescue community
5) Beliefs about out-of-home care	negative	positive if part of total treatment plan	positive for delin- quents/ negative for status offenders

Basic underlying differences in orientation, in turn, may drive responses to the kinds of problems that define service eligibility in each stream of care. For example, in the child welfare stream, which deals primarily with problems of abuse and neglect, parents are seen as the locus of the problem: they beat, batter, torture, sexually abuse, emotionally abuse, and neglect their children. Children entering the child welfare stream often have emotional or behavioral problems, of course, but these problems are generally viewed as resulting directly from their parents' maltreatment. The traditional focus of concern is *what has been done to children,* not what the children themselves have done.

In the mental health and juvenile justice streams, on the other hand, children are most often identified as needing services because of their own behavior. They are referred for treatment because they defy their parents, teachers, and others in authority; they exhibit bizarre behavior or thought patterns; they drink alcohol or take drugs; they try to kill themselves or to hurt other people. While many professionals in the mental health stream ascribe to theories of human development that see problem etiology in the parent/child interaction and, as a result, seek to include parents in the treatment process, it is the child's functioning, *what he/she has done,* that has traditionally been the focus of concern in the mental health stream.

In the juvenile justice stream, there is often even more concern with the child's behavior as a phenomenon separate from the family environment. Preeminent theories of causes of delinquency, on which policy responses have been based, have stressed social, structural, political, or even biological factors. As a consequence, parents are seldom involved in juvenile justice interventions, which have traditionally focused almost exclusively on punishment through containment to prevent repetition of past behavior.

As a result of these differences in orientation to problem location and focus of concern, out-of-home placement has historically served different purposes in the three streams of care. In child welfare, the purpose has been to separate child and parents to prevent further harm to the child. While a secondary purpose may be to give the child a more nurturant environment in which to grow and develop, there is almost always a preceding determination of physical risk. In the mental health stream, the purpose of placement away from home has traditionally been to contain the child for self-protection as well as to isolate him or her from the negative influences of home and community during treatment. In juvenile justice, the purpose of placement has been to remove the child from society, to protect the community from the actions of the child, as well as to punish the child and deny him or her the support and comfort of familiar surroundings.

As discussed in the introduction to this chapter, recent changes in attitudes and beliefs regarding the significant role of the family in child development and its potential contribution/obligation in the care of children with special needs have resulted in mandated efforts in all child-serving streams to decrease the incidence of out-of-home care of children. However, this social mandate has received differential responses from the three streams of care under discussion, often resulting in widely varying conceptualizations of the purpose and goals of family preservation in a total continuum of services to children and youth with special problems and needs.

Context and Models of Practice

Table 6.2 illustrates how the contextual characteristics of each child-serving stream discussed in relation to Table 6.1 may have influenced the development of models of intensive family preservation services across streams of care. For example, because of contextual differences in beliefs regarding the role and function of out-of-home care in each stream, outcome

Table 6.2 Comparative Characteristics of Intensive Family Preservation Services by Service Stream

	Service Stream		
	Child Welfare	*Mental Health*	*Juvenile Justice*
1) Goals of intensive family preservation services	prevent placement/stabilize family/enhance parenting skills	prevent unplanned placement/enhance family & child functioning	protect community/prevent future destructive behavior
2) Theory base for intensive family preservation services	crisis intervention/social learning/ecological	systems theory/theories of stress & coping/ psychodynamic (ego psychology)	systems theory/social learning theory
3) Focus of intensive family preservation services	family in crisis parent deficits/instrumental needs	interaction of individual, family, environmental systems	family system/ child behavior
4) Structure	30-60 days	6+ months	6+ months
5) Primary outcome measures	placement rates	family/child functioning	recidivism rates
Primary sources	Kinney et al. (1977) Kinney et al. in Whittaker et al. (1988) Pecora, Fraser, & Haapala (in press)	Reid, Kagan, & Schlosberg (1988) Dore (1988) Dore (1989)	Gordon et al. (1988) Tavantzis et al. in Merkin & Koman (1985)

goals of intensive family preservation services with regard to out-of-home placement can differ. For instance, placement prevention tends to be the primary, if not only, outcome goal of such services in the child welfare stream. While assurances may be sought that a child will not be further abused or neglected, little attention may be given to insuring positive long-term social and emotional outcomes for the child who remains in his or her family.

On the other hand, while family preservation and the prevention of placement in residential care are also important outcome goals of intensive family preservation services in the mental health sector, change in the child's functioning is often an equally important service outcome. If brief, planned treatment in a residential program or in an inpatient psychiatric facility is necessary to insure this change, then placement is viewed not as treatment failure, but as a facilitating action contributing to the outcome goal of resolution of intrapsychic distress and enhanced child functioning.

In the juvenile justice stream, community protection and prevention of behavior that threatens the social order are the mandated outcome goals. Those who advocate intensive family preservation services in that stream see enhanced family functioning as instrumental to this mandated outcome. Restoring the family's ability to manage and control its youthful member will allow the family to assume the social control function historically relinquished to the state.

Although a variety of intervention models are currently in use in intensive family preservation programs in the child welfare stream, perhaps none is as widely employed or enjoys as much institutional support as Homebuilders (Knitzer & Cole, 1989). This model of intensive family preservation services, developed in Tacoma, Washington, in the 1970s, is based on a combination of crisis intervention and social learning theories (Barth, 1988). It is purposefully designed to be a structured, short-term intervention of 30 to 60 days' duration (Kinney, 1989). During the treatment period, families are seen as frequently as necessary, most often in their own homes. A family is treated for whatever amount of time is required to stabilize the family system and teach family members, most often parents, new ways of addressing the problems generating the current crisis. For Homebuilders exponents, this crisis is viewed as resulting from the threat of out-of-home placement of a child (Kinney, Haapala, Booth, & Leavitt, 1988).

Based on the orientation of the child welfare stream to locating problems with parents, as illustrated in Table 6.1, it naturally follows that the most widely utilized model of intensive family preservation services, Homebuilders, would emphasize social learning theory, teaching parents new skills for child management. If the desired outcome goal is prevention of child placement, and the belief is that children are placed in out-of-home care because of what is being done, or may be done, to them by their parents, then focusing on changing parental behavior through a retraining process is a logical intervention strategy. Homebuilders-type programs do not claim to change overall family dynamics, but seek only to alleviate the immediate crisis and give parents a replenished repertoire of home and child management skills (Kinney et al., 1988).

The mental health stream has traditionally viewed emotional and/or behavioral problems as originating within the intrapsychic processes or, more recently, in the interaction between the individual and the environment. As a result, psychodynamic theories, theories of stress and coping, or systems theory are more likely to be employed to undergird intensive family preservation services in that stream of care.

One model of intensive family preservation services, the Pennsylvania model, currently in use in 20 sites throughout that state under the auspices of the Children's Division of the State Office of Mental Health, is based on systems theory, emphasizing interactions within the family as well as between the family and its social environment (Dore, 1989; Lindblad-Goldberg & Dore, 1989). The Pennsylvania model uses structural family therapy as its treatment approach, moving the focus of concern away from the individual child as the identified patient and onto the family and family/community interaction. This intensive family preservation model utilizes a six-month time frame, with initial intensive work focused on stabilizing families in crisis. In this framework, the crisis is seen as originating in family system interaction, not from the threat of child placement. In fact, in this schema, out-of-home placement of a family member is viewed as the mechanism whereby families resolve their intrasystem struggles and return to homeostasis. The goal of treatment in the Pennsylvania model is to expand the family's competence, both as a system and individually, by helping members change current patterns of transactions within the family and between family and community systems. In this way, a family is helped to make better use of its internal resources as well as resources in its environment (Lindblad-Goldberg & Dore, 1989).

Intensive family preservation services have a more limited history in the juvenile justice stream than in the mental health system and, especially, in the child welfare system. Available studies indicate that, while systems theory is the generally accepted theory base for the few such programs in juvenile justice, these often include a strong behavior change component, which engages parents in learning new techniques for managing deviant child behavior. Research on intensive family preservation models in the juvenile justice system indicates that brief, time-limited, crisis-oriented approaches are less successful, hence most programs in this stream are of at least six months' duration (Gordon et al., 1988; Gordon et al., 1988; Tavantzis, Tavantzis, Brown, & Rohrbaugh, 1985).

Research on Intensive Family Preservation Services in Three Streams of Care

The emerging body of research on intensive family preservation services clearly illustrates stream-of-care differences in designating outcome goals. The preponderance of studies of such services in the child welfare stream use prevention of out-of-home placement as the primary, if not sole, measure of program success. While some research, such as Fraser, Pecora, and Haapala's study of Homebuilders programs in Washington State and Utah, has employed measures of change in family and child functioning and in social support, in most reported studies, program success is equated with placement prevention (Frankel, 1988; Fraser, Pecora, & Haapala, 1988; Wald, 1988). For example, Bribitzer and Verdieck (1988) report on their evaluation of the Family Program, "an intensive home-based family centered program ... providing intensive in-home support and treatment to families with children in the custody of the county child welfare departments." This study defines successful outcome as "return of legal custody to parents or emancipation as deemed appropriate by the caseworker." Successful outcomes according to this definition were achieved in 55% of cases. Unsuccessful cases included those in which residential or foster care was continued, as well as those in which the child involved was placed in the custody of relatives (p. 261). The authors, like others who use placement as the single dependent variable, go on to identify characteristics of children and families that are associated with "outcome success," that is, return of legal custody to the family.

Like Bribitzer and Verdieck (1988), Szykula and Fleischman (1985) describe their research with a child protective service population "considered at risk for protective placement out of their natural homes because of abuse." This analysis of a social learning approach to family preservation, in which parents were taught "to apply noncorporal forms of discipline" and "to rely more heavily on positive reinforcement," describes two separate studies. In the first, families in which a parent or child was determined to have mental or emotional problems or a "significant handicap" were eliminated from the treatment group, and an A-B-A repeated treatment experimental design was employed. The sole dependent measure was data on overall placement rates in the agency before and after the intervention took place. Despite the clear behavioral change orientation of the intervention, there is no indication that the researchers measured changes in the experimental families' use of corporal punishment or positive reinforcement before and after the intervention took place.

In the second study reported on by Szykula and Fleischman (1985), Child Protective Services families were randomly assigned to experimental (social learning treatment) and control (usual CPS services) groups. These two groups were further divided into more difficult and less difficult cases, based on number of abuse reports and number of family problems. Again, child placement was the only outcome measured. While there were statistically significant differences in the number of children placed from the less difficult experimental (8%) and control groups (38%), there were no such differences found between placements from the more difficult cases in the two groups (64% versus 45%). In fact, slightly more experimental children than control children were placed.

Similarly, AuClaire and Schwartz (1986) failed to find significant differences in the number of post-treatment placements between control and experimental group adolescents in their study of family systems-based intensive family preservation programs in Minnesota. However, these authors did find significant differences in the number of placement days utilized by the two groups, with subjects who had received intensive family preservation services experiencing nearly 1,900 fewer placement days than control group members.

The AuClaire and Schwartz study suggests that placement as an event taken out of context is a poor indicator of the effects of intensive family preservation services, that absence of placement may or may not reflect more substantive changes in family or child functioning. AuClaire and Schwartz's findings indicate that it is not the event of placement, but its use in the context of treatment that may be significant in assessing treatment effectiveness. Indeed, the relationship between treatment and placement as negative outcome is unsupported in most current research. In some cases, increased numbers of planned, short-term placements may reflect greater clinical understanding and support of the family's need for respite and regeneration.

Although, as stated previously and as illustrated by Table 6.1, the traditional focus of concern in the child welfare stream is on what has been done, or may potentially be done, by parents to their children. Not a single study of intensive family preservation services outcomes with a child welfare population has reported determining occurrence of abuse or neglect in families during treatment. And while a number of studies have followed treated families over time, some for up to two years after termination of services, posttreatment placement, rather than subsequent incidence of neglect or abuse, is the dependent measure of choice. In states like Pennsylvania, where there must be actual physical evidence of abuse on which to found a protective services case, it is not difficult to imagine that there are many cases of abuse and neglect that do not result in out-of-home placement.

There is also a paucity of data on the effectiveness of the social learning component of brief, crisis-oriented treatment models such as Homebuilders. While developing new problem-solving and parenting skills are repeatedly cited as goals of Homebuilders treatment, none of the available studies of this model report specifically measuring changes in these behaviors (Kinney et al., 1988; Kinney, Madsen, Fleming, & Haapala, 1977).

On the other hand, an increasing number of studies of intensive family preservation services in the child welfare stream, including the Fraser et al. study of Homebuilders programs, are reporting using the Child Welfare League of America's Child Well-Being and Family Measurement Scales to measure changes in child and family functioning over time (see this volume: K. Nelson, Chapter 4; Pecora, Fraser, & Haapala, Chapter 1; and Yuan & Struckman-Johnson, Chapter 5). However, serious questions have been raised about the conceptual foundation as well as the construct and criterion validity of these scales (Seaburg, 1988). In addition, they have not been standardized on families outside the child welfare stream. Therefore, there are no clinical cutting scores on which to base understanding of degree of change over time.

The lack of an identifiable conceptual foundation for the Child Well-Being Scales is particularly relevant to the discussion here. If research on intensive family preservation services is to do more than answer the question of the efficacy of such services in preventing child placement, the outcome measures used must measure outcomes supported by an intervention's theoretical foundation. The Homebuilders model, for example, is based on crisis intervention theory and social learning theory (Barth, 1988). Crisis intervention theory postulates that crises have specific temporal parameters, that individuals and families in crisis are more open to outside intervention and to learning new coping mechanisms than when they are experiencing a steady state. The Homebuilders model uses this "window of opportunity" to engage families in structured learning of new child, self, and household management skills. The model reflects a belief that families get into trouble and children are placed, not because of underlying family pathology, but because they lack appropriate strategies for coping with the problems of daily life (Haapala & Kinney, 1988).

Outcome measures, then, must reflect that theoretical base. Testing the effectiveness of Homebuilders programs, using measurements developed from a different theoretical perspective, as, for example, using the FACES

III, which was developed to test Olson's Circumplex Model of family functioning, fails to link outcome with the intervention and gives no meaningful information about refinement or future applications of the model. For even if effectiveness of intensive family preservation services in preventing child placement can be solidly established, without in-depth understanding of how placement was prevented, the ability to adapt and apply such services is severely circumscribed.

Published research on intensive family preservation services in the mental health and juvenile justice streams is much more limited than in the child welfare stream. Data from one program site using the Pennsylvania model show that 77% of children identified as having severe emotional or mental problems at intake were still with their families at six-month follow-up (Lindblad-Goldberg, Stern, Stone, & Dore, 1989). However, descriptive information from that site reveals that some of these children had experienced brief, planned psychiatric hospitalizations on a nonemergency basis during treatment or in the follow-up period.

Preliminary data on 204 families treated in 18 intensive family preservation programs in Pennsylvania found a statistically insignificant increase in level of child functioning on the Global Assessment Scale, a clinician rating scale, between intake and termination, but highly significant improvements in family functioning in all areas of family interaction measured by the McMaster Family Assessment Device, a self-report measure completed by all family members above the age of 10 (Dore, 1990). Three-month follow-up data on a small proportion of the 204 families treated in the Pennsylvania programs found that about 25% of families had experienced an out-of-home placement in the mental health system either during treatment or since termination. However, these placements tended to be planned and of briefer duration than pre-treatment placements.

A retrospective study of outcomes for a sample of the 109 families served between 1984 and 1987, in an intensive family preservation services program at the Philadelphia Child Guidance Clinic, found that, in the one to three years since termination, only one identified patient had been hospitalized for psychiatric reasons. This program, which served as the prototype for the Pennsylvania model described earlier, serves low-income, minority families in one catchment area of West Philadelphia. Its primary goal is to stabilize families at risk of family breakdown, to prevent the psychiatric hospitalization of a child with identified mental or emotional problems, and to reintegrate into their families children returning from mental health placements. Indicators of family and child functioning, such as school attendance, employment, and stable living arrangements, show that 71% of these former mental health clients and their families had made positive post-treatment adjustment (Dore, 1988).

Again, the importance of tying outcome measures to program goals and to underlying conceptual theory regarding etiology of family breakdown must be stressed. In the mental health stream, where the family's elemental role in caring for special needs children is only beginning to be acknowledged and supported, it is critical that evaluation of intensive family preservation services reflects a systemic approach to the treatment process. New methods of evaluating family functioning in the context of its relationships with community systems must be utilized if fuller understanding of the family preservation process is to be gained.

In the juvenile justice stream, outcome studies of intensive family preservation programs have used various measures of recidivism as indicators of treatment success. One such study collected data on the number and severity of offenses during a two-year follow-up period (Gordon et al., 1988). Another surveyed social services and probation department referral sources to assess behavior changes and subsequent delinquent acts in treated youth (Tavantzis et al., 1985). Despite an expressed orientation to family systems theory and treatment models based on this theory, neither of these studies reported measuring changes in overall family functioning and its relation to child behavior and subsequent delinquency at termination or follow-up.

Homebuilders has also been used with youthful offenders. Haapala and Kinney (1988) describe the implementation of this model in a program serving 678 status offenders and their families in Washington State. A 12-month follow-up identified an 87% rate of placement avoidance. Again, however, there were no data on changes in family functioning (family conflict was present in 98% of referred families at intake) or on changes in the behavior of the status offending youth.

Conclusion

The development of intensive family preservation programs in the three child-serving streams discussed here provides a unique opportunity to study the influence of service system context on treatment model implementation and evaluation. Despite newly emerging social attitudes and public policies that call for a reorientation of children's services to focus on families, traditional service-stream perspectives influence how this mandate is implemented across streams of care. Recent research indicates that the problems of children tracked into the three service streams discussed here may be more similar than different, that it is often only demographic characteristics, such as income level or race, that determine in which stream a child enters the service system (Lerman, 1984; Schwartz et al., 1984). However, current research on intensive family preservation services suggests that treatment experiences for families and children may be very different across streams of care and that the historical orientation of each stream can influence how even a contemporary service initiative is adapted to fit complex institutional service environments. In turn, observation of the contextual effects on stream-specific implementation of the family preservation mandate can critically inform the next stage of research on the effects of intensive family preservation services.

References

Alexander, J. F., & Parsons, B. V. (1973). Short-term behavioral intervention with delinquent families: Impact on family process and recidivism. *Journal of Abnormal Psychology, 81,* 219-225.

AuClaire, P., & Schwartz, I. M. (1986). *An evaluation of the effectiveness of intensive home based services as an alternative to placement for adolescents and their families.* Minneapolis: University of Minnesota, Hubert H. Humphrey Institute of Public Affairs.

Barth, R. (1988). Theories guiding home-based intensive family preservation services. In J. K. Whittaker, J. Kinney, E. M. Tracy, & C. Booth (Eds.), *Improving practice technology for work with high risk families: Lessons from the "Homebuilders" social work education project* (Monograph No. 6). Seattle: Center for Social Welfare Research, University of Washington.

Bribitzer, M. P., & Verdieck, M. J. (1988). Home-based, family-centered intervention: Evaluation of a foster care prevention program. *Child Welfare, 67*(3), 255-266.

Curran, D. J. (1988). Destructuring, privatization, and the promise of juvenile detention: Compromising community-based corrections. *Crime & Delinquency, 34*(4), 363-378.

Dore, M. M. (1988). *Research on family-based services in a children's mental health program.* Unpublished manuscript, Philadelphia Child Guidance Clinic, Philadelphia.

Dore, M. M. (1989). *Annual report on the intensive home-base mental health services project.* Harrisburg: Office of Mental Health, Division of Child Services, Department of Welfare, Commonwealth of Pennsylvania.

Dore, M. M. (1990, March). *Current findings on the Pennsylvania family-based mental health services for children initiative.* Paper presented at the statewide meeting of county MH/MR coordinators, Harrisburg, PA.

Dore, M. M., & Guberman-Kennedy, K. (1981). Two decades of turmoil: Child welfare services, 1960-1980. *Child Welfare, 60*(6), 371-382.

Frankel, H. (1988). Family-centered, home-based services in child protection: A review of the research. *Social Service Review, 62*(1), 137-157.

Fraser, M., Pecora, P. J., & Haapala, D. A. (1988). *Families in crisis: Selected findings from the family-based intensive treatment project.* Paper presented at the annual program meeting, Council on Social Work Education, Atlanta, GA.

Friedman, B., & Algarin, A. (1989, Summer). CASSP—A fifth anniversary. *Update: Improving services for emotionally disturbed children.* Newsletter published by the Research and Training Center for Children's Mental Health, Florida Mental Health Institute, University of South Florida, Tampa, FL.

Galvin, J., & Blake, G. F. (1984). Youth policy and juvenile justice reform. *Crime & Delinquency, 30*(3), 339-346.

Gordon, D. A., Arbuthnot, J., Gustafson, K. E., & McGreen, P. (1988). Home-based behavioral-systems family therapy with disadvantaged juvenile delinquents. *The American Journal of Family Therapy, 16*(3), 243-254.

Haapala, D. A., & Kinney, J. M. (1988). Avoiding out-of-home placement of high-risk status offenders through the use of intensive home-based family preservation services. *Criminal Justice and Behavior, 15*(3), 334-348.

Kinney, J. M. (1989, October). *What is the Homebuilders program?* Paper presented at the annual meeting of the American Association for Marriage and Family Therapy, San Francisco, CA.

Kinney, J. M., Haapala, D., Booth, C.,& Leavitt, S. (1988). The Homebuilders model. In J. K. Whittaker, J. Kinney, E. M. Tracy, & C. Booth (Eds.), *Improving practice technology for work with high risk families: Lessons from the "Homebuilders" social work education project* (Monograph No. 6). Seattle: Center for Social Welfare Research, University of Washington.

Kinney, J. M., Madsen, B., Fleming, T., & Haapala, D. (1977). Homebuilders: Keeping families together. *Journal of Consulting and Clinical Psychology, 45*(4), 667-673.

Knitzer, J. (1982). *Unclaimed children.* Washington, DC: Children's Defense Fund.

Knitzer, J., & Cole, E. S. (1989). *Family preservation services: The program challenge for child welfare and children's mental health agencies.* New York: The Changing Services for Children Project. Bank Street College of Education.

Lerman, P. (1984). Child welfare, the private sector, and community-based corrections. *Crime & Delinquency, 30*(1), 5-38.

Levitan, S. A., Belous, R. S., & Gallo, F. (1988). *What's happening to the American family?* (Revised ed.). Baltimore: Johns Hopkins University Press.

Lindblad-Goldberg, M., & Dore, M. M. (1989, November/December). Home-based services widely used in USA. *Family Therapy News,* pp. 7, 26.

Lindblad-Goldberg, M., Stern, L., Stone, C. A., & Dore, M. M. (1989, October). *Home-based services to high risk families.* Workshop presentation at the annual meeting of the American Association for Marriage and Family Therapy, San Francisco, CA.

McGowan, B. G. (1988). Family-based services and public policy. In J. K. Whittaker, J. Kinney, E. M. Tracy, & C. Booth (Eds.), *Improving practice technology for work with high risk families: Lessons from the "Homebuilders" social work education project* (Monograph No. 6). Seattle: Center for Social Welfare Research, School of Social Work, University of Washington.

Nelson, K. (1990). Populations and outcomes in eleven family-based child welfare programs. In K. Wells & D. Biegel (Eds.), *Family preservation services: Research and evaluation.* Newbury Park, CA: Sage.

Patterson, G. R. (1980). Treatment for children with conduct problems: A review of outcome studies. In S. Feshbach & A. Fraczek (Eds.), *Aggression and behavior change.* New York: Praeger.

Pecora, P., Fraser, M. W., & Haapala, D. (1990). Intensive home-based family treatment: Client outcomes and issues for program design. In K. Wells & D. Biegel (Eds.), *Family preservation services: Research and evaluation.* Newbury Park, CA: Sage.

Reid, W. J., Kagan, R. M., & Scholsberg, S. B. (1988). Prevention of placement: Critical factors in program success. *Child Welfare, 67*(1), 25-36.

Schwartz, I. M., Jackson-Beeck, M., & Anderson, R. (1984). The "hidden" system of juvenile control. *Crime & Delinquency, 30*(3), 339-346.

Stroul, B. (1988). *Community-based services for children and adolescents who are severely emotionally disturbed. Volume 1: Home based services.* Washington, DC: Georgetown University Child Development Center.

Szykula, S. A., & Fleischman, M. J. (1985). Reducing out-of-home placements of abused children: Two controlled field studies. *Child Abuse and Neglect, 9,* 277-283.

Tavantzis, T. N., Tavantzis, M., Brown, L. G., & Rohrbaugh, M. (1985). Home-based structural family therapy for delinquents at risk of placement. In M. P. Mirkin & S. L. Koman (Eds.), *Handbook of adolescents and family therapy.* New York: Gardner.

Wald, M. (1988). Family preservation: Are we moving too fast? *Public Welfare, 46*(3), 33-38.

Yuan, Y. T., & Stuckman-Johnson, D. L. (In press). Placement outcomes of children served by intensive in-home care projects: The California experience. In K. Wells & D. Biegel (Eds.), *Family preservation services: Research and evaluation.* Newbury Park, CA: Sage.

7

Defining the Target Population for Family Preservation Services

ELIZABETH M. TRACY

Introduction

Intensive family preservation programs have experienced a dramatic increase in popularity as one way to strengthen families and prevent the out-of-home placement of children. These programs are characterized by intensity and brevity of service, coupled with accessibility and flexibility in meeting multiple family needs. Intensive family preservation programs provide a short-term infusion of clinical and concrete resources to families with children at risk of imminent placement. The goals of this service are multiple: (a) to protect children, (b) to maintain and strengthen family bonds, and (c) to stabilize the crisis situation that precipitated the child's referral to an out-of-home placement facility (Whittaker & Tracy, 1990).

Much of the current interest in family preservation, though, has centered around one goal, that of placement prevention. The underlying rationale for the development and expansion of intensive family preservation programs was to provide services earlier and more intensively to families so that children could be enabled to remain at home. Accordingly, intensive family preservation programs have defined their target populations in relation to children at risk of imminent placement.

AUTHOR'S NOTE: Special acknowledgment is extended to Selma Gwatkin, Bellefaire/Jewish Children's Bureau; Earl Landau, Cuyahoga County Department of Human Services; and Jill Kinney, Behavioral Sciences Institute for their review of earlier drafts of this chapter.

A clear statement of the target population—to whom services should be directed—is critical to the design and evaluation of any social service program. A clear definition assists in determining if the program is reaching those clients for whom it was intended to serve and for whom the services are thought to be most effective. It also enables practitioners to compare case outcomes across the life of the program and in contrast to other programs providing similar or different services (Feldman, 1988). Inadequate specification of the target population can result in inappropriate referrals, thus making poor use of staff time and frustrating referral agencies.

The task of defining the target population for intensive family preservation services is not as easy as it might seem. This is due to the fact that intensive family preservation programs serve families and children from a variety of different service streams, funding sources, and referring agencies, each often using its own definitions of the target population. Achieving a statement as to which families are considered eligible for intensive family preservation is at once an ethical, programmatic, and research issue (Wells, in press). From an ethical point of view, it is important to provide services to those families genuinely in need. This requires an ability to assess accurately the need for placement and to ensure equal access to appropriate services. From a programmatic point of view, it is important that intensive family preservation programs reach those families for whom they were intended and who can benefit from the services provided. This requires an ability to establish both appropriate selection criteria for entrance into service and referral procedures that maintain appropriate focus.

From a research perspective, it is important to note that efforts to define the target population broadly may inadvertently include the selection of groups at less immediate risk of placement, and thereby threaten the research to determine whether programs are preventing placement. Some have argued that the cost-effectiveness of intensive family preservation programs is only achieved when these services are reserved for families at risk of imminent placement. Extensions of the service to other families, who may benefit from service but who would not be likely to need placement services, is believed to compromise the fiscal grounds upon which these programs are based (D. Nelson, 1989).

To date, intensive family preservation services have been extended to a number of other populations: children returning from foster care and residential settings, children in adoptive homes that have the potential to disrupt, emotionally disturbed children, delinquent youth, and substance abusers. The extent to which these client populations are at risk of imminent placement, as well as the extent to which they compare with the traditional target group for family preservation services, is unknown. Unless programs can accurately specify and select appropriate target groups, their effectiveness in preventing placement cannot be determined.

The purpose of this chapter is to explore the current definition of the target population for intensive family preservation programs in the child welfare system and to discuss the major factors influencing this definition. A number of conceptual, definitional, and programmatic issues will be discussed as they relate to assessing the need for placement, establishing selection criteria, and implementing referral procedures.

Throughout the chapter, reference will be made to a detailed but non-representative survey of the intake and referral procedures of six family preservation programs in child welfare, some of which are represented in this volume (see Table 7.1). Each of the programs surveyed share general criteria for intensive family preservation services recently established by the Child Welfare League of America (1989), that is, highly intensive service provision (8 to 10 hours per week), caseload size from two to six families, and a service duration of 4 to 12 weeks. Individual programs, though, vary in the intensity of service and design. Each of the six program directors was asked to provide information regarding target population, referral procedures, selection criteria, and relationships with referral sources. Factors used to assess the appropriateness or inappropriateness of referrals were also identified.

Conceptual and Definitional Issues

There is no clear uniform description of families at risk of placement (Magazino, 1983). Many different kinds of problems can precipitate a referral for placement. Children served by intensive family preservation programs in the child welfare stream may receive referrals of children from the child welfare, mental health, or juvenile justice systems. Thus, intensive family preservation programs may serve children at risk of abuse and neglect; children adjudicated as status offenders or delinquents; emotionally disturbed children; children with incapacitated, emotionally disturbed, or cognitively impaired parents; children with developmental disabilities; and adolescents in conflict with family and the community (Bryce, 1982).

While the majority of intensive family preservation programs accept referrals from a wide variety of sources, there are a number of programs that target specific populations at risk, usually based on the source and availability of funding (The National Resource Center on Family Based Services,

Table 7.1 Definition and Selection of the Target Population: Selected Family Preservation Programs

	Homebuilders[a]	Utah family preservation[b]	New Jersey family preservation[c]	Pact Bellefaire[d]	Beech Brook[d]	Parmadale[d]
Definition of target population	–imminent danger of placement –# and type of previous placements –previous use of less intensive services –severity and duration of family dysfunction	–imminent risk of placement –family in crisis –previous use of less intensive services –child(ren)'s safety not jeopardized by remaining in home	–imminent risk of placement –previous use of less intensive services –child(ren)'s safety not jeopardized by remaining in home	–imminent risk of placement –previous use of less intensive services –reunification –stabilization of adoption	–imminent risk of placement –child in danger to self or others –previous use of less intensive services –stabilization of adoption –reunification	–imminent risk of placement –previous use of less intensive services
Time frame for imminent placement	time frame not specified (within 5 days for NY)	within 2 weeks	within 24 hours	time frame not specified	time frame not specified	time frame not specified
Who determines risk of placement	referring workers (child protective services, family reconciliation services)	referring workers (juvenile court, youth services, protective services)	referring workers (division of youth & family services, crisis intervention unit, emergency mental health)	referring workers (division of human services, insurance providers, mental health professionals Bellefaire intake committee)	referring workers (division of human services, juvenile court, mental health board, Beech Brook intake team)	referring workers (HB 440 programs, other county agencies)
Risk assessment models used	Washington State matrix (none in NY)	Utah risk assessment (protective services only)	Illinois matrix (division of youth and family only but not required)	none used	juvenile court uses risk assessment model	juvenile court uses risk assessment model
Family in crisis	imminent placement viewed as crisis	imminent placement viewed as crisis	imminent placement viewed as crisis	family does not need to be in crisis	most families have past crisis period due to time to process referral	not necessarily

continues

141

Table 7.1 continued

	Homebuilders[a]	Utah family preservation[b]	New Jersey family preservation[c]	Pact Bellefaire[d]	Beech Brook[d]	Parmadale[d]
Use of secondary screening	–by intake coordinator –by worker within 3 visits or 3 days	–by FP supervisor –by external screening committee –by worker within first 72 hours	by FP intake worker –by external screener or screening committee (depends on county) –by worker within 3 days	–by program director's review of referral information –by worker after initial interview	–by program director's review of referral information –by worker after initial visit	–by FP director's review of referral information –by worker and supervisor after initial interview
Inappropriate referrals	–child not at risk of placement –no parent/family member willing to participate –child in placement and not returning within 7 days –goal is to keep family together until placement can be secured	–after 72 hours, parent still refuses to participate –child/family safety cannot be guaranteed, e.g. suicidal, unpredictable violence –goal is to keep family together until placement can be secured –sex abuse case if no adjudication and perpetrator in home	–risk of placement due to homelessness –referral source has not tried other less intensive services –no parent willing to participate –case of heavy drug use, psychotic parent	–child not at risk of placement –violent unsafe families –severely mentally retarded parents –if perpetrator of sexual abuse remains in home –no parent/family member willing to participate –actively psychotic or drug-abusing parents	–safety of child cannot be guaranteed –active drug abuse –severe mental illness or retardation –parents not willing to participate –older adolescent does not want to participate	–home is unsafe to enter –family refuses to participate –services beyond scope of FP program are required –active substance abuse by referred/identified client
Family commitment to participate	at least one parent or one family member (e.g. adolescent)—by allowing worker in home	at least one adult—by verbal contract	at least one adult—by verbal contract	at least one parent and identified child by verbal contract	at least one parent and child (if adolescent)—by written contract	at least one parent and identified child—by written contract (sometimes)

continues

142

Table 7.1 continued

Parental functioning as selection criteria	–not factors in screening	–not factors in screening; drug use and endangering factors assessed on a case by case basis	medical status	psychological/emotional factors and drug use are assessed on a case by case basis	substance abuse parents must be willing to address issue and must be sober; mental illness and retardation should not interfere significantly with parenting	substance abusing parents must be willing to enter treatment, mentally ill parents must comply with medication, mentally retarded parents must be able to meet child's basic needs
Safety	cases of extreme danger to family/worker screened out after they have been assessed in the home	cases representing severe safety risk to child even with FP services screened out—cases of sexual abuse screened out unless adjudicated by court and/or perpetrator out of home	supervisor participates in first visit to assess safety—safety issues are planned for—sexual abuse handled in same manner	–safety contracts used between worker and family –violent families are screened out –sexual abuser cannot be home unless participating in treatment	–cases with past history of violence accepted on case by case basis –willingness of parent to protect child from sexual abuse considered –when safety of child at risk, protective services referral made	supervisor and worker determine safety of situation on case by case basis
Catchment area	geographical or county based	geographical boundaries	county-based	any family within 45 minutes drive	county-based	county-based
Reunification services	if child returning home within one week of first visit	provided for some cases of interrupted reunification including adoption disruption	not provided, but have worked to prevent further placement after one child in family has been placed	if child returning home from foster home, hospital or residential treatment –provides service to threatened adoptions and foster placements	if child returning home within week of initiating FP service	as requested by referring agency

continues

143

Table 7.1 continued

	Homebuilders[a]	Utah family preservation[b]	New Jersey family preservation[c]	Pact Bellefaire[d]	Beech Brook[d]	Parmadale[d]
Referral procedures	–phone contact with intake coordinator –recent contact with family noted but not required –joint meeting of referring worker, FP staff and family can be requested but not required –family need not be new to referring agency	–phone contact with intake coordinator –phone contact with screening referral committee –recent contact with family noted but not required –joint meeting of referring worker, FP staff and family can be requested but not required –family need not be new to referring agency	–phone contact with FP intake –FAX referral information forms to FP program –referral source must have had contact with family within past 24 hours –joint meetings/case conferences not done routinely –family need not be new case to referring agency	–phone contact with program director –referral source must have had recent contact with family –joint meeting of referring worker, FP worker and family –family need not be new case to referring agency	–phone contact with program director –referral source must have had recent contact with family –joint meeting not always possible	–phone contact with FP director –recent contact with family not required –family need not be new case to referring agency –joint meetings held when practical
Relationship between FP program and referring agency	contact maintained as requested by referring worker—closing document sent	contact maintained as requested by referral source–termination letter including recommendations sent –beginning, midpoint and end of services report provided where ongoing worker involved	referral source kept up-to-date –termination letter and recommendations sent	–initial assessment, 30–60–90 day reports, and treatment recommendations sent –phone contact as needed	–initial assessment –weekly written reports sent –termination report with recommendations sent	–varies according to agency policy

[a] Serves nine counties in Washington State and operates a program in the Bronx, NYC
[b] Reported for two districts served during 1985-87
[c] Provides services via contracts with eight private agencies.
[d] One of five contracted service providers for Cuyahoga County Division of Human Services (Cleveland)

144

1988). For example, a number of programs are designed to prevent the need for psychiatric hospitalization, residential treatment, and therapeutic group care. Other programs are designed to prevent the need for juvenile detention of delinquent youth; some provide intensive supervision in lieu of detention. A smaller number of programs focus on training and support services to maintain developmentally disabled children in their homes. Some programs are specifically designed for substance-abusing youth. Whatever the specified clientele, each program must define the subgroup of its potential service population and design its intake processes for selection of client families who meet the eligibility criteria as specified by the funding source.

A major influence on the target population is the stated program goal (Frankel, 1988; Magura, 1981; Nelson, Landsman, & Deutelbaum, 1990). This chapter deals primarily with those programs serving families with children at risk of imminent placement and whose primary goal is to prevent out-of-home placement. These programs provide home-based services for families whose children *must* be placed unless some immediate improvement can be effected. It is assumed that families served by these programs face more acute crises and experience a greater number of chronic problems than families served by broad-based preventive programs (Kadushin & Martin, 1988).

Thus, intensive family preservation programs are often conceptualized as placement prevention programs. At the point of referral to family service, "risk of imminent placement" means that someone with authority to place has indicated that the placement process will be initiated unless intensive services are provided. Accurate assessment of "risk of imminent placement" consists of providing answers to several separate questions. First, is removal of the child a necessity, given the child, family, and surrounding circumstances? Second, is removal of the child a certainty at this time? Finally, what is the most appropriate placement and can it be secured immediately? It is also important to point out that placement may represent the best clinical decision for some children and families and should not always be considered as failure. Prevention of what would be an *unnecessary* placement, then, while ensuring the safety of the child within the home, reflects a more accurate goal of family preservation services (Edna McConnell Clark Foundation, 1985).

In fact, the most important single factor defining the target population across all family preservation programs is the child's being at risk of imminent separation from the family. Of the 333 programs listed in the 1988 edition of the National Resource Center's *Annotated Directory of Selected Family-Based Services Programs,* 217 programs identify family preservation as a primary goal (see Table 7.1 as well). This goal may include placement prevention, delay of placement, or shortening of the duration of placement. In addition, many programs require that the family first exhaust all other less-intensive services that might prevent placement, and be in "crisis" at the time of referral (K. Nelson, 1988).

There are, however, a number of difficulties with the current definition of "risk of imminent placement." First, the extent and intensity of the precipitating crisis are not specified, nor are criteria available for assessing the nature of the crisis event. This means that referring workers must assess crises based on their own definitions and judgments. It is assumed that threat of placement constitutes a crisis for the family. Crisis intervention theory holds that crisis increases amenability to change, especially when services are delivered intensively and concurrent with the crisis period (Kinney, Haapala, Booth, & Leavitt, 1989). It is arguable, though, whether the family must be in crisis to benefit from these services (Barth, 1989). It would be helpful, however, if intake standards for defining crisis were available to guide referring agencies.

In practical terms, though, it is often difficult to refer families precisely at the point of crisis. In some programs, especially those in public agencies, cases must be screened by supervisors, resource managers, and/or placement screening committees prior to the family preservation referral. This process can take several weeks, during which time some of the precipitating crisis events may appear to have been resolved, or families may have learned to adjust to them and are no longer motivated to work toward change. In other situations, the family preservation program may be full at the time of referral, with no openings for new cases. This has led some programs to establish waiting lists for family preservation services. The concept of a waiting list is antithetical, however, to the stated purposes of these programs.

Similarly, the concept of "imminent placement" is difficult to implement in practice. An "imminent" event is one that is likely to occur at any moment, but imminence of placement is typically difficult to determine. Family preservation programs must either specify time frames for imminence or else be at the mercy of varying standards of different referring agencies. Is an imminent placement one that will occur within one to two days, within one week, or within one month? Among the programs surveyed in preparation for this chapter, four out of six programs had no specified time frames for determining imminency (Table 7.1).

No placement can be imminent, though, unless it can be secured immediately, and it is becoming increasingly difficult to locate appropriate placements in a timely manner. For this reason, referrals made merely to keep the family together until an out-of-home placement can be arranged are generally considered inappropriate for family preservation services (Haapala, Kinney, & McDade, 1988).

Ideally, families referred to intensive family preservation services will have utilized or exhausted all other less-intensive services. In other words, less-intensive services, such as parent aides or parent groups, have been tried but have not been successful in averting the need for placement. Few programs specify to what extent other services should have been accessed, for how long, and at what intensity. Originally, family preservation services were the service of last resort. This can no longer be assumed. Maryland's "Intensive Family Services" intervenes with high-risk families before protective services are involved and the need for placement has been determined (Kamerman & Kahn, 1989). A county in Pennsylvania makes use of family preservation services early in the life of a case, that is, within six months of intake. Families with problems of a more chronic nature, known to the agency for an extended time period, are not considered eligible for preservation services.

The resulting target population, then, consists of children and families in which placement is not necessary at this time, given appropriate amounts and intensity of services. Intensive family preservation services may be better conceptualized as an alternative to placement than as placement prevention per se. From their inception, family preservation programs were characterized as alternatives to placement. It was evident that children often entered placement by default due to lack of viable options. In other situations, "traditional" services were not sufficient to meet the child's and the family's needs. It was felt that many more children could be enabled to remain at home if services were available, accessible, and offered early and intensively.

The distinction between risk of placement and risk of unnecessary placement is an important one for conceptualizing the target population for family preservation programs. At issue is the representativeness of children served by family preservation services, as compared with children in out-of-home placements. There is some evidence to suggest that family preservation services, as currently designed, are an alternative to placement for only a portion of the population of children at risk of out-of-home care (Wells, 1989).

It is very difficult to contrast and compare characteristics of children and families in out-of-home care with those receiving family preservation services. This is due to different record keeping and reporting methods, making comparisons problematic. No doubt children served by family preservation programs and those children in placement share a number of characteristics, including the predominance of single-parent (female-headed) households, lower socioeconomic status, extensive service history, and the extent and multiple nature of presenting family and child problems (K. Nelson, 1988; Pecora, Fraser, Haapala, & Bartlome, 1987). However, Wells (1989) and Wells and Whittington (1988) concluded from reviewing characteristics of children in placement that commonly employed selection criteria and referral procedures for acceptance into family preservation services might exclude a number of children now in placement from receipt of these services. It is important, therefore, to consider the ways in which particular programmatic features may influence the definition and selection of the target population.

Two final factors influencing the definition of the target population of family preservation programs involve both the distinguishing of at-risk populations from those children in need of placement and the placement decision-making process itself. Until recently, there were few standardized assessment tools or checklists for determining the need for placement. Programs often relied exclusively on worker judgment. Since a number of public agencies have authority to place children, the need for placement and the timing of it may be defined differently by different referral sources. The fact of the matter is that placement represents a complicated process, responsive to a number of worker, agency, child, family, and community factors. Recent and dramatic instances of abuse occurring in a child's home may create a prevailing tendency to place children. On the other hand, instances of abuse that occur in foster homes or group care settings tend to discourage placement of children.

The community context also impacts both the definition of risk of placement and the likelihood that placement will occur. Child and family situations that may trigger a referral for placement in one community may not in another community because of available resources and services. In a resource rich environment, families and social service agencies may have less need to resort to placement. Some examples: Provision of an adequate supply and quality of housing may reduce the number of placements that occur due to homelessness and poor living conditions; drug/alcohol treatment programs that provide day care or respite care may offer a better chance for parents and children to remain together during recovery; and neighborhoods with rich traditions of informal helping may offer types of support of immediate benefit to averting the need for placement.

Programmatic Issues

Selection Criteria

Selection criteria operationally define the rules for screening clients in or out of programs. Selection criteria most often refer to characteristics of the child, family, or surrounding conditions that must exist for the referral to be accepted by a particular program. A number of frequently cited selection criteria and referral procedures are discussed in the following sections as they relate to the types of families served by intensive family preservation programs (Haapala, et al., 1988; Pecora et al., 1987). In addition, Table 7.1 documents the variety of selection criteria employed, even within the limited number of programs surveyed, including such factors as parental functioning, family commitment, and safety issues, among others.

Commitment to Participate

Because family preservation workers provide services in the family's home, all programs require that at least one adult agree to participate in the program (see Table 7.1). Some programs require all family members to agree to participate or, at a minimum, one adult and a child who is an adolescent. Written contracts are often used to make expectations and services clear to all parties and to obtain client commitment. Initial contracts are also frequently used to ensure safety for all family members. For example, the contract may ask family members to refrain from physical violence or to remove weapons during the time period of the intervention.

While family preservation services are voluntary by nature, most families realize that this service represents a last resort to placement, and so may feel coerced to participate in order to keep their child at home. In some areas where funding is available, families may be ordered by the court to participate (e.g., 17% of the families in K. Nelson's study [1988] were court ordered). Finally, a number of programs surveyed (see Table 7.1) indicated that the first contact with the family should be a three-way meeting among the family, the referring worker, and the family preservation worker, in which purposes and goals of the intervention could be clarified.

Child at Risk in the Home

Unless the program is working toward family reunification, most programs require the child either to be in the home or to be returning shortly from an out-of-home placement. The agreed-upon goal for all concerned must be to keep the family together. Family preservation programs typically do not work with families while the child is in placement. In fact, for some programs, placement of the child in certain types of settings, and for specified time periods, would be considered a reason to terminate work with the family.

Parental Functioning

Some programs make an individual assessment on a case-by-case basis of parental functioning, and may exclude those cases in which active substance abuse, mental illness, or cognitive functioning will impair the parent's or parents' ability to participate in the program. In regard to substance abuse, some states (e.g., Maryland) require that substance-abusing parents participate in a detoxification and rehabilitation program prior to their referral for in-home services.

Catchment Area

Some family preservation programs are only funded for referrals from a defined geographic catchment area (e.g., county-based). Often programs consider the travel time involved to reach families and define their catchment area in relation to the worker's accessibility to the family. This is done to achieve accessibility and responsiveness, with most programs ideally wanting the assigned worker to live within less than one hour's drive from the family.

Inappropriate Referrals

Situations that are generally considered inappropriate for referral to family preservation programs include: (a) when the safety of the child cannot be guaranteed or would be jeopardized by remaining in the home; (b) when the child and/or family are unwilling to agree to the service; (c) when the family is homeless since programs do not have the resources to locate emergency housing; (d) when the child is not at risk of placement; and (e) when the safety of the worker cannot be ensured (Haapala et al., 1988). Individual programs may also exclude children over or under particular age groups; children with multiple previous placements; families who have previously received family preservation services; and/or families involved in court proceedings that are likely to result in an order for placement (Feldman, 1988). Feldman points out that newly developed family preservation programs often exclude more families; as their staff competencies grow, they become more comfortable accepting a wider variety of referrals or families with seemingly more complex problems.

Safety

Safety—of the child and of the worker—is an important selection criterion, as well as a reason for termination. Families involved in family preservation programs are typically informed that if the child is in clear danger, staff will make a protective services report and advocate for out-of-home placement. Family preservation staff must achieve a balance between the goal of family preservation and ensuring that the child's safety and treatment needs are met (Wald, 1988). While worker safety is always an issue for social service programs, the issues are heightened for family preservation staff. This is because family preservation staff work flexible hours and in clients' homes versus office settings. They are frequently responsible for dealing with crisis situations on the spot and for independent decision-making.

Organizational Factors

The reality of delivering intensive family preservation services is that selection criteria are often difficult to apply in a consistent manner. One complicating factor has to do with staff changeovers among referral sources, with resulting shifts in program goals. Over time, referring agents may develop "program myths" about whom the program is intended to serve and which referrals are appropriate. Shifts may be real or perceived but, in any event, may result in changes in the number and types of referrals. Shifts may be due to recent experiences with one or more clients—a dramatic success or failure—as well as to rapid or persistent referring staff turnover.

Other complicating factors are a result of funding patterns and sources of funding. Selection criteria may be more stringent, depending on the source of funding. For example, programs have considerably more leeway in accepting families who are eligible for third-party payments. Privately contracted family preservation programs may also have more latitude in accepting a wider variety of family problems than do public agencies. It may be possible to accept families at earlier stages of risk for whom placement is not imminent but likely in the future. The status of the case within the referral source may also be factor. Some states only offer family preservation services after a substantiated protective investigation; other states offer help prior to an investigation (McGowan, 1989).

Without clear selection criteria, it is very difficult for family preservation programs to allocate their scarce resources. Programs are often presented with referrals of families who have compelling needs for *some* type of intensive service, but it is questionable whether that service is family preservation. Likewise, there may be compelling reasons to accept cases—to provide more variety of clinical experiences for family preservation workers, to keep caseloads high, or to foster a positive relationship with a potential referral source—which are not based solely on clinical factors. These are issues that family preservation program administrators face on a day-to-day basis; the decisions reached significantly impact the types of families served by these programs.

Referral Procedures

While selection criteria serve as screening mechanisms, referral procedures specify who can refer clients and under what conditions. Clear referral guidelines result in timely, appropriate referrals that are comparable across time and across different referral sources. Referral procedures can also assist in validating the need for placement by requiring case review or supervision by others, both internal or external to the referring agency.

The nature of the link between the family preservation program and its referral source is very important to the effectiveness of the program. A number of strategies have been developed to foster good working relationships with referral sources (Feldman, 1988; Haapala et al., 1988). Table 7.1 documents the referral procedures and the nature of the relationship with the referring agency, as reported by the six family preservation programs surveyed for this chapter.

Education and Training

Referring workers need accurate and current information about family preservation programs in order to make appropriate referrals. Information is needed about selection criteria, types of families served, and the exact referral procedures to follow.

Screening/Assessment Tools

Common screening and assessment tools can facilitate more consistent referrals across workers and agencies. Of particular importance is the process and criteria for determining risk of placement. In spite of the availability of decision-making tools, family preservation programs and those agencies who refer families to them rarely make explicit use of these procedures in their selection and referral process. All too often risk of placement is assessed only by the referring worker. Many programs find it difficult to know with any certainly whether referred children would have actually been placed (Kinney, Madsen, Fleming, & Haapala, 1977). The result is that the concept of "risk of imminent placement" has been difficult to operate in a clear, consistent manner, both within and across programs (Frankel, 1988; Stein, 1985).

In one county, a consortium of contracted family preservation programs is beginning to use a common referral information sheet, requesting the same types of family information from each referring agency (S. Gwatkin, personal communication, June, 1989). This assists the referring agency in determining appropriate referrals and ensures that the family preservation worker has an accurate picture of the family prior to the first visit. In addition, some programs require the referring worker to have had recent contact (e.g., within 48 hours) with the family prior to the referral in order to ensure that information about the family is current. This time frame is predicated on the assumption that families are in crisis and cannot wait for service.

Secondary Screenings

Many programs employ a second-stage screening, by either the referring agency or the family preservation program. This secondary screening ensures that the family is at risk of placement, either has exhausted other less-intensive services or no other services are appropriate, and meets specific eligibility criteria for family preservation services. Secondary screening within the referring agency generally consists of supervisory reviews or placement screening committees.

Intensive family preservation programs typically screen for client eligibility through an intake worker's telephone contact with the referring worker or through supervisory review of the intake information. In addition, many programs rely on the initial home visit as a means of screening for appropriateness, and often set time limits (e.g., within so many visits) for the worker to determine case appropriateness (see Table 7.1). The problem with this procedure, however, is that families who are considered inappropriate for service—due to safety issues, for example—are sometimes considered treatment failures by the referral/funding source.

Relationships with Referring Workers

While these procedures ease the referral process, they do not take the place of clear agency goals, explicit eligibility criteria, and ongoing networking among referral sources and service providers. Although most programs pay a great deal of attention to these issues during the start-up phase, it is becoming increasingly clear, as programs enter their second generation, that the link with referral and funding sources is of ongoing importance. Finally, well-trained referring staff, who are knowledgeable about existing programs and committed to maintaining family strengths and integrity, can do much to facilitate referrals and motivate families to participate in intensive family preservation services.

Summary Discussion and Implications for Research

This chapter has discussed a number of factors impacting the definition of the target population for family preservation programs: conceptualizing and determining the need for placement, establishing selection criteria, and implementing referral procedures. Each factor necessarily depends on the others, and together ultimately they determine the appropriateness of services for at-risk families. Without a clearly defined program goal, standardized methods for assessing risk, consistent criteria for program eligibility, and efficient referral mechanisms, it is difficult for family preservation services to reach and serve their intended client population. A number of practical problems relating to staff changeover, program changes over time, referral sources, and funding patterns were discussed because these too impact the target population served.

The result is that the concept "risk of imminent placement" has been difficult to operationalize in a clear, consistent manner. This has been due both to the various definitions employed as well as to the community context in which placement decisions are made. The target population can be defined and understood in relation to: (a) the social service system that originates the referral, (b) the selection criteria used by individual family preservation programs, and (c) the legislative, policy, and community contexts that mandate preventive services. Family preservation programs may be best thought of as an alternative to unnecessary placement. It is important for researchers and program administrators to understand the practical limitations inherent in specifying, identifying, and selecting children in danger of placement. In addition, different programs may be serving children at varying levels of risk due to the individual selection criteria employed.

As family preservation programs expand, there will be a number of emerging issues in relation to the defined target population. Some issues stem from the increasing number of programs and the growing base of funding and referral sources. Other questions arise from the nature of family problems, which may be becoming more complex due to the larger numbers of families experiencing extreme deprivation, homelessness, and substance abuse. Future research on intensive family preservation services can inform and further refine the definition of the target population by focusing on the following five areas.

1. More detailed comprehensive information is needed on the types of families served by different family preservation programs, including the selection criteria and referral procedures employed, the community context, the services provided, and the responsiveness of families to these services.

2. More information is needed about family characteristics at each point in the continuum of service. Comparative studies of children and families served by family preservation, foster care, and residential services would be helpful in addressing the representativeness of the target population.

3. Much more information is needed on the referral procedures used within different service streams and how these procedures impact the target population. There may be differential access to family preservation services, depending on how the child happens to come to the attention of service providers and which agency makes the referral (Edna McConnell Clark Foundation, 1985). In addition, more information is needed on the types of families referred from different service streams, including presenting problems, success rates, and responsiveness to various forms of intervention. It would also be helpful to contrast and compare family preservation programs within various service streams; for example, family preservation services as contrasted with the delivery of family-focused delinquency prevention projects. More information is also needed on the impacts of different ages and developmental stages.

4. The experiences of minority families served by family preservation services needs documentation. Referral patterns can be examined to determine whether minority families experience differential access to family preservation programs (Hawkins & Salisbury, 1983). The flexibility and accessibility of family preservation services would appear to be highly responsive to the service needs of many minority families who might otherwise be reluctant to participate in or lack access to more traditional social services. In fact, Fraser, McDade, Haapala, and Pecora (1989) report that minority families tended to have higher success rates in family preservation programs, as compared with

non-minority families; however, this was observed only in the Washington State sites.

5. The use of research information on treatment success and failure in defining the target population must be explored. A number of recently completed research projects on the effectiveness of family preservation programs have yielded important information regarding factors associated with treatment success and failure (Nelson, this volume; K. Nelson, 1988; Fraser, Pecora, & Haapala, 1988). For example, Fraser et al. (1989) report from their two-state evaluation of the Homebuilders model, an intensive family preservation program, that older children who had more extensive histories of out-of-home placement, truancy, drug/alcohol involvement, delinquency, noncompliance in the home, and participation in mental health service programs were at greater risk of failure.

In addition to child characteristics, there have been a number of family factors associated with treatment failure. Fraser et al. report that less cohesive "disengaged" families were nearly four times more likely to experience service failure. In addition, parents whose parenting behaviors had resulted in injury to the child were at increased risk of service failure.

It is tempting to use information on factors associated with treatment failure to screen out referrals for intensive family preservation services on the basis that this represents a more equitable allocation of scarce resources. This might result in targeting family preservation services for families just entering the child welfare system, without prior placement experience, or excluding adolescent clients in order to achieve the highest possible success rates. Families might be subject to an assessment period in order to determine their suitability for family preservation services.

Fraser et al. (1989), however, caution that our ability to predict who will benefit from family preservation services is not very accurate. They suggest that a more ethical use of this information is to improve and refine programs and to identify those families and children for whom supplemental services and different therapeutic techniques may need to be developed (p. 3).

Through careful documentation of what services work for which types of families, family preservation programs may be able to refine their services for different family configurations, as well as define appropriate target populations for specific types of programs. For example, the research evidence cited above seems to suggest that family preservation services be configured differently for noncompliant, acting-out adolescents. Special strategies for engagement of the family in service may be needed, as well as more intensive networking and linkage with ongoing supportive resources once service is completed (Stroul, 1988). As we learn more about the experiences of different families, it may be possible to develop packages of family preservation services responsive to different presenting problems and target populations.

References

Barth, R. P. (1989). Theories guiding home-based intensive family preservation services. In J. K. Whittaker, J. Kinney, E. M. Tracy, & C. Booth (Eds.), *Reaching high-risk families: Intensive family preservation in human services* (pp. 89-112). New York: Aldine.

Bryce, M. E. (1982). Preplacement prevention and family reunification: Direction for the 80's. In E. S. Saalberg (Ed.), *A dialogue on the challenge for education and training: Child welfare issues in the 80's* (pp. 77-82). Ann Arbor: National Child Welfare Training Center, University of Michigan, School of Social Work.

Edna McConnell Clark Foundation. (1985). *Keeping families together: A case for family preservation.* New York: Edna McConnell Clark Foundation.

Feldman, L. (1988). Target population definition. In Y. Y. Yuan & M. Rivest (Eds.), *Evaluation resources for family preservation services* (pp. 1-18). Washington, DC: Center for the Support of Children.

Frankel, H. (1988). Family-centered, home based services in child protection: A review of the literature. *Social Service Review, 62*(1), 137-157.

Fraser, M., McDade, K., Haapala, D., & Pecora, P. (1989, February). Assessing the risks of treatment failure in intensive family preservation services. Presented at the *Second Annual Research Conference, Children's Mental Health Services and Policy: Building a Research Base.* Tampa, FL.

Fraser, M., Pecora, P., & Haapala, D. (1988). *Families in crisis: Findings from the family based intensive treatment project.* Federal Way, WA: Behavioral Sciences Institute.

Haapala, D., Kinney, J., & McDade, K. (1988). *Referring families to intensive home based family preservation services: A guide book.* Federal Way, WA: Behavioral Sciences Institute.

Hawkins, J.D., & Salisbury, B.R. (1983). Delinquency prevention programs for minorities of color. *Social Work and Abstracts, 19,* 5-12.

Kadushin, A., & Martin, J. A. (1988). *Child welfare services* (4th ed.). New York: Macmillan.

Kamerman, S., & Kahn, A. (1989). *Social services and youth and families in the United States.* New York: Columbia University School of Social Work. The Annie E. Casey Foundation.

Kinney, J. M., Haapala, D., Booth, C., & Leavitt, S. (1989). The Homebuilders model. In J. K. Whittaker, J. Kinney, E. M. Tracy, & C. Booth (Eds.), *Reaching high-risk families: Intensive family preservation in human services* (pp. 31-64). New York: Aldine.

Kinney, J. M., Madsen, B., Fleming, T., & Haapala, D. (1977). Homebuilders: Keeping families together. *Journal of Consulting and Clinical Psychology, 45*(4), 667-673.

Magazino, C. J. (1983). Services to children and families at risk of separation. In B. G. McGowan & W. Meezan (Eds.), *Child welfare: Current dilemmas, future directions* (pp. 211-254). Itasca, IL: F. E. Peacock.

Magura, S. (1981). Are services to prevent foster care effective? *Children and Youth Services Review, 3,* 193-212.

McGowan, B. G. (1989). Family-based services and public policy: Context and implications. In J. K. Whittaker, J, Kinney, E. M. Tracy, & C. Booth (Eds.), *Reaching high-risk families: Intensive family preservation in human services* (pp. 65-87). New York: Aldine.

National Resource Center on Family-Based Services. (1988). *Annotated directory of selected family-based services programs.* Iowa City: School of Social Work, The University of Iowa.

Nelson, D. (1989). Recognizing and realizing the potential of "family preservation." In J. K. Whittaker, J. Kinney, E. M. Tracy, & C. Booth (Eds.), *Reaching high-risk families: Intensive family preservation in human services* (pp. 13-30). New York: Aldine.

Nelson, K. (1988). *Family based services: Factors contributing to success and failure in family based child welfare services: Final report.* Iowa City: The National Resource Center on Family Based Services, The University of Iowa, School of Social Work.

Nelson, K., Landsman, M. J., & Deutelbaum, W. (1990). Three models of family-centered placement prevention services. *Child Welfare, 69*(1), 3-31.

Pecora, P. J., Fraser, M., Haapala, D., & Bartlome, J. A. (1987). *Defining family preservation services: Three intensive home based treatment programs.* (Research Report Number 1, Family-Based Intensive Treatment Research Project.) Federal Way, WA: Behavioral Sciences Institute.

Stein, T. J. (1985). Projects to prevent out-of-home placement. *Children and Youth Services Review, 7,* 109-121.

Stroul, B. A. (1988). *Volume I: Home based services.* (Series on community-based services for children & adolescents who are severely emotionally disturbed). Washington, DC: CASSP Technical Assistance Center, Georgetown University Child Development Center.

Wald, M. S. (1988, Summer). Family preservation: Are we moving too fast? *Public Welfare,* 33-38.

Wells, K. (in press). Family preservation services in context; Origins, practices and current issues. In I. Schwartz (Ed.), *Family and home based services.* Lincoln: University of Nebraska Press.

Wells, K., & Whittington, D. (1988). *Characteristics of children referred to out of home care.* Cleveland: Bellefaire/Jewish Children's Bureau.

Whittaker, J. K., & Tracy, E. M. (1990). Family preservation services and education for social work practice: Stimulus and response. In J. K. Whittaker, J. Kinney, E. M. Tracy, & C. Booth (Eds.), *Reaching high-risk families: Intensive family preservation in human services* (pp. 1-11). New York: Aldine.

8

Measuring Outcomes

MARY ANN JONES

Introduction

All human service interventions share a common goal—to have a beneficial effect on the persons served. But how do we know if that goal has been achieved? That is the task of outcome measurement. And the task is daunting. Measuring the outcomes of service is at once the most important and the most difficult aspect of evaluating an intervention program. Coulton and Solomon (1977) contend "if the procedures used to measure the dependent variable [the impact of the intervention on the client] are not valid indicators of the concept, then the rigorous [research] designs are of little more than aesthetic value" (p. 4).

The struggle between the importance and the difficulty of outcome measurement ensures that it is an issue that never gets settled. By way of illustration, 50 years have passed since the Institute of Welfare Research (IWR) was established at the Community Service Society of New York City and undertook as its major work the measurement of client change in response to social casework interventions. Over a period of many years the efforts of well-known researchers and methodologists, such as John Dollard, O. H. Mowrer, J. McVicker Hunt, Margaret Blenkner, Leonard S. Kogan, and Ann W. Shyne, were enlisted in the development of the CSS Movement Scale, a scale designed to track a client's movement, or change, in four areas of social functioning (Hunt & Kogan, 1950). The efforts failed, however, to produce a measure that gained wide acceptance, and now one rarely hears mention of the Movement Scale except, as here, in a historical context.

Many researchers and methodologists have taken up the challenge of client outcome measurement in the past 50 years, and yet we seem no closer to a measure or a set of measures that has a wide following for measuring outcomes in the human services generally or in family preservation services specifically. And it is neither intended nor foreseen that this chapter will lead the family preservation field toward consensus on outcome measurement. What is intended is to suggest some ways to think about outcome measurement for family preservation services that might be useful. To this end, the chapter contains discussion of the logic of outcome measurement, the nature and dimensions of change, a conceptualization of the domains of change goals, the types of change measures with potential relevance for family preservation programs, and recommendations regarding outcome measurement for those services. Several specific measures of various types are noted in the chapter, but no attempt has been made to present an exhaustive list of potential measures or to evaluate those that are mentioned. Other excellent sources are available for those purposes (see, for example, Ciarlo, Brown, Edwards, Kiresuk, & Newman, 1986; Jacob & Tennenbaum, 1988; Magura & Moses, 1986; New York State Council on Children and Families, 1988; Weiss & Jacobs, 1988).

The chapter focuses on outcomes at the level of the individual case or the program; and while efforts have been made to identify issues of particular relevance for intensive, short-term, crisis-oriented family preservation programs, much of the chapter is more broadly applicable to family intervention programs in general.

The Logic of Outcome Measurement and the Nature of Change

Logic of Outcome Measurement

This venture begins with the consideration of what is an outcome. An outcome is the result of something. The "something" that is of interest here is the intervention of family preservation programs. Since there is no way to detect a result that is not represented by a change, the concept of change is implicit in the notion of an outcome. Putting these ideas together, then, the focus of this chapter becomes the measurement of the change that results from participation in family preservation programs.

Change is the "difference between two states" (Group for the Advancement of Psychiatry [GAP], 1966, p. 380), "a divergence from uniformity or constancy in any quality, quantity or degree" (*Webster's Second New International Dictionary*). The change that is implicit in the idea of program outcomes is the discrepancy between the condition or situation of a person (or family or other target of intervention) who received the services of the program, compared to their condition or situation had they not received the service. This, of course, is unknowable since a person cannot both receive and not receive the same service. It is important, however, to underscore this point that seems largely to have been ignored in the logic of outcome measurement: The change that represents the efficacy of a service is *not* the discrepancy between the before and after states of the individuals receiving the service, but the unavailable discrepancy between their condition at the same point in time with and without the service.

And so we attempt as best we can to simulate this implicit comparison. We do this with before-after designs, which presume that the course of events for the subjects is discernible based on the before state (usually a steady state is presumed), and control or comparison designs, which presume that the only difference between persons who receive the service and persons who do not is the service itself. In any given instance, these presumptions may or may not be warranted. If they are not warranted they threaten the internal validity of the study (Campbell & Stanley, 1963). The threats of history and maturation (and the more commonly known concept of spontaneous remission) speak to the potential for error in before-after comparisons. Maturation and spontaneous remission are particularly important sources of error when families enter a service program due to a crisis, or when entry into the service program itself represents a crisis. This is because one of the characteristics of a crisis state is disequilibrium and disorganization of the family's usual state (Hill, 1958; Parad & Caplan, 1960); and the normal response, with or without outside intervention, is for equilibrium to be reestablished. By definition, all families in intensive family preservation services enter the program in a state of crisis, making the issue of before-after comparisons particularly problematic. It is not sufficient proof of the efficacy of the service that the families are functioning better after the service than they were before. The proper questions are: Does the service enable them to achieve a higher level of functioning than they would have achieved without the service (magnitude of change); and does the service accelerate their achievement of improved functioning (rate of change)?

The control group approach is much stronger than the before-after approach for attempting to simulate the comparison of persons with and without a service at the same point in time. The strength of the approach, however, depends on the extent to which the presumption of equivalence of the two groups is a reality. The best chance of making this a reality is through random assignment of cases to experimental and control conditions; or if a crucial background factor has been identified, random assignment of matched pairs.

Dimensions of Change

The job of providers of family preservation services is to induce change, and the job of evaluators of the service is to measure the change that is induced. There are six dimensions of change available for measurement (GAP, 1966) that hold potential for assessing family preservation services:

Occurrence

This is the most fundamental aspect of change. Has change occurred or not? This is the one dimension that can be measured for all types of change. The answers are in the form of "yes" or "no," presence or absence. In order to be counted as a change, the change must be perceptible.

The calibration of the measurement instrument is crucial to the determination of whether change has occurred. Measurement instruments that require a lot of change before change is detected will underestimate the occurrence of change. For example, a change measure that requires abstinence before a change in alcohol abuse is noted will miss all change that falls short of that. On the other hand, instruments that are very finely calibrated may overestimate change by registering insignificant or transient changes.

A related issue is that scales are sometimes more finely calibrated at one end of the continuum than at the other. The Family Risk Scales (Magura, Moses & Jones, 1987), for instance, have a ceiling of "adequate." A family cannot score better than adequate on any of the component scales. Improvement in an area in which a family is already functioning at an adequate level will, therefore, not be detected by the scale. More frequently, however, for child welfare cases, it is the inadequate side of the scale that is insufficiently developed. Just as the Family Risk Scales have a ceiling of adequate, some scales have a floor of adequate, and all or most of the calibration is reserved for levels of enhanced functioning beyond adequate. This will mean that change in poorly functioning families that still does not bring them up to an adequate level of functioning will not be detected.

Before they select their measures, programs should consider the type of client population they serve and the nature and amount of change that they can reasonably expect and wish to detect.

Direction

This is the next most fundamental aspect of change: What is the direction of the change against some referent? Movement along a continuum with definable end-points is implied. One has more or less of some quality or condition than was true previously. In family preservation programs, the end-points of the relevant continua usually represent some notion of improvement or deterioration. Not all change is directional. Some change represents alteration without a sense of movement along a continuum; for example, moving from Ohio to New York, getting married, changing jobs (of course these changes could also be evaluated to see if they represented positive or negative change). One of the vexing issues in evaluating family preservation services concerns the directionality of placement into foster care. Should placement into care be regarded as a negative outcome, and averting placement a positive outcome? This measure will be discussed in some detail later in this chapter.

Magnitude

The additional dimension of amount of change may frequently be measured. Magnitude implies some quantification of the amount of change. This determination permits the comparison of people and programs on the amount of change achieved.

Rate

The rate of change adds the element of time to the amount of change. A problem in measuring the rate of change is to distinguish between the object and the field: a specific family's recovery from crisis, for instance, from the normative rate of crisis resolution.

Duration

The question this dimension of change poses is: How durable or permanent is the change, how lasting are the effects? A crucial implication of duration (and its companion concept, reversibility) for outcome measurement is the timing of the measurement. The assessment of a program can range from wildly successful to unsuccessful, based on when the outcome measures are taken. This influence can be seen in Table 8.1 from the five-year follow-up of a group of preventive services programs in New York City (Jones, 1985, p. 88).

Table 8.1 Data for Children Entering Foster Care, by Number of Months Since Assignment and Research Assignment[a]

	Research assignment					
	Experimental (n=175)			Control (n=68)		
Number of months since assignment to study	Children entering care during interval					
	n	%	Total %	n	%	Total %
1-3	16	9	9	12	18	18
4-6	4	2	11	5	7	25
7-12	7	4	15	4	6	31
13-24	12	7	22	2	3	34
25-36	6	3	26	5	7	41
37-48	9	5	31	2	3	44
49-60	3	2	33	0	0	44
61-72	2	1	34	0	0	44
73-84	0	0	34	0	0	44
Median number of months before entering care[b]	12.6 months			4.4 months		

[a]The Lee-Desu statistic, which is used to test the significance of the difference in the survival rates of different samples, equalled 4.01, a value significant at the .05 level.
[b]For those who did enter care

Clearly, one's view of the success of the program in preventing entry into foster care rests to a large extent on when the assessment was made. Three months after assignment to the programs, only 9% of the children in the experimental group had entered care, but by the end of six years, one-third of the children had spent some time in care. This erosion of success in placement prevention is not surprising and is, of course, not limited to these preventive programs. As the editors of this book discuss in the "Introduction" to this volume, for example, follow-up studies of intensive family preservation programs reveal that initial rates of placement prevention programs are not being sustained. The success of the preventive programs, relative to the service-as-usual control group, also changed over time. The gap between the two groups in the percentages of children entering foster care was proportionately much greater at the end of the first year than it was at the end of the sixth year. It is apparent that one of the effects of preventive services is to postpone foster care rather than to prevent it. The merit of this outcome—postponing entry into care—is a complex matter and beyond the scope of this discussion; but without a sufficient length of follow-up and the experience of a control group for comparison, one does not even realize the extent to which a program may be having this effect.

Another issue concerning the duration of change is particularly relevant for family preservation programs that target families in a state of crisis and then work to resolve the crisis. The authors of a monograph on the assessment of change in psychotherapy (GAP, 1966, p. 389) comment that Freud believed readily induced change was more likely to be short-lived than change that was hard-won. They comment further that, since individuals in crisis are more susceptible to change for good or for ill, their change will be less durable. This argument may represent the wishful thinking of long-term psychotherapists espousing a "no gain without pain" philosophy, or it may be correct. This writer is unaware of empirical evidence bearing on this issue.

Sequence

Another aspect of change, but one rarely looked at in family preservation services, is the matter of the sequence of complex changes. Since many of the changes that family preservation services are attempting to achieve seem to be complex, this might be a productive area for investigation in an effort to better understand the nature of the change that a program is trying to foster.

Summary

Any effort to assess outcomes or change resulting from family preservation services must be concerned, at a minimum, with the first three of the dimensions of change enumerated here: occurrence, direction, and magnitude. The last three dimensions—rate, duration, and sequence—are more complex notions that are interrelated and provide a picture of the dynamic quality of change. These are potentially fruitful areas of investigation for preventive services evaluators, but ones that are rarely broached, probably because of constraints of time, money, and measurement technology. Unfortunately, for those of us whose business it is to evaluate family preservation services, the nature of the changes are more complex and dynamic than are our measures.

Locus and Level of Change Goals

Intervention programs are predicated, explicitly or implicitly, upon the idea of desired areas of change, or change goals. One issue a program must decide on is the locus of the intended change. Who or what does the program wish to change? Intervention programs may have as their goal changing, among other things, public opinion, policy, community conditions, institutions, and individuals. The principal locus of change for family preservation programs is at the family and individual level.

The term *level* of change goals is meant here to distinguish between those goals that are fundamental and intrinsically desirable and those that are merely the means to a desirable end. The former might be called terminal, ultimate, or end goals, and the latter might be called enabling, triggering, intermediate, or means goals. Examples of end goals are improved parental functioning, marital satisfaction, increased self-esteem, sense of self-efficacy, cessation of substance abuse. Examples of means goals are attending job training, receiving public assistance or mental health services, using birth control, or keeping a log of target thoughts, feelings, or behaviors. These latter goals are not inherently desirable. They are only desirable if they lead to the desired end goal. To use what may seem a prosaic analogy, these two types of change goals are like spot bowling and pin bowling. The ultimate goal for both types of bowlers is to knock down all the pins, but some bowlers find that they are better able to achieve that goal if they ignore the pins altogether, pick a spot on the alley, and bowl to that spot. The spot becomes the enabling goal. But there is nothing inherently virtuous in hitting the spot. Hitting the spot is only virtuous if it is preliminary to knocking down the pins. If one consistently hits the spot but continues to have lousy bowling scores, one has picked an infelicitous enabling goal and needs to change one's spot! In sum, an enabling goal is only as good as its link to an ultimate goal.

The distinction between ultimate and enabling change goals is important for both practitioners and evaluators. Both should, insofar as is possible, identify ultimate goals that are expected to result from the service and concentrate on the accomplishment and measurement of change toward these goals. When the ultimate goals are beyond the time frame of the program's involvement with the family, it may be necessary to identify enabling goals that are believed to be related to the ultimate goal; but unless the link between the enabling and ultimate goals has already been proven, it is a hypothesis that awaits testing.

Another approach to addressing ultimate goals beyond the scope of a program's time frame is to break the goal into smaller components or steps that can be accomplished more quickly. The terms *distal* and *proximal* goals (Heller, Price, & Sher, 1981) may be useful here. Distal goals are those that are at some remove, and proximal goals are the components or steps that, if continued, would result in the more distant goal. Let us think of a child who is socially isolated. Making one friend, where before he had none, could be identified as a proximal goal, or a "down payment," toward the larger goal. Participation in an after-school program, in contrast, would be an enabling goal. The distinction between proximal and enabling goals is subtle but important. Proximal goals are inherently desirable steps toward the ultimate goal, while enabling goals are believed to lead to ultimate goals but are not valuable in and of themselves. Participating in an after-school program may well have a salutary effect on the socially isolated child, but it remains to be seen. Making a friend, however, is inherently desirable for the child and may also lead to additional friends. In terms of level, then, there seems to be a hierarchy of importance in change goals for the practitioner to accomplish and for the evaluator to measure. In descending order of importance, the hierarchy is: ultimate-distal; ultimate-proximal; and enabling.

Content of Change Goals

Another important aspect of change goals is their content, or what some have called "domains of concern." These are defined as "areas where change may be observed over time as well as targets for intervention" (National Center for Clinical Infant Programs (NCCIP), 1987, p. 21). The relevant domains of concern to a great extent reflect the professional and intellectual perspective of the program. Two main perspectives guiding family intervention/family preservation services are child development and child welfare. Programs with a child development perspective emphasize, as the term implies, the enhancement of the child's development and have traditionally relied upon IQ and other cognitive measures to assess the program outcomes. Some aspects of parental functioning, primarily those that concern the parents' contribution to the child's development in roles such as stimulator, educator, and communicator, are of interest to child development specialists. Programs with a child welfare perspective, in contrast, tend to have a remedial orientation. They focus to a much greater extent on the functioning and role performance of the parent, but at a very basic level, such as providing adequate physical care for the child and refraining from abusing or neglecting the child. Here the emphasis is not on the parent as an enhancer of the child's environment, but as the provider of basic needs—food, shelter, safety, medical care, and education. In a family preservation program with a child welfare perspective, the child himself may actually receive little direct attention from either the practitioner or the evaluator.

Child development goals can seem precious to someone from a child welfare perspective, and child welfare goals can appear unambitious to child development specialists. Reacting to an item from the Childhood Level of Living Scale (Polansky, Chalmers, Buttenwieser, & Williams, 1978), a child welfare professional of many years said to the author, "What do you mean, 'Planned overnight vacation trip is taken by family?' The question is whether the mother will even allow the child to go on an outing organized and supervised by the school!" In another conversation, a child psychologist who ran a family intervention program for CPS cases in a suburb of Phila- delphia reacted to an outcome item about the child's staying in school by saying to the author, "I don't want these children simply staying in school, I want them going to Bryn Mawr and Haverford."

There are indications, however, that some adherents of either perspective wish to broaden their view to include some of the emphasis of the other. In a 1979 survey of nearly 200 child welfare agencies in the United States and Canada (Magura & Moses, 1980), respondents most frequently selected the child as the most important focus for the development of new outcome measures. A monograph by the National Center for Clinical Infant Programs [NCCIP] (1987) on evaluating family intervention programs attempts to broaden the perspective of its largely child development audience: "It is our view that all of the factors relevant to the functioning of a family or a parent are also ultimately salient to the well-being of a child" (p. 21). Upshur (1988) points out that even programs specifically designed to enhance child development learned in the 1960s and 1970s that they had to take the parents into account. This conviction resulted from two findings: that children's IQ scores are linked to their family's socioeconomic status; and that parental involvement is an important predictor of the maintenance of IQ gains in compensatory education programs such as Head Start. Since that time, parental involvement has become an important component of intervention programs for young children. Despite this increased interest in parents, however, Upshur reports that a meta-analytic review of 162 early interven- tion studies revealed that only 5% of 1,665 outcome indicators for which effect sizes could be calculated concerned someone other than the target child.

Drawing on three recent works about outcome measurement and evalua- tion of family and child intervention programs, one from a child welfare perspective (Magura & Moses, 1986) and two from a child development perspective (Weiss & Jacobs, 1988; NCCIP, 1987), five domains of concern for such programs may be identified: the child; the parent; parent-child interaction; family systems; and family resources. The NCCIP monograph outlines the domains and discusses other issues relevant to evaluating family intervention programs. The Weiss and Jacobs book contains chapters by various authors reviewing measures associated with each domain. The Magura and Moses book is principally devoted to describing the Child Well-Being Scales, but it also reviews other recommended measures for child welfare programs. The remainder of this section contains discussion of the five domains and associated measures.

Child Outcomes

The child development field has not only expanded its interest in areas of parental functioning, but has also expanded its view of relevant areas of child functioning. NCCIP observes, "There is more to influence and more to observe than a child's IQ" (p. 21), and points out that intervention programs for children and their families are of two sorts: those in which the children are disabled in some way and for whom the program goals therefore focus on "the facilitation of adaptive behavior and developmental competence" (p. 23); and those in which the children are not disabled but are receiving service because of family problems. For the children in this second group, normative development is possible, and the service goals are the "prevention of developmental or behavioral deterioration" (p. 23). NCCIP (1987) enumerates eight sub-domains under child outcomes: physical health; temperament, including responsiveness-engagability and general adaptability-coping; physical appearance and dominant mood; motor development and activity; social/emotional functioning; cognitive functioning; language; and play.

Hauser-Cram and Shonkoff (1988), authors of the chapter "Rethinking the Assessment of Child-Focused Outcomes" in Weiss and Jacobs (1988), agree that child outcomes have focused too narrowly on measures of cognitive development and IQ. They believe that these measures, although appealing for their relative objectivity, ease of administration, and compatibility with conventional statistical analyses, have produced few compelling social implications and have failed to capture the scope and richness of the impact of family intervention programs on children. They comment:

The growing attention to broader, more ecologic domains presents an exciting opportunity for reconceptualizing the child-oriented impacts of family services. As the burden of demonstrating program effectiveness is distributed more evenly across multiple dependent variables, opportunities arise for greater creativity in assessment. (p. 73)

Hauser-Cram and Shonkoff recommend two new areas of child-focused outcomes that they believe look particularly promising for evaluating family intervention programs: social competence and self-regulatory behaviors. The authors admit that the definition of social competence remains vague and elusive, but that most agree it is a quality expressed both in and out of the school setting. Some evaluators have constructed indices of school adjustment, including such areas as achievement, attendance, classroom behavior, and use of school-related services. Others have observed the interaction of the child with peers; and still others have used parent or teacher rating scales, such as the Child-Behavior Checklist or the Vineland Adaptive Behavior Scales. By *self-regulatory behaviors,* the authors are referring to problem-solving skills that focus on "approaches taken to tasks, rather than on the attainment of correct solutions or the acquisition of new knowledge" (p. 85). They mention specifically attention, motivation, and curiosity and discuss measures that address these attributes, while commenting that few have been developed with adequate reliability and validity. The authors conclude their review of child-focused measures with the following observation: "Past approaches to assessing program impacts on children focused on attributing importance to what was measurable. Future efforts must be directed more toward measuring what is important" (p. 90).

Parent Outcomes

NCCIP (1987) enumerates five subdomains under the heading of parent outcomes: general health, socio-emotional functioning, cognitive functioning, life-course development, and parental functioning. They see parental functioning as including physical caregiving, parent's attitudes about himself or herself as a parent, psychological availability, appropriate communication, and parent as teacher. Upshur (1988) identifies four types of parent variables that may represent targets of intervention: attitudes, behavior, knowledge, and self-development. Since it is parental behavior (omission, commission, or quality) that brings most families to the attention of family preservation programs, behavior or functioning will be the area of most immediate—and perhaps only—concern to evaluators of these programs. There tends to be little consensus in the measures selected for assessing parental outcomes. Magura and Moses (1980) found no two agencies using the same parent measure in a 1979 survey of nearly 200 child welfare agencies in the United States and Canada, and Jones (1989) found the same in a survey of 92 preventive services programs in New York State. Three measures, however, that have been used in evaluations of family preservation programs are described below:

- The Child Well-Being Scales (CWBS) (Magura & Moses, 1986) are a set of 43 areas on which a caseworker, or other person familiar with a family, rates the adequacy of the functioning of the parents or the children. Each of the 43 areas has from three to six levels of performance, ranging from adequate to increasing degrees of inadequacy. Each level is described by observable conditions or actions, which serve to anchor the ratings. The scales were selected to represent a broad range of issues that might necessitate intervention, particularly issues of child protection. Examples are physical health care, nutrition, supervision of children, parental relations, and parental acceptance of/affection for children.

  The seriousness of each area for the welfare of the child was assessed through a survey of 765 child welfare professionals across the United States, and a seriousness score was assigned to each area on the basis of those judgments. The seriousness scores are used as weights in the calculation of an overall Child Well-Being Score or as subscales of interest (such as the three factor-based subscales constructed by Magura and Moses of Household Adequacy, Parental Disposition, and Child Performance).

  The Child Well-Being Scales were used by two of the studies reported in this book (the California study by Yuan and Struckman-Johnson, and K. Nelson's assessment of 11 family-based programs). Nelson's chapter contains a discussion of and response to some of the psychometric issues that have been raised about the scales.

- The Family Risk Scales (FRS) (Magura et al., 1987). With the Child Well-Being Scales as a starting point, the Child Welfare League of America researchers, in consultation with preventive services providers, designed 26 items believed to be dimensions relevant to the risk of entering foster care, such as habitability of residence, adult relationships, parent's physical health, physical punishment, and child's school adjustment. Each item is rated by the caseworker at two or more times during the life of the case. Once again, there are from four to six possible ratings for each item, ranging from adequate to successive levels of inadequacy, and each rating is illustrated by a brief description. Seriousness scores have not been developed for the Family Risk Scales, but the authors recommend the calculation of three factor-based composite scores—Parent-Centered Risk, Child-Centered Risk, and Economic Risk—which were constructed from the use of the scales with 1,158 families in preventive services programs in New York City and New York State in 1983. (The Family Risk Scales were used by the Utah-Washington study reported in this book by Pecora and colleagues.)

- The McMaster Family Assessment Device (FAD) (Epstein, Baldwin, & Bishop, 1983) was developed to provide family therapists and researchers with "reliable information about family functioning on a wide variety of clinically relevant dimensions" (p. 171). The FAD covers six dimensions of family functioning: problem solving, communication, roles, affective responsiveness, affective involvement, and behavior control. Each family member rates his or her agreement or disagreement with 53 statements representing these six dimensions. Mean scores are calculated for each of the six subscales and an overall scale of general functioning. The scale takes 15 to 20 minutes to complete, and the internal consistency and discriminate validity results are quite promising. A companion scale, the McMaster Clinical Rating Scale (CRS), has been developed to obtain the perceptions of clinicians.

Other parent functioning scales that a program might wish to consider have been reviewed by Magura and Moses (1986), notably Geismar's Family Functioning Scale and Polansky and colleagues' Childhood Level of Living Scale (Urban Version). Because of their child and family welfare focus, these scales are often overlooked in reviews of instruments with a more psychological or family systems perspective and are mentioned here for that reason.

Parent-Child Interaction

The boundaries of this domain are not as clearly defined as the others. NCCIP, for instance, includes under this domain only measures that have an interactive component, while Howrigan (1988), in her review of the measures addressing this domain, includes many aspects of the parenting role. Also, measures from this domain are more typically the antecedent or intervening variables believed to influence the outcome variables than they are the outcome variables themselves. In terms of change goals, then, this domain tends to concern enabling goals rather than ultimate or end goals.

NCCIP identifies five subdomains of parent-child interaction: mutuality and reciprocity of child and parent; dominant affective tone and intensity of engagement; frequency of interaction; modes of communication; and play. Howrigan does not attempt to define the domain of parent-child interaction, but does give examples of what she considers to be parent-child interaction measures, among which she mentions parental attitudes, perception, and knowledge about child rearing; parental perceptions and expectations of child development; accuracy of the mother's expectations for her child's behavior, maternal activity choices, and "childmindedness." Howrigan seems to give special significance to measures of attachment between child and mother, and indeed this is the only area that appears to be truly interactive; the others could just as easily be classified under parent outcomes.

Family Systems

This domain, an outgrowth of family systems theory and family therapy, concerns family dynamics and patterns that cut across individual family members and concern the social environment for the whole family. Walker and Crocker (1988) include in this domain such things as family rules, communication patterns, structures and alliances, intergenerational influences, and family development patterns. NCCIP identifies four family level variables that may have relevance for family preservation services: informal social support, marital relationship, family cohesion, and family adaptability.

Family systems theory is based on the idea that there are patterns of family interaction that characterize and encourage good or optimal family functioning and also patterns that are dysfunctional. As was noted for the parent-child interaction domains, the variables in this domain tend to represent enabling rather than ultimate goals.

Walker and Crocker (1988) conducted an extensive review of the literature on family systems measures and identified the seven most widely used measures. Five are self-report measures and two are observation/rating scales. By far the most popular of the self-report scales is Olson and colleagues' Family Adaptability and Cohesion Evaluation Scales (FACES). The other self-report family measure that one occasionally encounters in evaluations of family intervention programs is Moos and colleagues' Family Environment Scales (FES). As reported in Walker and Crocker (1988), the Family Environment Scales assess the "social climate" of the family, including the interpersonal relationships among the members, the types of personal growth valued in the family, and the family's basic organizational structure. Both FACES and FES are easy to administer and score. Readers wishing more information on these and other family systems measures are referred to Walker and Crocker.

An additional set of measures that seems appropriate here are those concerning family stress and coping. Readers interested in measures of this domain are referred to Krauss (1988), who has reviewed them and has identified several that might be relevant for family preservation programs.

Family Resources

The final domain of concern is the external or environmental resources that are available to a family. Major among these are money, employment, housing, mental or physical health care, education, transportation, day care, and self-help groups such as Alcoholics Anonymous. The problems here may concern inadequate resources in the community or the family's inability to use the resources that are available.

Another issue that could be considered here is a family's social support network. Family intervention programs may have as a goal in many cases the shoring up of a family's social network both to overcome a sense of social isolation and loneliness (Polansky, 1985) and to build in more supports and assistance. Cleary (1988) briefly reviews the literature on the influence of social support and concludes:

> [T]he relevance of social support to a number of health-related processes is now well established. . . . Many studies also link social support to psychological health and psychiatric morbidity. . . . Specific types of support, such as emotional support and perceived availability of support, may buffer the impact of stressful life events. (p. 196)

Cleary observes that a family intervention program could be interested in measuring social support both as a pre-existing condition that may mediate the effects of the program and as an outcome measure of program effectiveness. Social support could represent a desirable goal in itself or an intervening variable that might lead to other, more distal outcomes. Two of the major dimensions that one may measure about social supports are structure (size of network, strength, density, dispersion) and function (instrumental, informational, appraisal, and emotional). Other issues about social support concern the perception of support versus its actual availability; availability versus actual use; and the extent to which the degree of social support is a function of the individual or of the environment.

Cleary reviews many measures of the structure and function of social support networks, as well as measures of confiding relationships and family social support measures. One example of a measure that could be relevant for family preservation programs is the Social Support Questionnaire. It measures tangible, informational, and emotional support by presenting the respondent with situations and asking who he or she could count on to help. For more information on this measure and others, see Cleary (1988).

The Measurement of Change

Types of Measures

There are three major types of measures appropriate for family preservation services: case events, family or individual change, and client satisfaction.

Case Events

Case events are objective, officially recorded changes in the status of a family or of its members. Two case events of particular relevance to family preservation services are entry into foster care and the substantiation of a report of child abuse or neglect.

Case events have compelling strengths and weaknesses as outcome measures. A major strength is that they are objective measures requiring little or no interpretation or judgment on the part of the data collector. A second strength is that they often embody the major, explicit goals of a service and can therefore be highly relevant indicators of the success of the program.

On the negative side of case events as measures of outcome, they are, taken as a group, the type of measure least amenable to change as the result of intervention at the case level. Many of the casework effectiveness studies cited in the early 1970s as evidence for declaring social casework a failure (see, for example, Fischer, 1973; Grey & Dermody, 1972; Mullen & Dumpson, 1972) used case events, such as arrests, court appearances, institutionalization, divorce, and termination of public assistance, among their outcome measures. Beck and Jones (1973) pointed out that the very nature of the outcome measures might be one of the reasons for the disappointing findings of some of these studies:

> To achieve their goal of objective criterion measures, some of the investigators selected types of outcomes possibly not achievable and in any case of greater concern to the wider community than to those receiving the service. . . . Such goals often originate outside the client and may never be accepted by him as in his interest. (p. 13)

The advent of meta-analytic procedures produced evidence that the type of outcome measure used influences the findings on a program's effectiveness. Smith and Glass (1977) performed a meta-analysis of 375 controlled studies of the efficacy of psychotherapy. Two findings from their analysis bear upon this discussion. The independent variable having the largest correlation with effect size (a standardized measure of the superiority of the experimental group over the control group on a given outcome measure) was the level of "reactivity" or "fakeability" of the outcome measure. Reactivity was scored at the lowest level for such things as physiological measures and grade point average and at the highest level for nonblind therapist ratings. The correlation between reactivity and effect size was .30. The next largest correlation was .19, and only one other correlation was greater than .10. The positive correlation means that the more reactive or "fakeable" the measure, the more positive the results, and, conversely, that the less reactive the measure, the less positive the results.

The other finding of relevance in the Smith and Glass (1977) study is that the content of the outcome measure is also associated with the effect size. Outcome measures concerning fear/anxiety reduction or self-esteem had average effect sizes three times those of school or work achievement measures (.97 and .90, respectively, versus .31). "Adjustment" measures fell in between with an average effect size of .56. Taken together, these findings provide compelling evidence that nonreactive, behavioral measures, of the type that case events usually are, yield the poorest findings in outcome evaluations. Such measures then will usually produce a conservative estimate of the effectiveness of a program.

On the other hand, case events, since they are by definition official events, are very sensitive to system-wide effects. A reduction in the number of clients receiving public assistance may attest to the success of a job-training program, or it may reflect an upswing in the economy. The success of a program in preventing entry into foster care may signal a successful program or a locality in which foster care has fallen into disfavor. In the parlance of Campbell and Stanley (1963), case events are particularly susceptible to the threat of history (events external to the study, but affecting the outcomes of the study). The effect of history on case event measures can go in either direction. A program can look either very successful or very unsuccessful, depending upon the influence of the historical events. The best antidote to the threat of history is knowledge of the experience of a randomly assigned control group. The crucial matter to ensure is that case events reflect the impact of the program, not the impact of external events.

Magura and Moses (1980) identify other weaknesses of case events as outcome measures. The identification of the event with the outcome presumes that the event has the same fundamental meaning in all cases, and this is, of course, not the case. Many observers have criticized the use of entry into foster care as an outcome measure of family preservation services for this reason. Entry into care can be a good or a bad thing, depending on the circumstances. The real issue, they argue, is the aptness of the worker's judgment. The real outcome measure is "good entry into foster care" versus "bad entry into foster care"; but when one adds the evaluative qualifier, one is no longer talking about an objective case event.

Other weaknesses of case event measures are that they are insensitive to the nature and amount of improvement or deterioration (if any) that preceded and perhaps precipitated them, and that they provide no knowledge of changes that do not result in a change in case status (the calibration problem again). And, finally, case events that are dependent upon decisions of the service providers have the undesirable quality of being subject to their conscious or unconscious manipulation. A worker who knows that his or her program is being evaluated on the basis of the number of children who enter foster care may wittingly or unwittingly have his or her judgment and decisions compromised by the unintended "demand characteristics" of the outcome measure. Magura and Moses comment: "Outcome measurement should help inform agency decision making, not be identical with it" (1980, p. 61).

Family or Individual Change

This is the type of measure that one usually thinks of when one thinks of outcome measures. It includes a wide range of content, such as individual and family functioning, behavior, attitudes, skills, knowledge, and role performance, much of which has already been discussed in the section on content of change goals.

Since some form of change in the family or in its members is the heart of the matter for family preservation programs, the major strength of measures of family and individual change is their salience. A major weakness, however, also concerns salience: Precisely which domains of concern are the salient areas to target for change? Some areas are fairly clear. They tend to be aspects of parental behavior that place the child at risk of physical or emotional harm. Other areas are more nebulous. The domains that were identified as primarily the province of enabling goals (parent-child interaction, family systems) are particularly subject to ambiguity. Are they or are they not the proper targets for change? One hears program advocates complain that disappointing evaluation findings were the result of outcome measures that did not address the domains that were the goals of the service. This can happen when the program and the evaluator fail to identify the correct targets for change, or when someone has become enamored of an outcome measure, regardless of its appropriateness.

A second weakness of family and individual change measures is the quality—reliability and validity—of the measures. The dilemma in terms of quality is that reliability, a necessary but not sufficient condition for validity, is enhanced by the objectivity of a measure, but validity often is not. It is very hard to identify measures of family and individual functioning that are both objective and valid. To illustrate this point, one could render aspects of parental functioning more objective by counting the number of times that things occur, for instance leaving a child unattended. But confronted with actual cases, one quickly learns that a parent's presence does not equal supervision, and a parent's absence does not equal neglect (Jones, 1987). We can improve the "countability" of the concept, but often at the sacrifice of the meaning. Levine and Luborsky (1981), in an article concerning their efforts to measure the content of psychotherapy patients' core conflicts, comment on this tradeoff: "There has often been an inverse relationship between the consensus that could be obtained and the importance of the concept to be judged" (p. 501).

Client Satisfaction

The third type of measure one finds used in intervention programs is client satisfaction. In fact, in a recent survey of voluntary preventive services programs in New York State (Jones, 1989), client satisfaction measures were the type of measure the agencies reported using most frequently in their efforts to evaluate their services. Although the distinction is not always made clear, client satisfaction measures are a subset of client self-report measures. Client self-report measures may concern the whole array of a client's background, conditions, problems and functioning. Client satisfaction measures, on the other hand, focus more narrowly on the client's reactions to the service provided, either in a global fashion (e.g., "In general how satisfied were you with the service you received?") or more specifically service by service. Client satisfaction measures are then perhaps more akin to measures of process than of outcomes (Ciarlo et al., 1986, also make this point). Often, however, if an agency goes to the trouble of asking clients for their reactions to the service, they will also ask some outcome questions (e.g., "How are things now, compared to when you first came to the agency?"). So, in fact, client satisfaction measures may be a portion of a larger client self-report outcome procedure, or they may be the primary intention of the procedure, with a few global measures of outcome added in. They are included in this conceptualization as a type of outcome measure because they represent one of the major ways in which family preservation programs can and do measure the effects or impact of their service.

Client satisfaction measures are no substitute for outcome measurement. A satisfied client does not necessarily mean an improved client, and an unsatisfied client does not necessarily mean an unimproved client. Such measures can, however, fill in a piece of the puzzle about the overall effectiveness of a program. The major contribution of client satisfaction measures (in the strict sense of the term) is to screen for gross patterns of dissatisfaction and to identify, through open-ended items, problems from the client's perspective that might not otherwise be apparent (e.g., not enough parking places on Thursday afternoons).

Sources of Data

There are three sources of data available to evaluators of family preservation programs: the family; the caseworker (directly or through the case record); and third parties or collaterals, such as CPS, schools, day care centers, an so forth (either directly with the individuals or through records about the family or child). A recent survey of preventive services programs in New York State (Jones, 1989) found that caseworkers (either directly or through agency records) were overwhelmingly the most frequent source of information on family and individual change measures (82% of the measures were based in whole or in part on information from the caseworker); followed by the client (53% of the measures); and trailed by third parties (12% of the measures). (The figures exceed 100% because a measure may use more than one source of data.)

It is understandable that most outcome measures used in family preservation programs are based on information obtained from the clients or the caseworkers. These are readily accessible data sources and the two sources that have the most information about what is going on. The other sources, however, should be more widely exploited. Official records are the source of most case event measures, and programs should find a way to capture this information routinely about their cases. Third parties are very useful as an independent check on what is happening with the child or family. These are harder to come by because of issues of confidentiality and the burden imposed on the third party.

Generalized versus Individualized Measures

Generalized measures are those that are held constant for all clients in a program. Any standardized measure would be an example. All clients would get a score or rating on the same measure. An individualized measure is one that is tailor-made for the specific case. Examples of each are the Global Assessment Scale (Endicott, Spitzer, Fleiss, & Cohen, 1976) for the generalized measure, and Goal Attainment Scaling (Kiresuk & Sherman, 1968) for the individualized measure.

The Global Assessment Scale is a single rating scale used to assess the overall psychological health or sickness of an individual. It is measured on a scale from 1, representing the psychologically sickest individual, to 100, representing the healthiest. The scale is broken into ten 10-point intervals, accompanied by a vignette characterizing the functioning of a person who should be rated within that interval. Each person is then given a single rating score between 1 to 100, representing his or her degree of psychological health.

Goal Attainment Scaling is a technique rather than a measure. The caseworker or therapist, with or without the involvement of the client, develops one or more outcome scales tailored to the specific problems and goals of the case. Observable outcomes representing various levels of accomplishment are established for each target of change. The expected level of outcome is established and given the score of zero. Four other levels of accomplishment are established: two are better than expected and are scored +1 and +2, and two are worse than expected and are scored -1 and -2. At some specified time, a rater rates the accomplishment of the goals yielding a score for each change target and an overall score for all of them taken together.

The strength of Goal Attainment Scaling is that it is tailored to each client, so that progress is assessed only on the basis of relevant problems, and the magnitude of the change can be pegged to reasonable expectations for the client. The weakness of the measure is that it yields no sense of the status of functioning of a client or a group of clients against some absolute standard, nor does it offer a satisfactory way of aggregating information about change or functioning across clients. The Global Assessment Scale, in contrast, does allow for the comparison of functioning against an absolute standard, but it does not allow for tailoring the goals or possible levels of accomplishment to a given case.

Reflections on Outcome Measurement
in Family Preservation Programs

There are two purposes for measuring outcomes of family preservation programs: program accountability and service improvement. Program accountability is a justification process that addresses the question: "Of all the competing demands for public money, why should some of it go to family preservation programs?" Service improvement, in contrast, poses the question: "How can we improve upon the service that we provide in family preservation programs?" These motives are quite different and have different implications for program evaluation and outcome measurement.

The motive for evaluating or monitoring the results of family preservation programs has much to say about the type of outcome measurement that will be relevant. If the motive is accountability, certain case event measures will be of utmost importance. The obvious ones are entry into and exit from foster care and CPS reports. A publicly funded program created expressly to avert the need for foster care cannot adequately account for itself without information on the accomplishment of that goal. The CPS reports are an important adjunct to that measure, because implicit in the goal of keeping children with their families is the requirement that this be done safely.

Case event measures of this sort do not, however, tend to be very instructive for service improvement. An agency doesn't learn much about improving service from looking at the number of cases in which entry into foster care or a CPS report took place, compared to a comparison group, but rather by looking at what led up to entry into care or the filing of the report, what efforts were made, and what became of them. Service improvement efforts require getting behind the simple facts of foster care and CPS reports, and getting behind those facts will involve some form of outcome measurement that assesses individual or family functioning.

The motive driving an evaluation of a family preservation program also has implications for the best sponsor for the evaluation. Accountability efforts should be under the aegis of budget directors, policymakers, and public administrators. These are the persons charged with the responsibility for determining the allocation of public funds among competing claims, and the persons who have ready access to the systemwide data essential for monitoring entry into foster care and CPS reports. Service improvement evaluations, on the other hand, seem best suited to program planners. It is the program planner who has the knowledge to identify the meaningful, unresolved questions about service delivery. What service models should family preservation programs be offering? Are some modalities or techniques more efficacious than others? Do some models of service work better with some families or problem configurations than others? If these questions sound familiar, it is not surprising. They have been posed by program planners and evaluators for years; but because of the preoccupation with accountability issues, little progress has been made in answering them. Relieved of the burden of conducting accountability studies, program planners could focus their attention on identifying salient issues for service improvement—such as intensity, duration, technique, and modality.

There are two investigative strategies for service improvement. One is the experimental comparison of service options mentioned earlier. This method requires uniform outcome measures across cases. Multiple measures, multiple sources of data, multiple sites, and multiple investigators are highly recommended for this type of study. The answers are too important to willingly tolerate bias from any of these sources. Even the allegiance of the evaluator has been found to be a source of bias (Berman, 1989).

This type of experimental research, however, is costly, lengthy, and incapable of addressing all of the potentially important combinations of background, problem, and service variables. We also need, therefore, smaller scale strategies for measuring outcomes to improve services. Here we are talking at the level of the individual case. We need to better understand the change processes within cases. This may be done by the practitioner through single subject design methods or intensive case analysis, or it may be done by researchers through process research methods. In the practitioner-based methods, the practitioner looks at his or her cases to ascertain progress and how it is accomplished. In such a close-up look at the change in a given case, the many dimensions of change discussed earlier in this chapter—occurrence, amount, direction, rate, duration, and sequence— can all be identified and analyzed. This is far beyond what is possible in group designs. Individualized outcome measures, such as Goal Attainment Scaling, would be very appropriate for this type of research.

For the second strategy toward better understanding change at the individual case level—process research—it is useful to turn to psychotherapy research, where much of this work has been going on. Psychotherapy researchers have taken as their mission the understanding of psychological and behavioral change: when it occurs, why it occurs, and why not. They have brought to awareness the understanding that there is no end-point to what we may call an outcome. An outcome is merely a cross-sectional view of a dynamic change process (Greenberg, 1986). Consequently, some psychotherapy researchers have abandoned investigations of outcome research that they found disappointing in favor of investigations of change during the psychotherapy process (see, for example, Mahrer & Nadler, 1986). A variety of new procedures has been developed to support these interests, such as videotaping psychotherapy sessions for intensive analysis; debriefing patients immediately after a session to obtain their reactions to what went on during the session; and interviewing patients for their between-session events and feelings. These ideas take client feedback far beyond client satisfaction. There is much more to be learned from clients than just what they thought of the service they received (see, for example, Mayer & Timms, 1970; Pelton, 1982).

Focusing on individual cases also brings one more into the realm of qualitative research. In *Exploring Clinical Methods for Social Research,* Berg and Smith (1985) decry "significant results with trivial importance" (p. 190) and urge greater use of qualitative methodologies in order to learn "more from fewer cases" (p. 207). Hauser-Cram and Shonkoff (1988) indict past approaches to assessing program impacts on children for attempting to "attribute importance to what was measurable," rather than attempting to "[measure] what is important" (p. 90). Mayer and Timms (1970) observe:

> It is our impression that exploratory studies have relatively low status in social work research circles. In a mistaken view of the manner in which scientific knowledge accumulates, social work researchers have tended to identify research exclusively with the techniques required to carry it out, especially those needed for rigorous quantitative studies. . . . [A] preoccupation with technical matters . . . has seemingly drawn attention away from the study of clients, at least insofar as exploratory, loosely formulated studies are called for at this point. The invidious distinctions attached to different research procedures have, it would appear, left clients unstudied. (pp. 16-17)

How should our evaluation efforts and resources be divided between the motives of accountability and service improvement? As it now stands, most of the resources have gone into the accountability motive. The time may be ripe for an infusion of new energy and curiosity in understanding what is accomplished in family preservation programs and how it is accomplished, for greater vitality in program improvement, and for evaluators to design evaluations and select outcome measures that will have something useful to say to practitioners.

References

Beck, D. F., & Jones, M. A. (1973). *Progress on family problems: A nationwide study of clients' and counselors' views on family agency services.* New York: Family Service Association of America.

Berg, D. N., & Smith, K. K. (Eds.). (1985). *Exploring clinical methods for social research.* Beverly Hills, CA: Sage.

Berman, J. S. (1989, June). Investigator allegiance and the findings from comparative outcome research. In V. Shoham-Salomon (Chair), *Beyond the competition: Are some therapies better for some clients?* Panel Session 26 at the annual meeting of the Society for Psychotherapy Research, Toronto.

Campbell, D. T., & Stanley, J. C. (1963). *Experimental and quasi=experimental designs for research.* Boston: Houghton Mifflin.

Ciarlo, J. A., Brown, T. R., Edwards, D. W., Kiresuk, T. J., & Newman, F. L. (1986). *Assertive mental health treatment outcome measurement techniques* (DHHS Pub. No. ADM 86-1301). Washington, DC: National Institute of Mental Health.

Cleary, P. D. (1988). Social support: Conceptualization and measurement. In H. B. Weiss & F. H. Jacobs (Eds.), *Evaluating family programs* (pp. 195-216). New York: Aldine.

Coulton, C. J., & Solomon, P. L. (1977). Measuring outcomes of intervention. *Social Work Research and Abstracts, 13*(4), 3-9.

Endicott, J., Spitzer, R. L., Fleiss, J. L., & Cohen, J. (1976). The Global Assessment Scale: A procedure for measuring overall severity of psychiatric disturbance. *Archive of General Psychiatry, 33,* 766-771.

Epstein, N. B., Baldwin, L. M., & Bishop, D. S. (1983). The McMaster family assessment device. *Journal of Marital and Family Therapy, 9*(2), 171-180.

Fischer, J. (1973). Is casework effective? A review. *Social Work, 18*(1), 5-21.

Grey, A. L., & Dermody, H. E. (1972). Reports of casework failure. *Social Casework, 53,* 534-543.

Greenberg, L. S. (1986). Change process research. *Journal of Consulting and Clinical Psychology, 54*(1), 4-9.

Group for the Advancement of Psychiatry, Committee on Research. (1966). *Psychiatric research and the assessment of change* (Vol. VI, Report No. 63). New York: Group for the Advancement of Psychiatry.

Hauser-Cram, P., & Shonkoff, J. P. (1988). Rethinking the assessment of child-focused outcomes. In H. B. Weiss & F. H. Jacobs (Eds.), *Evaluating family programs* (pp. 73-94). New York: Aldine.

Heller, K., Price, R., & Sher, K. (1981). Research and evaluation in mental health. In R. Price (Ed.), *Prevention in mental health: Research, policy, and practice* (pp. 285-414). Beverly Hills, CA: Sage.

Hill, R. (1958). Generic features of families under stress. *Social Casework, 39*(2-3), 139-150.

Howrigan, G. A. (1988). Evaluating parent-child interaction outcomes of family support and education programs. In H. B. Weiss & F. H. Jacobs (Eds.), *Evaluating family program* (pp. 95-130). New York: Aldine.

Hunt, J. McV., & Kogan, L. (1950). *Measuring results in social casework.* New York: Family Service Association of America.

Jacob, T., & Tennenbaum, D. L. (1988). *Family assessment: Rationale, methods, and future directions.* New York: Plenum.

Jones, M. A. (1985). *A second chance for families—five years later: Follow-up of a program to prevent foster care.* Washington, DC: Child Welfare League of America.

Jones, M. A. (1987). *Parental lack of supervision: Nature and consequence of a major child neglect problem.* Washington, DC: Child League of America.

Jones, M. A. (1989). [Survey of use of case outcome measures in New York State preventive services programs.] Unpublished raw data.

Kiresuk, T. J., & Sherman, R. E. (1968). Goal attainment scaling: A general method of evaluating comprehensive community mental health programs. *Community Mental Health Journal, 4,* 443-453.

Krauss, M. W. (1988). Measures of stress and coping in families. In H. B. Weiss & F. H. Jacobs (Eds.), *Evaluating family programs* (pp. 177-194). New York: Aldine.

Levine, F., & Luborksy, L. (1981). The core conflictual relationship theme method: A demonstration of reliable clinical inferences by the method of mismatched cases. In S. Tuttman, C. Kaye, & M. Zimmerman (Eds.), *Object and self: A developmental approach* (pp. 501-526). New York: International Universities Press.

Magura, S., & Moses, B. S. (1980). Outcome measurement in child welfare. *Child Welfare, 59,* 595-606.

Magura, S., & Moses, B. S. (1986). *Outcome measures for child welfare services: Theory and applications.* Washington, DC: Child Welfare League of America.

Magura, S., Moses, B. S., & Jones, M. A. (1987). *Assessing risk and measuring change in families: The family risk scales.* Washington, DC: Child Welfare League of America.

Mahrer, A. R., & Nadler, W. P. (1986). Good moments in psychotherapy: A preliminary review, a list, and some promising research avenues. *Journal of Consulting and Clinical Psychology, 54*(1), 10-15.

Mayer, J. E., & Timms, N. (1970). *The client speaks: Working class impressions of casework.* New York: Atherton.

Mullen, E. J., & Dumpson, J. R. (1972). *Evaluation of social intervention.* San Francisco: Jossey-Bass.

National Center for Clinical Infant Programs (NCCIP). (1987). *Charting change in infants, families and services: A guide to program evaluation for administrators and practitioners.* Washington, DC: NCCIP.

New York State Council on Children and Families. (1988). *Taxonomy of outcome statements, measures, and data collection instruments and methods for preventive programs serving youth* (2nd ed.). Albany: New York State Council on Children and Families.

Parad, H. J., & Caplan, G. (1960). A framework for studying families in crisis. *Social Work, 5*(3), 3-15.

Pelton, L. H. (1982). Personalistic attributions and client perspectives in child welfare cases: Implications for service delivery. In T. A. Wills (Ed.), *Basic processes in helping relationships.* New York: Academic Press.

Polansky, N. A. (1985). Determinants of loneliness among neglectful and other low-income mothers. *Journal of Social Service Research, 8*(3), 1-15.

Polansky, N. A., Chalmers, M. A., Buttenwieser, E., & Williams, P. (1978). Assessing adequacy of child caring: An urban scale. *Child Welfare, 57,* 439-449.

Smith, M. L., & Glass, G. V. (1977). Meta-analysis of psychotherapy outcome studies. *American Psychologist, 32,* 752-760.

Turner, C. P., & Martin, E. (Eds.). (1984). *Surveying subjective phenomena* (vol. 1). New York: Russell Sage Foundation.

Upshur, C. C. (1988). Measuring parent outcomes. In H. B. Weiss & F. H. Jacobs (Eds.), *Evaluating family programs* (pp. 131-152). New York: Aldine.
Walker, K. E., & Crocker, R. W. (1988). Measuring family systems outcomes. In H. B. Weiss & F. H. Jacobs (Eds.), *Evaluating family programs* (pp. 153-176). New York: Aldine.
Weiss, H. B., & Jacobs, F. H. (Eds.). (1988). *Evaluating family programs*. New York: Aldine.

9

From Chicago to Little Egypt:

Lessons from an Evaluation of a
Family Preservation Program

JOHN R. SCHUERMAN
TINA RZEPNICKI
JULIA LITTELL

Introduction

In this chapter we consider a number of issues that arise in the evaluation of family preservation programs. Our observations are drawn largely from our early experience in the evaluation of the family preservation program in Illinois. That program, and our work with it, are now only one year old, but we think we have learned a number of important lessons in that short time. We begin with a brief description of the service program and its evaluation, and then turn to a discussion of some issues we have faced. We consider problems in the definition of outcomes and of the target group, the exploration of the nature of the intervention, and difficulties in gathering data on a large program. Finally, we discuss our efforts to implement a full-scale

AUTHORS' NOTE: We are grateful to Diane Yost and Barry Colvin of the Illinois Department of Children and Family Services; to Harold Richman, Penny Johnson, and Steve Budde of the Chapin Hall Center for Children; and to the editors of this volume for helpful comments on an earlier version of this chapter. Hundreds of staff members in DCFS and in the provider agencies, from the Wisconsin border to Little Egypt, have assisted us in this project, and we are most indebted to them. Finally, our colleagues on the evaluation staff provide not only diligent effort but insightful observations into our work. This paper grew out of lively interchanges among all of us.

randomized experiment on this program. We raise a number of problems, suggest a few solutions, and hope that others will join with us in the task of providing more complete answers.

The Illinois program, called Family First, consists of several components. The first component, implemented in 1989, is designed to prevent the out-of-home placement of abused and neglected children. As this is being written, a program for reunifying families with children in foster care is being instituted, and a program to help maintain adoptions is planned. The State Department of Children and Family Services (DCFS) contracts with private agencies to provide the services. Families with children who are at risk of placement are referred to these private agencies by DCFS personnel in the course of investigations of abuse or neglect. Services are to be short-term (90 days or less), intensive, and home-based. In planning its initiative, Illinois chose to give the private agencies a great deal of freedom in designing their programs. No particular "model" was prescribed, although specifications were provided for certain program features such as length of service.

The Illinois program is large. In its first year (beginning in January 1989), it involved more than 30 private agencies throughout the state. It covered Chicago, the rest of Cook County, and a number of other counties in the state. Through December 1989, approximately 1,000 families had been served by the program. Beginning in January 1990, it will cover the entire state and involve more than 60 agencies.

The evaluation is also large, in terms of both its staff size and its ambitions. Chapin Hall, a children's policy research center at the University of Chicago, was awarded the contract for evaluation following a competitive bidding process. The evaluation contains two main components: the collection of data on case characteristics and outcomes, and the collection of data on how the program is implemented by both the public and private agencies. The objectives of the evaluation are to provide a description of the program and the families it serves and an estimate of the effects of the program on families and children, effects during the period of service and during a follow-up period of at least one year. We also hope to provide preliminary answers to the classic question of evaluation: "What works with whom?"

In its initial conceptualization of the evaluation, with the encouragement of representatives of the private sector, DCFS envisioned a rigorous experimental design. During the first year of the program, we have worked with DCFS on plans to implement such a design. Many obstacles have arisen to implementing an experiment, but it now appears that such a study will be possible. We discuss some of the obstacles below. While we await implementation of the experiment, we are gathering data on cases served in the family preservation program and on two unmatched samples. The unmatched samples include cases in which placement occurred in the investigation stage and cases in which the intact family is being served in the home. These data cannot be used to estimate the effects of the program, but they allow us to describe cases in the program as compared to other cases that enter the child protective system.

We believe that the study of the implementation of the program is a particularly important part of our work. This study involves description of the programs of the private agencies, of the interaction between the public and private agencies, and of the ways that personnel in the public and private agencies make decisions about cases. We use questionnaires to gather quantitative data from agency personnel on their views of the program and their activities. We are also attempting to develop, through frequent unstructured interviews with staff of both the public and private agencies, an intensive, qualitative understanding of how the program works. Each of the private agencies and offices of the public agency is assigned to a Chapin Hall staff member, who spends most of his or her time visiting these offices. These staff members gather information about how things are working in the field and also serve as liaisons between the agencies and the evaluation office. They are important in interpreting our needs for the "hard" data on cases that the agencies must provide us.

A range of information is being sought on case characteristics, services provided to cases, and case outcomes. As discussed below, we are collecting data on a variety of outcomes at several points in time. We hope to follow cases for at least one year following the completion of services. Demographic variables and data on child and family functioning, together with information on services, will be used to try to understand variations in outcomes. Data on case characteristics and case outcomes come from three sources: (a) an instrument we designed that is completed by the private agencies at the time a case is closed to provide information on problems in the family, services delivered, and outcomes; (b) various DCFS forms that must be completed on cases; and (c) the DCFS computer files on cases. In designing our data requirements, we attempted to be sensitive to the burden we were placing on operating personnel, hence we attempt to make as much use as possible of data that are gathered for other purposes by using existing DCFS forms and computer systems.

The large scale of the program necessitates our substantial dependence on others for data on cases. We discuss below some of the problems this dependence has created. At a later point, we hope to interview a sample of parents who have taken part in the program, using interviewers under our supervision, in order to provide an additional, independent source of information.

The Problem of Outcomes

The objective of family preservation programs is the maintenance of family units while assuring the safety of children. The target group for such programs is families in which there is likelihood of placement of children. The principal outcome variable is, therefore, whether children are placed. A case may be considered a failure if a child in the family is placed in substitute care during the period of service or during a specified follow-up period; otherwise, the case may be considered a success. Other outcomes might be measured; but in family preservation evaluations, this variable is overwhelmingly dominant.

It would appear that this outcome variable is remarkably clear, straightforward, and easy to measure. In fact, in the evaluation of social programs, evaluators are rarely presented with such a clear and dominating outcome variable. But we will discuss a number of problems with placement as outcome.

The concern with placement arises out of a belief that placement of a child in substitute care is damaging to the child; it is better for the child to grow up in his or her birth family. The premise of family preservation programs is that abusing and neglectful parents can become adequate caretakers so that the birth family can be preserved. The problem is that there are limits in the technology for working with families, and some birth families cannot be made safe for children. Obviously, a child should not be allowed to die or suffer serious injury while his or her family is being preserved. Hence, placement may mean several things; it may mean that the service was flawed, or it may mean that no service could have kept the family together while protecting the child from harm. In family preservation work, maintaining the child at home is a proxy for the presumed benefits of growing up in one's own family, while placement also represents a benefit, the benefit of reduced risk of future harm.

Thus, as an outcome variable, placement is a curious thing. In the aggregate, reduced placement rates are desirable, hence placements are "bad." In the individual case, placement is, in some sense, "good," unless an error in judgment has been made by the decision maker. Certainly the decision maker believes that placement is in the best interests of the child. This is unlike outcome variables in other kinds of programs. Working is almost always "better" than unemployment; so if a client of a job-training program fails to get a job, the outcome cannot be considered "good" in that case. While placement might be the result of poor execution of the technology, of limits in the technology, or of errors in the selection process for the program, it is, nonetheless, thought to be the best thing for the child in the individual case.

In the face of this dilemma, placement is retained as an outcome measure because it is used in the aggregate and comparatively. Growing up in one's birth family is usually (though not always) the best thing for a child. Hence, if a family preservation program results in fewer placements than the old way of doing things, it is thought to be better. The new program has presumably prevented unnecessary placements that would have been made by the old program.

But does this comparison of placement rates make for an adequate outcome measure? We have talked with many people in both the public and private agencies in Illinois who appear to think it may not. They cite situations that may dilute the meaningfulness of placement as an outcome, even in the aggregate. They suggest that family preservation programs may serve a "case-finding" function. Intensive work with families means that families are observed closely, that is, there is a substantial "surveillance" component of these programs. Abusive behavior that might otherwise go undetected may be observed, and a child placed as the result. To the extent that this phenomenon exists, placement rates in family preservation programs may be increased. Of course, these situations are ones in which the outcome for the child is presumably beneficial; the child has been protected from harm, so the placement statistic includes those "good" outcomes.

At times, such an outcome may even be the one expected by the public agency. We have been told of cases in which the public child protection agency believed that a child should be placed, but did not think that it had enough evidence to make that judgment stand up in court. Some of these cases are referred to family preservation agencies in the hope that they will develop evidence sufficient to take custody of the children. It is also believed that the family preservation program may result in "better" placements when they occur. We are not sure what this means, but we assume that it includes cases in which parents and children are better prepared for placement and in which plans for placement are better developed than those that would have been developed by the public agency. As yet, we have no hard evidence that family preservation programs result in more case-finding or in "better" placements.

The intensity of family preservation work may also cause another problem in the interpretation of placement as an outcome variable. The increased surveillance may suppress abusive or other undesirable behavior for the time being. As a result, placement may merely be postponed. The possibility of such effects makes it even more important that the evaluation include adequate follow-up.

The problems in using placement as an outcome variable may be related to conflicts in the values governing practice in child welfare today. Among those values are the importance of the birth family, permanency, least restrictive alternative, the notion of making "reasonable efforts" to avoid placement, and the safety of the child. In some cases, these values come into conflict and must be weighed. Some risk to the child may be tolerated in order to maintain the family unit. The performance of reasonable efforts to avoid placement in some cases may delay a permanent plan. Sometimes prolonged efforts to maintain the family may culminate in a more restrictive alternative than would have been necessary had placement been made earlier. We believe that evaluators must be sensitive to these value conflicts and attempt to understand the ways in which workers and the system deal with them. Beyond that, each of these values suggests different outcome measures.

Still another important value is that of costs. Anticipated reduction in foster care costs is a major reason for the support of legislators for these programs. Ideally, evaluations should compare total costs with and without the family preservation program.

The Definition of Placement

Even accepting placement as an outcome measurement, problems arise in its definition. When is a placement outside the birth home a placement? Placements for short lengths of time, placements with relatives, and informal placements cause difficulties in the definition of "placement." While any placement may cause some trauma to the child and family, should a placement for only two days be considered a placement for purposes of evaluation? If not, where does one draw the line? In Illinois, as in many states, the public child welfare agency may take "protective custody" of a child for a maximum of 48 hours, at which time a court must order "temporary custody." Hence, one solution is to use a court-ordered placement as a criterion.

What about placements with relatives? In Illinois, as in many states, there is currently much emphasis on placement with relatives, on the theory that such placements are better for the child. Apparently, the idea is that a relative's home is "closer" to the birth family. The child is likely to know the relative, the culture of the relative's home is likely to be similar to that of the birth family, and contact with the birth family is likely to be facilitated. As a result, placement with relatives is sometimes thought to be "not really a placement," or at least to be different enough that it should not be considered in the same category as other substitute care placements. The problem is that relative placements vary in their effects on children and their families (as do other kinds of placements). Some may have "family preservation" effects, while others may be as disruptive as placement in a non-relative foster home or institution. A pervasive concern of some practitioners for relative placements is the safety of the child. In a family with multigenerational abuse, it may not be wise to place a child with a grandmother who abused her daughter. In addition, relatives may not adequately protect a child from a perpetrator. In still other cases, custodial relatives may interfere with efforts to achieve reunification.

How should relative placements be counted in evaluation of family preservation programs (see Pecora, this volume)? Placing a child with a relative is not the same as leaving the child in the birth family, so it seems these placements should be counted in some way. One criterion might be the formality of such placements. Some relative placements involve licensing and payments from the state; others are sanctioned by the state without licensing or payment; while still others are quite informal arrangements, which may not even be known to the state. It is tempting to define "placement" as a formal arrangement, but we believe that would be a mistake. The formality of a relative placement is unlikely to be highly associated with its impact on the child and family. Of course, informal placements other than with relatives are utilized sometimes and also cause problems in the definition of "placement."

Measurement of Child and Family Functioning

No extensive program evaluation involves only one outcome measure (see Jones, this volume). Programs have multiple effects, and a particular effect may be measured in several ways. It is usually assumed that a thorough evaluation should attempt to detect these multiple effects and should include multiple measures of important effects. Outcome measures in our evaluation include length of placements; subsequent reports of abuse or neglect, and whether these reports are substantiated; degree of involvement of the family in service efforts; and various measures of change in child and family functioning, including changes in assessed levels of risk of harm to the child. It has been argued that these measures of outcome should be on a par with placement.

Agencies, particularly the private agencies in our study, hope to do more than simply prevent placement and assure the safety of children. They hope to improve the lives of children and families by helping them to improve their functioning. But questions have been raised about the appropriateness of some of these measures in family preservation evaluation. The principal function of the state child protective agency is to protect children from physical harm. Some areas of functioning may be quite unrelated to risk of physical harm. Using a measure such as school functioning as an outcome variable in family preservation evaluation implies that facilitating improvement in school functioning is a responsibility of the state. When a state agency takes custody of a child, it has responsibility to provide the best possible environment for the child. But that does not mean that, in working with intact families, the agency should take on similar responsibilities. State child welfare agencies are severely taxed as it is without assuming vast new areas of responsibility. We believe that in selecting and interpreting outcome measures, evaluators should consider their implications for the child welfare agency.

If such other measures of outcome are accepted as legitimate for study, the problem of how they are to be interpreted remains. What overall conclusions might be drawn from various patterns in the outcome data? For example, what if a program can be shown to have important positive effects on the functioning of children and families, but has only marginal effects on placement rates? Does that justify continuation of the program, when it has been created primarily to reduce placements, and sold to legislators largely on the basis of anticipated reductions in foster care costs? Researchers might be inclined to leave such questions to policymakers, but they are likely to be pressed on this point; and we believe that it is their responsibility to at least provide some analysis to aid the policy-making process.

Other Outcomes

The implementation of a family preservation program, particularly when it is done on a large scale as in Illinois, has effects beyond those observable at the level of individual children and families. In particular, it may have substantial effects on the operations of the public agency, private agencies, courts, state's attorneys, and other organizations and individuals. In fact, it could be argued that this is the most important effect of family preservation programs: a shift in the "culture" of child welfare away from depending on placement for the protection of children from harm and toward the value of maintaining intact families wherever possible. That observation leads to the question of whether a family preservation program that results in workers having a family orientation could be considered a success even if it has only marginal impact on placement rates.

The detection of system effects is a major challenge for family preservation evaluators. Documenting system change requires comparisons, and obtaining adequate comparative data is often difficult. Evaluators are usually not in a position to study a system for very long before a new program is implemented, so a comparison with a "baseline" may not be possible. Comparisons with areas in which the program is not implemented are likely to be unconvincing because of the difficulty in establishing similarities in important characteristics of the areas. Areas for implementation of a program are usually not chosen randomly; and the reasons for choosing them will often affect the implementation and its outcomes.

We believe that one way to focus examination of system effects is to examine the decision making of key individuals, particularly child protective workers, judges, and state's attorneys. The implementation of a family preservation program is likely to have significant effects on a wide range of decisions about children, including such things as the assessment of risk and the criteria for taking custody of children. Our study of such matters is facilitated by the fact that Chapin Hall conducted a number of previous studies in DCFS, including a study of decision making by child protective workers in Chicago. Thus we have some "baseline" data available for comparison. The discussion of system effects brings us back to the issue of placement as an outcome variable. There are likely to be system effects beyond those of program implementation that will have an impact on such things as placement rates. Prime examples of influences having such effects are the availability of foster homes and media coverage of child deaths. Such "macro" factors may cause increases or decreases in placement rates quite apart from the effects of family preservation programs.

Definition of the Target Group

The objective of preventing placement of children leads directly to the specification of the target group for the program. In most family preservation programs, the target group is defined as "families in which there is imminent risk of placement of one or more children." As with the specification of placement as outcome, that criterion appears to be straightforward but, in fact, contains many difficulties. Workers do not appear to use a well-articulated set of rules for reaching the judgment that a child is in need of placement (for discussions of systems of rules in child welfare intake, see Stein & Rzepnicki, 1983, 1984; Schuerman, 1987; Schuerman, Mullen, Stagner, & Johnson, 1989). In addition, it is generally recognized that not all cases in need of placement are appropriate for referral to family preservation services. As noted above, some children would not be safe, even with the provision of services. Other criteria, such as likely cooperativeness of the family with services, are often established. All of these criteria involve uncertain and imprecise judgments, judgments that must often be made on the basis of incomplete and uncertain information.

Exactly what is meant by "imminent risk of placement" is not clear. It would seem that it should mean that the child would have been placed in the absence of the family preservation program. It is evident that few workers making these decisions are willing to adhere to such a rigorous definition. It appears that there are many "borderline" cases being referred to family preservation programs in which placement would not have been taken in the absence of the program. In addition, many cases in which placement is not imminent, but in which there exists risk of placement in the future, seem to be accepted into these programs. Of course, it could be argued that serving these families will reduce future rates of placement and that should be considered a benefit of the program. The problem with such an argument is that it depends on the prediction of human behavior in the future, and such predictions are notoriously imperfect. The technology for accurately predicting the abuse of a child within the next six months or one year simply does not exist (Frankel, 1988; Stein, 1985).

Beyond that, in Illinois some cases referred to the program are not considered by anyone to involve much risk of placement, either now or in the future. We suspect that this may be the case in other family preservation programs. It is evident that the group receiving services includes cases in which placement would not have occurred in the absence of the program. These cases may well receive benefit from the program, but their presence creates great difficulties in the interpretation of placement rates. A low rate of placement may well be due in part to the fact that many of the children would not have been placed anyway. Unfortunately, it is impossible for the evaluator to identify with any precision the cases in which placement would not have occurred in the absence of the program.

Even if referral workers were scrupulously adhering to a criterion of referring only cases in which placement is thought to be imminent, difficulties would remain. These difficulties revolve around the effects of a new program on the decision-making process mentioned above. The existence of a family preservation program as an alternative may well have subtle, sometimes unconscious, effects on the assessment of risk to a child. Cases in which the worker would not consider placement may nonetheless be deemed to be at imminent risk of placement in order to secure family preservation services. Hence, the group that receives services in a family preservation program will include cases in which placement would not have occurred in the absence of such a program.

Still another problem with the definition of the target group is that advocates for family preservation efforts assume (implicitly or explicitly) that many placements today are unnecessary, or at least would be unnecessary if family preservation services were available. As with all judgments, those regarding placement will include some "false positives" and some "false negatives." However, we know of no data that would provide an estimate as to the size of the unnecessary placement group. Hence, a firm basis cannot be provided for estimates of the potential demand for family preservation services.

All of these considerations make it particularly important that rigorous experiments be conducted on the effects of family preservation programs. Other quasi-experimental designs are simply unable to provide adequate estimates of effects in the face of uncertainties as to the character of the group served, in particular whether all families (or even most families) in the group would have experienced a placement in the absence of services. We return to this issue later in the chapter.

Problems in Evaluation of Program Implementation

As indicated in the introduction, a major part of our evaluation involves an examination of the implementation of the program by the state and private agencies. This involves the collection of standardized data from private agency personnel on their attitudes and activities. In addition, we conduct intensive, unstructured interviews with personnel at various levels in both the public and the private agencies. Through this work we hope to be able to describe the private agency programs; the interaction of the state agency and the private agencies; and the decision-making processes in both sectors. In this section we are able to present some beginning findings from our qualitative work. We believe these findings demonstrate the benefits of intensive efforts to understand how the programs work.

At this point, our dominant finding is that there is considerable variation among individuals in the state agency and in the private agencies in their views of the program and how they are going about implementation. At the beginning of the project, we asked various officials and supervisors in the state agency what they expected from the program and what they expected the program would accomplish. We received a variety of responses to these questions, ranging from the belief that the program was the only hope for the Department to manage its overwhelming responsibilities to the view that the program constituted a diversion of resources from more promising approaches. Some people, in both the public and private agencies, believed that the program would, in fact, live up to its billing, reduce placements and allow many cases that would have been served for an extended period of time by the public agency to be closed. At the other end of the continuum, other people, particularly those who were concerned with the limitations of the 90-day period of service, believed that the program simply provided an "extended assessment." This assessment might result either in placement or in more extensive case planning than could have been accomplished by the public agency.

While people with operating responsibility are often nervous about evaluation, informants at the "conservative" end of the continuum were particularly concerned. One goal of the program is the prevention of placement in 85% of the cases served. These informants were worried about a now-familiar scenario: A program that is oversold must eventually answer to the evaluation data. Many staff were concerned with how we, the evaluators, would deal with this situation. Would they get a sympathetic hearing for their efforts to explain results that did not meet earlier expectations? There were attempts to shift the goals of the program (we were urged to take a "broader" view of outcomes) away from the prevention of placement. As we suggested above, evaluators must find ways to think about such "other" outcomes of programs, outcomes that may be beneficial but not those that were promised.

Our examination of the relationship between the public and private agencies has focused on four processes: the selection of referrals by the public agency; the process of handing cases over to the private agencies; the involvement of the public agency during service by the private agency; and the process of handing cases back to the public agency at the end of service (at 90 days, unless the case is extended or closed). Regarding referral practices, as might be expected, there are variations around the state in kinds of cases referred. Referral practices appear to have evolved considerably in the year since the program began. Public agency workers have developed notions about the capacity of particular agencies to deal with particular kinds of clients, and these notions affect referral practices. For example, some agencies are thought to be unable to handle cases of drug abuse, but might be adept at dealing with other cases, such as teenage mothers. In addition, there appears to be a considerable degree of informal negotiation between the public agency and the private agencies regarding the kinds of cases referred. All private agency contracts provide for "no decline" of referrals; but agencies sometimes ask DCFS not to send any more of a certain kind of client for a while, and DCFS appears to honor this request. More generally, understandings develop as to certain kinds of clients that are inappropriate. Obviously, formal contracts cannot contain all of the understandings that exist between agencies. Evaluators are faced with the problem of assessing such informal arrangements and perhaps judging their appropriateness.

The process of handing cases back to DCFS is also of interest. A goal of the program is to close cases at the end of the 90-day service, but often cases stay open under DCFS supervision (during the first months of the program about 75% remained open after the termination of family preservation services). The reasons cases remain open vary. Some continue to receive services from organizations that are paid by DCFS, and this payment could not continue if the case were closed. Others are kept open for ongoing monitoring by DCFS, and still others remain open simply because the risk to the child is deemed to remain high.

What is done with these still open cases varies greatly. The private agencies are authorized to provide "family maintenance" services for some cases, while others are returned to DCFS for ongoing services. Regular DCFS follow-up services often involve referrals to private agencies, perhaps the same agencies providing family preservation services. Some clients continue to receive services similar to those provided in the family preservation program; in fact, it might be wondered when the program terminates for them. Others experience a dramatic change in their relationships to the child welfare system. Evaluators must find ways to deal with the fact that, for many clients (perhaps most), the end of the program does not mean the end of services. We should try to determine what services clients receive post-termination and how those services affect the interpretation of follow-up data.

In our study of private agency programs, we examine structural elements (e. g., length of service, whether teams of therapists and case aides are used, size of caseload), services provided, and attitudes of workers (how they view the program and its clients). We also try to gain some understanding of the interaction between workers and clients, although we have not attempted direct observation of those interactions. The ultimate task in this work is to identify those program aspects that make a difference in outcome. We believe that, unfortunately, the aspects of service that have the most impact may not be those that are easily identified and measured. For example, while structural aspects and the adherence to stated protocols (such as the length of service) may have some relationship to outcome, we suspect they are not the most important elements in service. We believe that the particular package of services provided may also not be strongly related to outcome. Instead, we think that more elusive elements may be more important, such as the "zeal" of workers, their ability to manage the "cognitive dissonance" that arises out of the recognition of program limitations, and their skill in "working the system" on behalf of clients. Success in any endeavor requires that one believes in it and in one's efficacy. The intensity of family preservation work demands an unusual level of energy and investment. It also requires considerable optimism, belief in client potential for change, and facility in identifying client strengths.

The measurement of such factors is a major challenge for evaluators of family preservation programs. We have made beginning attempts to address this problem, but much work remains. Our experience so far confirms the importance of a substantial investment in an intensive qualitative study of the work that goes on in these programs.

Problems of Data on Cases

As indicated above, we depend heavily on workers in the public and private agencies for data on cases. The size of the program and the limitations in the evaluation budget require this approach. Our case data come from forms we have designed that are completed by workers in the private agencies, from existing DCFS forms, and from DCFS computer files.

We have very little control over the conditions under which these data are provided and thus their quality. We depend to a very large extent on the diligence and goodwill of workers to provide us with good data. There are many threats to the quality of the data. Workers are burdened with many pressing tasks; completion of forms is often put off and they are sometimes completed hurriedly and late, when memory has dimmed. Many items require judgment, and there will be variations in the way such judgments are made, no matter how precise the instructions. Many of these judgments are subject to reactivity: They may be seen as reflecting on the work of the individual making the judgments. Beyond all that, we have problems in simple compliance: Some forms are not completed or not all items on them are completed.

As indicated above, we have sought to minimize the data collection burden on staff of the agencies by utilizing the Department's computer files for as much data as possible. These are very large and complex databases, requiring a great deal of sophisticated programming on our part to make them usable for our purposes. It might be thought that data in the computer files would be more accurate than those gathered in other ways, but that is not the case. Data in the computer files are provided by the same personnel as other data we use and are subject to the same limitations in reliability, validity, and completeness. We depend on the computer files particularly for data on the "hard" outcomes, such as confirmed reports of subsequent abuse and neglect, the placement of a child, and the length of time in placement. While these data eventually become available in the computer, we often have to wait a considerable time until they are entered.

Solace in the face of problems of data quality might be sought in the assumption that they are randomly distributed and lead primarily to an increase in "within groups" variation. Hence, they might contribute to "Type II" error, but not to the affirmation of false conclusions. However, it is unlikely that such a sanguine thought is sustainable. The errors arising from these factors are likely to differ systematically among regions and programs.

What can be done about the data quality problem here? Except for information obtained from the computer files, the data require coding and data entry by our staff. We perform periodic reliability checks on samples of coding and data entry, but this does not get at the reliability of the information provided to us. For some data, we have multiple sources of information. For example, information on confirmed reports of abuse and neglect during the course of service is obtained from both private agency workers and the computer files. That presents the problem of resolving discrepancies, for which we are in the process of devising solutions. As to the "softer" data on such things as identification of problems families face and the assessment of risk, we may be able, in our qualitative study, to get a sense of how variations in orientation affect judgments, thereby enabling us to better understand the limitations in the data.

We think it likely that the problems in data quality that arise in a large-scale evaluation, in which the researchers must depend on others for data, will lead evaluators to emphasize "harder" data such as placements and subsequent reports, data which can be assumed to be "better," though far from perfect. This will cause chagrin to operating personnel who believe it important to examine subtler outcomes. At the urging of agency staff, we have attempted to include information on the subtler aspects of service and its outcomes, but variations in approaches to the work and in interpretations of terms have substantial effects on the resulting data. Much work remains to be done on the use of both existing data and data obtained from operating personnel in the evaluation of large-scale family preservation programs.

Problems in Implementing Experimental Designs

In issuing the Request for Proposals for the evaluation of the family preservation program in Illinois, DCFS displayed great foresight in calling for a rigorous experimental evaluation. Members of the private agency sector encouraged the Department to conduct an experiment. As indicated above, we are convinced that a rigorous experiment is the only design that will provide convincing evidence for the effects of family preservation programs. A major consideration leading to this conclusion is the ambiguity of the specification of the target group and the attendant uncertainty as to what outcomes would have been in the absence of the program. A number of nonexperimental designs have been proposed, including before-after comparisons of areas in which family preservation programs are implemented; comparisons of supposedly comparable areas of the state, some having family preservation services while others do not; and case matching designs. None of these designs adequately controls for selection bias and other threats to interpretation of results.

During the first year of the evaluation, we have worked with the Department on plans for implementation of an experiment. We have not pushed for an immediate implementation of the experiment because we believe that it is not appropriate to subject a program to experimental evaluation in the first months of its existence. Programs should be allowed time to settle in and develop some proficiency. How long programs should be given before beginning an experiment is a matter of debate.

We are planning to implement the experiment in only a few selected areas of the state, because of the need to adequately supervise the case assignment process and other aspects of the research. Our criteria for selection of areas for the experiment are adequacy of numbers of cases, feasibility of implementation, geographic variation, and quality of the programs. We believe that it is desirable to choose programs that are thought to be good, since one can learn more from good practice. Of course, the fact that we are limiting the experiment to selected areas means that we will be limited in the conclusions that we will be able to draw from the results. Our conclusions will apply to areas and programs like those we study. Our estimates of the effects of family preservation will not apply to all programs in the state, but will be likely to represent the "high end" of practice in Illinois.

Although top executives in the Department and leaders in the private agency field have supported the idea of an experiment from the beginning, other staff have been more skeptical; and these are staff upon whom we must depend for actual implementation. Concerns have included common arguments against experimentation, particularly the ethics of denying services to those selected for the control group, and possible legal liability of the Department if the experiment is implemented. Of course, control group families will not be denied services altogether; they will receive the regular services of the Department. Various members of the Department appear to disagree as to how disadvantaged these families will be.

There is also concern about the effects of the experiment on numbers of cases served by the private agencies. Staff worry that it might not be possible to keep private agencies' programs full because of the need to divide the eligible pool between the experimental and control groups. There is also the frequently observed phenomenon of referrals "drying up" when an experiment is implemented, although they usually return to normal levels later on.

The issue of informed consent of subjects has been a topic of many conversations with the Department. At present, the Department has determined to proceed with the experiment without obtaining the informed consent of subjects. There are two principal reasons for this decision. First, and most important, is the view that free informed consent is not possible in a situation involving potential coercive actions of the state. If subjects agree to be in the experiment, they would be put into either the experimental group, where they would receive services designed to maintain the family intact, or into the control group, where they would receive regular services and the child might be removed from the home. If subjects did not agree to be in the experiment, they would receive regular services and the child might be removed from the home. It is felt that this choice implies threats that are inconsistent with the idea of informed consent.

Second, there is concern with the feasibility of the informed consent procedures. It is important that the random-assignment process occur after the decision is made that the case is eligible for family preservation services and consent is obtained. Therefore, the worker, together with a supervisor and possibly a program liaison, must make an eligibility decision, obtain informed consent from the client, consult the random assignment process, discuss the assignment with the family, and finally make the referral either to the family preservation program or to the regular services program. This would require additional visits to the family by staff who are already overburdened. There is also concern with maintaining the quality of the informed consent process when it must be conducted by many workers throughout the state.

There is precedent in not obtaining informed consent in experiments such as this. Federal Department of Health and Human Services regulations on research on human subjects provide for an exemption for studies conducted by states and the federal government on public programs (for discussions of these issues see Breger, 1983; Rivlin & Timpane, 1975).

Although an experiment is the only way to obtain estimates of the effects of a program such as this, the interpretation of data will not be unequivocal. Some threats to generalization of results will remain, even with an experiment. There are the effects on the system of instituting the program discussed earlier. Decision making about cases in both the experimental and the control groups, for example, whether to take custody of a child at risk, is likely to differ from decision making before the implementation of the program. For example, workers may be less likely to take custody in certain kinds of cases. These effects may not be the same in the experimental and control groups. Worker decisions may be affected by their beliefs about the effects of their decisions on the outcome of the evaluation. In addition, the character of regular (control group) services may change. On the one hand, there may be "contamination," in that regular services may become similar to family preservation services. On the other hand, workers in regular services may become demoralized by the existence of new services that are supposedly superior. Still another problem in generalizing from the results of an experiment is that of possible effects of the experiment on selection of cases for the experimental pool. The processes of selecting cases for the experiment are unlikely to be the same as those that would be used in an established, proven program.

As to the objective of finding out what works with whom, additional problems intrude. While we may be able to institute random assignment of cases to experimental and control groups within regions, we will not be able to randomly assign cases to various private agency programs in those regions. Where there is a choice of program for a case assigned to the experimental group, that choice will be made by DCFS personnel. This may result in associations between case characteristics and service characteristics such that the effects of each cannot be sorted out because of the collinearity. There is also the problem of obtaining adequate numbers of cases in cells representing particular combinations of case and service characteristics. Despite these difficulties, we hope to bring some data to bear on the problem of specifying approaches for particular groups of clients.

Conclusions

Family preservation is both a set of services and a movement. When a program is implemented, its planners seek not only to provide new options for services for families but also to reform the system in dramatic ways. They seek changes in the way families are thought of, in the way services are conceived, in the ways of doing bureaucratic business, and in relationships among agencies. Evaluators are accustomed to focusing on individual and family level outcomes and must learn how to provide accounts of these system level effects. In addition, some of the family level effects that are sought are difficult for evaluators to examine. For example, we know of no "empowerment" index. Finally, those outcomes that appear to be relatively straightforward may turn out to be rather complex, as we have illustrated with our discussion of placement as an outcome variable.

The institution of family preservation services comes at a time of severe strain on public child welfare systems (Monroe & Isherwood, 1988). Reported incidents of abuse and neglect are increasing, and these systems are increasingly asked to take on new responsibilities, such as abuse prevention and the investigation of psychological harm to children. Many observers believe that cases are becoming more complex: There is widespread substance abuse and now the daunting problem of pediatric AIDS. Family preservation services may be seen as one way to help these systems cope with increased demands, but they will also create new demands of their own. For example, some observers have suggested that the availability of family preservation services may cause an increase in the protective service caseload. Evaluators must find ways to cope with this complex of forces.

In this chapter, we have also provided illustrations of other challenges in the evaluating of a large-scale family preservation program: the conceptualization of placement as an outcome, the definition of the target group, the examination of implementation, the quality of data, and issues in the design of randomized experimental studies. We are confident that these challenges will yield to careful analysis.

References

Breger, M. J. (1983). Randomized social experiments and the law. In R. F. Boruch & J. S. Cecil (Eds.), *Solutions to ethical and legal problems in social research.* New York: Academic Press.

Frankel, H. (1988). Family-centered, home-based services in child protection: A review of the research. *Social Service Review, 62,* 137-157.

Monroe, A. D., & Isherwood, J. T. (1988). *The changing DCFS workload: 1976-1986.* Carbondale: Illinois State University.

Rivlin, A. M., & Timpane, P. M. (Eds.). (1975). *Ethical and legal issues of social experimentation.* Washington, DC: The Brookings Institution.

Schuerman, J. R. (1987). Expert consulting systems in social welfare. *Social Work Research and Abstracts, 23,* 14-18.

Schuerman, J. R., Mullen, E., Stagner, M., & Johnson, P. (1989). First generation expert systems in social welfare. *Computers in Human Services, 4,* 111-122.

Stein, T. (1985). Projects to prevent out-of-home placement. *Children and Youth Services Review, 7,* 109-121.

Stein, T., & Rzepnicki, T. (1983). *Decision making at child welfare intake.* New York: Child Welfare League of America.

Stein, T., & Rzepnicki, T. (1984). *Decision making in child welfare services: Intake and planning.* Boston: Kluwer-Nijhoff.

10

The Public Policy Implications of Family Preservation

DOUGLAS W. NELSON

As this volume attests, a great deal is being learned about family preservation. The research is helping us understand what family preservation is, who it may serve effectively, who it might not, and what it costs to provide such services. The findings are already sufficient to enable the rejection of extreme or overblown policy inferences. Family preservation is neither a magic bullet that can uniformly reverse family dysfunction nor a systemic panacea that will soon supplant the need for placements. Neither, however, is it merely a naive or sentimental affirmation of the ideals of family and prevention, without any practical or policy import.

Instead, it may be fairest to say that what we have learned about family preservation to date both raises a high level of policy-relevant promise and still leaves a number of key research questions begging for clearer answers.

A variety of reports, for example, gives us reason to believe that brief, intensive in-home services can effect measurable change in the environment, attitudes, and behaviors of at least some severely stressed dysfunctioning families—and that, for at least a fraction of these families, the change achieved is sufficient to allow the protection, treatment, or correction of the children involved without an immediate need for placement (Fraser, Pecora, & Haapala, 1988; Fuqua & Thieman, 1989; Haapala & Kinney, in press; Jones, Magura, & Shyne, 1981). What we have not learned, however, is precisely how these interventions produce the evidenced changes; in what types and percentages of cases they are actually effective; which characteristics of interventions and families best correlate with "success" or "failure"; or how durable are the improvements wrought by these time-limited interventions.

In a similar way, available studies, as well as cost reports from existing programs, provide a sound basis for concluding that the average direct public cost of providing most types of family preservation services has been and will continue to be lower than the direct cost of a typical placement in most states (Behavioral Sciences Institute, 1986; Haugaard & Hokonson, 1983; Kinney, Haapala, Booth, & Leavitt, 1988; National Resource Center on Family-Based Services, 1983). The significance of this finding for conclusions about cost-effectiveness, however, must be tempered by an admission of the limitations of available research. We do not, for example, have any studies that fully track the indirect or follow-up costs that may be associated with "successful" placement prevention; nor do we have any analyses that carefully discriminate between cases in which placement is postponed and those in which the need for separation is permanently averted.

The foregoing are but a few of the many examples cited in this book of both the achievement and the incompleteness of existing research into family preservation. We note this mixed state of the research here in order to frame the central question that drives this chapter. Put simply, it is: In what ways and to what degree can the currently available research on family preservation be responsibly used now to influence basic decisions and directions in public policy toward at-risk children and families?

Some observers have suggested that much more has to be learned and confirmed about family preservation before it can be conscientiously advanced as a major lever for reassessing and reforming public responses to children in need (Wald, 1988). Others contend that, even with the imperfection and limits of existing research, what we have observed about family preservation is already sufficient to have a powerful impact on how we think about, criticize, plan, and shape the future delivery of a whole range of protective, mental health, and rehabilitative services to families and children.

This chapter, it should be stressed, is grounded in a strong commitment to the latter view. Indeed, the principal intent of the arguments that follow is to draw out the implications of what we have already learned of family preservation and urge their aggressive application to pressing questions of human service policy, practice, and delivery.

To that end, we begin with an examination of what may be the most concrete potential application of family preservation research—that is, the potential of time-limited, intensive interventions to help states and communities "manage" the escalating and costly reliance on placement to meet the protection, treatment, and correction needs of children. This is followed by a discussion of the potential impact of family preservation research on the operational meanings given to some pivotal existing public policy principles, particularly on the practical definitions and standards applied to "reasonable efforts," "least restrictive environment," and the "best interests of the child." A third section reviews the possible implications that our knowledge of the actual delivery of family preservation services has for the practice, delivery, and organization of broader social and therapeutic services to families. The chapter concludes with a brief speculation, suggesting how some of the key premises underlying family preservation might usefully serve as a foundation for posing some more sweeping questions aimed at redefining basic public responsibilities and responses to families.

The Implications of Family Preservation for the More Effective Management of Public Resources

It is no longer news that powerful economic and social forces are increasingly challenging the capacity of a growing number of American families to provide durable, secure, and supportive environments for the healthy development of their children. Declines in earning power, teenage pregnancy, single-headed households, two-earner families, drugs, persisting high school dropout rates, conflicting social values, inadequate supplies of affordable housing, eroding income support programs—these are but some of the labels we give to the underlying conditions that are contributing to increased family vulnerability, dysfunction, and illness. Throughout the country, the impact of these forces is now being measured in ever more reports of child abuse and neglect; startling growth in the incidence of parental and infant addiction; and increases in intrafamily conflict, violence, and emotional disorder. The public response to these consequences can, in turn, be gauged in growing protective service caseloads; in dramatic and accelerating foster and group care placement rates; in renewed pressure for the incarceration of delinquents; and finally in the rapid expansion of residential and in-patient treatment of child and adolescent mental health problems.

All of these trends, of course, are clearly impacting public costs. Since the mid-1980s, the annual increases in the cost of child placements have grown at the state level in increments of tens of millions; nationally, the growth is counted in the hundreds of millions and, soon, in the billions (Center for the Study of Social Policy, 1988a; County Welfare Directors Association of California, 1990; Tennessee General Assembly, Select Joint Committee on

Children and Youth, 1988). Unaltered, these trends foreshadow nearly a tripling in the real dollar expenditures for the protective and mental health placement of children within less than a decade.

For better or for worse, it is this context that gives the potential of family preservation its most concrete and immediate relevance to public policy. If, for example, family preservation could be counted on to postpone or prevent placements that otherwise would be made, and if it could be expected to do this without sacrificing children's interests and without adding net additional public costs, then the value and benefit of expanding family preservation ought to be fairly easy to convey in the current environment of system crisis.

Of course, the actual power of family preservation's promise in this regard turns on how confidently we can answer some obvious questions. The most basic of these is whether family preservation can actually do what its name implies—that is, can it really preserve families who would otherwise be temporarily or permanently separated at public cost.

If we are careful not to equate persuasiveness with precision, then it is fair to say that the evidence on this issue is fairly strong. The records of Homebuilders, the longest-running family preservation model, suggest that more than 70% of the families they serve remain together one year after their intervention. What gives this significance is that independent assessments of the referral patterns and case histories of Homebuilders' clients indicate that *the majority* of these families were at genuine risk and would have experienced separation without the assistance provided. Evaluations of other family preservation programs in several states are producing findings comparable to the Homebuilders experience. Typically, researchers report that between 50% and 90% of the families served by family preservation do not experience a placement for at least some time (e.g., three months to one year) following the intervention (Fuqua & Thieman, 1989; Johnson, 1987; Pearson & King, 1985). More recent studies are also beginning to utilize a variety of methods—such as family risk scales, case characteristic analysis, worker interviews, and, occasionally, control group comparisons—to confirm that a considerable fraction of the "preserved" families would very probably have experienced a placement but for the intervention.

None of this is intended to suggest that the research now available is definitive. We still lack the experience and research that would enable us to gauge what percentage of *the total population of families at risk of placement* might be safely kept together through brief and intensive in-home services. Furthermore, even the findings we have regarding "percentages of placements avoided" lack a desirable standard of precision. More control group studies (that can factor out contextual variables such as availability of placement resources) would certainly offer a more accurate and unassailable estimate of family preservation's real potential effectiveness rate.

While these are significant limitations, they are not crippling enough to preclude prudent policymakers from drawing important inferences from the available research. Chief among these is the reasonable conclusion that, where properly executed, family preservation can prevent the necessity for placement in a good share of the families determined to be eligible for assistance; and further, that these families "look a lot like" a substantial fraction of the total number of families that are now being separated across the country.

This finding, by itself, has obvious policy import. Given the nation's express commitment to fostering family survival, wherever practical and consistent with the child's rights, and given the widely endorsed standard of least-restrictive setting for the treatment and correction of children, an increased reliance on evidently effective models of family preservation would appear to have a strong ethical base in already existing social policy values.

The available research, however, suggests that family preservation may not only be "the right thing" to try on behalf of at-risk families, but it may also be the most fiscally prudent response. A growing number of studies and analyses indicate that the per family costs of providing most types of family preservation interventions are lower than the public cost of predictable placements for the same type of family in the same jurisdiction. In Iowa, Vermont, and other states, for example, the costs of providing family preservation have been reported to run about $3,000 per family, while the costs of supporting "typical" placements in those states ranged from $6,000 (for foster care) to $40,000 or more (for treatment or correctional placement) (Bruner, 1988; Johnson, 1987; Office of Evaluation, Florida Department of Health and Rehabilitative Services, 1982). Even if one assumes that family preservation programs will succeed in preventing placement in only 60% of the families served (a rate below Homebuilders' experience), the intervention would appear to "save" more than it costs.

Assertions about "saving" money, like the one offered above, require some qualification. The contention here is not that the introduction of family preservation will necessarily lower the absolute cost of serving at-risk families, or even that the expansion of such programs will, by itself, lower the number of child placements made in a given jurisdiction. In fact, a whole host of variables determines costs and placement rates, including such things as court behavior, community attitudes, economic circumstances, the prevalence of drug abuse, the cost of placement services, and the supply of placement resources. What the proponents of family preservation actually argue is simply that there is a good basis in existing research for assuming that competent and well-targeted short-term interventions can reduce placement rates and total system costs *from what they otherwise would have grown to* without such diversion efforts.

Some advocates of family preservation have generalized such calculations into expansive estimates of the long-run cost efficiency of a system-wide commitment to intensive placement prevention. By asserting that well-designed intensive services can avert the need for placement in a large percentage of all the families at risk of separation *and* by pointing to family preservation's alleged capacity to prevent not only the immediate placement risk, but also subsequent placements of siblings, these advocates are prepared to assert that a systemic investment in family preservation is likely to reduce dramatically what otherwise would be the total future public costs of providing child welfare services.

Ultimately, however, such claims turn on how carefully family preservation can be targeted. If family preservation is to create a bona fide future cost saving, a substantial percentage of the families referred to the program must be at real and imminent risk of separation. Put plainly, they must be families who would experience a placement without the attempt at family preservation. To the extent that family preservation is expanded to families who would not be separated (however justifiable that may be on other grounds), it will simply add costs to the system rather than reduce them.

The logic of the foregoing is plain enough, but the practical question remains: Is it realistic to assume that a state or community can initiate, expand, and maintain a family preservation capacity that is disciplined enough in its targeting to actually realize its cost-effectiveness potential? The answer, based on what we currently know, is probably yes. A number of recent state initiatives suggests that it is possible to establish, enforce, and refine referral policies and procedures that target family preservation to families who are at bona fide risk of placement (AuClaire & Schwartz, 1986; Fuqua & Thieman, 1989). Furthermore, the growing research into the characteristics of families successfully and unsuccessfully served by intensive in-home services should enable continual improvement in the identification of families for which family preservation is both most likely and least likely to be efficacious. At the same time, practice-level research is contributing to an increased understanding of the conditions, therapeutic methods, and skills that appear most relevant to making intensive interventions effective. Taken together, this growing body of experience and research adds up to an already adequate, and an improving, basis on which to build a responsibly targeted and thereby cost-effective reliance on family preservation services. When this is joined with a recognition that the typical per family costs of most existing family preservation programs have grown in the past few years far more slowly than average placement-related costs, an even more powerful argument can be made for the realistic cost-containment potential of placement prevention.

In short, one of the expectations arising from what we now know about intensive in-home services is that, from a public cost perspective, the burden of fiscal arguments should be shifting away from those who advocate the development of a targeted family preservation capacity and on to those who still question its affordability. While the data about family preservation's precise cost containment impact may still be incomplete, the evidence is utterly unmistakable that taking no action to alter placement trends will be very costly indeed.

These fiscal implications have a special bearing on federal policy-making. Since the mid-1980s, federal spending under Title IV-E and Medicaid has grown at an ever-accelerating rate, reflecting, in part, the increasing nationwide reliance on out-of-home care to meet the protection and treatment needs of children (U.S. Congress, House Committee on Energy and Commerce, 1988; U.S. Congress, House Committee on Ways and Means, 1989). Although the federal stake in containing these entitlement costs has been frequently asserted, there has been virtually no national leadership in providing states with the fiscal incentives or supports to develop responsible alternatives to placement. Medicaid and Title IV-E remain far easier for states to access on behalf of children in foster care or restrictive treatment settings than they are for services to the same children while still in their homes. At a minimum, it would appear fiscally prudent to extend at least some federal entitlement funding to state and local in-home programs that are expressly designed to prevent federally matchable placement costs.

All of the foregoing discussion has been cast—somewhat awkwardly, but nonetheless deliberately—in the context of public costs. This is, in part, because costs are the most immediate objection raised against investment in any new programmatic capacity and, in part, because the cost-containment potential of family preservation is one of the more compelling political reasons for policymakers to attend to the research on intensive in-home services. These considerations notwithstanding, however, the implications of what we are learning about family preservation go far beyond its role as a potential gatekeeper and substitute for future placement expenditures. Indeed, they more importantly go to informing and reinforcing some of the central policy principles that are intended to govern public responsibility to children and families. An overview of some of these implications is the subject of the next section.

Implications of Family Preservation for Improving Conformance to Public Policy Goals and Values

Perhaps the most significant implications arising from the experimentation with family preservation are those which touch on the basic policy values and legal standards that currently govern the delivery of child welfare and mental health services. The political and social frameworks in which these values are embedded are, of course, elaborate and complex; and no attempt to summarize them is pretended here. It suffices for our purposes to note that much existing public policy and law toward children turn on a few critical standards, among them: that "the best interests of the child" is the paramount standard for state intervention and action; that "reasonable efforts" to keep children with their family is a precondition to a justifiable placement; and that "the least restrictive setting" consistent with need is a key criterion for defining the most appropriate locus for the mental health and rehabilitative treatment of children and youth.

Of course, nothing we have learned about family preservation calls any of these core principles into question. On the contrary, what the experience with intensive in-home services may do is provide powerful examples and options that can give refined and more concrete reference to these underlying standards.

However much we might wish it otherwise, the practical meanings of our conceptions of "reasonable efforts," "least restrictive environment," or "best interests" are ultimately *relative* ones. What constitutes a "reasonable effort" to keep a family together depends in large part on what options are available and how practical those options are plausibly judged to be. Similarly, the benchmarks of "least restrictive environment" take on different meanings depending on what particular continuum of settings can be shown to be consistent with effective treatment.

Even more manifestly relative is the definition of a child's "best interests." Almost all such determinations involve the weighing of the benefits and costs of one action against the benefits and costs of all the *other* choices that are known and available to decision makers.

The point of all this, put plainly, is that what we are learning about family preservation can and should be influencing the interpretation and application of these key public policy standards. As noted before, family preservation has been shown to be a practical and responsible way of keeping a significant fraction of at-risk children with their families. Accordingly, it seems eminently reasonable for judges, administrators, advocates, and clients to begin to see the availability and, where warranted, the use of intensive in-home interventions as a commonsense standard or minimum test for what constitutes "a reasonable effort" to prevent placement. This does not mean that family preservation efforts would be presumed to precede all placement decisions, but simply that the ability to provide such services in appropriate cases ought to become a minimum benchmark of a state's or community's capacity to comply with reasonable efforts requirements.

A parallel case can be made for advancing a more rigorous interpretation of the least restrictive principle as it applies to mental health treatment settings for children. The increasing number of child and youth admissions to residential and inpatient settings for mental health care are presumably justified on the grounds that less restrictive alternatives "consistent with need" are not available or practical. The growing evidence of the practicality and efficacy of intensive in-home, family-centered therapy, however, suggests that less disruptive and far less costly options could be found to address the treatment needs of an important share of the children and youth now being placed (Behavioral Sciences Institute, 1981; Hinckley & Ellis, 1985).

The implications of family preservation may be even more significant for how courts and communities calculate "the best interests" of a child. Although it is often understated, it is nonetheless well known that the removal of a child extracts and entails a significant human cost. Stated plainly, children who are separated from their families can be expected to suffer. In addition to foregoing the elusive but real human benefits of family continuity and membership, children who are placed away from home are subject to dislocation, fear of the unknown, guilt, stigmatization, loss of identity, and exposure to sometimes serious risks from caretakers who have no familial obligations. In most placement decisions, the judgment is presumably made that these known and predictable risks are outweighed by the benefits of the protection, care, and/or treatment that can be secured through removal. Placement, in such cases, is said to reflect the child's best interests.

In many instances, however, what we are learning about family preservation points to a different calculus. The acceptable costs of removal become unacceptable as soon as it can be plausibly argued that the objectives of placement could be secured without the need for placement as the means.

This, of course, is precisely what family preservation appears to offer in a substantial fraction of the crisis situations in which the state is asked to determine a child's best interests.

The preceding discussion provides a basis for a general summary observation. For at least a decade, commitments to keep children with their families, to make reasonable efforts to prevent their removal, and to seek the least restrictive settings for care and treatment have been largely unchallenged as goals and standards for public services to children. Despite this, the recent prevailing trends have been toward increased separation and placement as well as a growing reliance on more structured out-of-home settings for treatment. The prevailing explanation for this departure of system performance from system goals is that there is no practical alternative to the current pattern of responding to the contemporary needs of children and families. The evidence and experience around intensive in-home services, however, is growing to the point where the plea of "no alternatives" is fast becoming more of an excuse to be challenged than an explanation to be accepted.

The Implications of Family Preservation for More Effective Service Delivery to Families

In the preceding pages, fiscal and policy arguments have been advanced in favor of a public commitment to employ family preservation as a more systemic response to families in crisis. Were those arguments to be widely embraced, the resulting expansion of family preservation services could materially alter the locus and character of current protective and treatment responses to at-risk children; and it could do so within the foreseeable future. At a minimum, a commitment to expand family preservation—to making it routinely accessible for at-risk families—would yield a system less reactively reliant on placement and more affirmatively committed to natural families as the context for securing the safety and health of vulnerable children.

It should be added that these potential effects on service delivery systems might also bring with them some equally important indirect impacts. The child welfare and treatment benefits of family preservation are most often (and understandably) envisioned in terms of the children whose removal is prevented. But family preservation may also enable an improvement in the care and treatment of children in placement. By virtue of its ability to reduce what otherwise would be the number and incidence of removals, a strong family preservation capacity could moderate the pressure on a state's available out-of-home resources. This, in turn, ought to increase the probability of sustaining a true continuum of care, of making prompter and more appropriate placements, of finding placement settings closer to home, and of assuring better supervision and treatment of those children in care (Center for the Study of Social Policy, 1988b). In short, a commitment to family preservation contains within it at least some potential to enhance and improve the public response to the needs of children in placement.

The potential of family preservation to prevent significant numbers of future child placements is what gives the intervention its *strategic* importance. In the end, however, the implications of what we are learning about family preservation may extend well beyond its strategic role. That is, it may be not only what the intervention does, but also *how it does it* that gives broader relevance to the research on family preservation. Stated simply, the reasons that family preservation works—the design and practice characteristics that make it effective—may well prove to have important implications for a much wider range of human service delivery issues.

As presented in other chapters, several elements set existing models of family preservation services apart from most other forms of service provision to families and children. These distinguishing characteristics include: a family-centered approach to assessment and treatment; use of the home as the primary delivery and treatment setting; cultivation of an intense and egalitarian professional-client communication; a deliberate limitation in the duration of the intervention; and, finally, an expressly broad, flexible, and generalist response to the multiple problems presented by the families served (Kinney, Haapala, Booth & Leavitt, 1988; Pecora, Fraser, Haapala & Bartlome, 1987). Considered collectively, these five elements define family preservation. What makes these particularly worthy of study—both individually and interactively—is the apparent effectiveness and efficiency in achieving desired outcomes with some of the most challenging of human service client populations. The families targeted for family preservation interventions are usually in extreme crisis. Many have endured a long history of problems as well as multiple prior episodes of service or treatment from human service agencies. The fact that family preservation interventions are sometimes capable of enabling such families to regain and maintain an adequate level of functioning lends credibility to the methods and practices they employ.

Although each of the family preservation practice elements may have relevance to other arenas of treatment and practice, the characteristic with the broadest implications for human service delivery is the non-categorical or generalist approach brought to family problems by family preservation workers. In this regard, family preservation services are unlike most human service delivery systems, which are organized and financed around particular clusters or categories of problems: income needs, drug abuse, disability, housing, protective supervision, acute health care, delinquency, and so on. Instead of assuming such a categorical orientation, family preservation programs are predicated on the assumption that a multiplicity of different and interacting problems most frequently disable family functioning. Accordingly, family preservation workers are deliberately charged with a responsibility for recognizing and responding to a range of presenting needs. This often means that workers are directly involved in practical problem-solving (e.g., transportation, emergency income, home management), simultaneous with their counseling and instructional assistance to address inappropriate behaviors or intrafamily conflicts. Family preservation staff also help families use more specialized resources, such as health care or alcohol treatment, and they try to link them with ongoing programs, like Medicaid or job training, where these are needed to create or maintain adequate family performance. This integrated approach to problem-solving is seen by many analysts as critical to family preservation's effectiveness in quickly, but durably, upgrading family capacity to care for children.

Of course, what makes this approach more broadly significant is that the presence of multiple and interactive problems is by no means limited to those families experiencing a placement-threatening crisis. In fact, it is well understood that many families who demonstrate a need for a particular kind of help also often experience other related but separate problems. Serious drug abuse in an adult family member, for example, commonly correlates with a heightened probability of family conflict, inadequate parental supervision, and adjustment problems in children. Similarly, families headed by a single teen mother display a higher likelihood of having parenting education and early childhood health care needs as well as a need for income support.

In today's human service context, however, there is rarely a single agency or even entry point in the system that is organized or financed to assume responsibility for helping resolve the multiple and interactive problems of such families. Drug treatment programs may address the addiction problems of a family member, but the household's related needs for income security or improved parental supervision are outside the treatment counselor's jurisdiction. Welfare offices can determine a teen parent's eligibility for AFDC, but historically they have not been equipped or expected to assess or address the need for nutrition education, parenting support, or alcohol treatment. These remain the responsibilities of other parts of the system.

The irony here is that it may take a placement-threatening crisis before such multi-need families encounter an individual professional who seeks to address the range of factors that undermine adequate family functioning. And even that occurs only in those exceptional places where a true family preservation capacity has been established. Some alternative to this pattern seems compelling. The answer probably does not lie in the wholesale extension of family preservation to non-crisis situations, but it does seem appropriate to borrow the breadth of the family preservation worker's responsibility as a standard for the redesign of intake points, needs assessment, service planning, and case management that someday should be more routinely available to families in various stages of need.

At the heart of this implication is a basic challenge to the categorical character of current human service funding and delivery. Family preservation works, in some measure, because its workers assume responsibility for the *broad range* of problems that may threaten family capacity, and because they have the training and resources to respond to multiple and often changing needs. Application of that model to family services generally would inescapably entail more comprehensive methods of need assessment and new vehicles for service coordination and continuity. At a minimum, it points to the long-sought but rarely achieved consolidation of intake and assessment for families and children in need of assistance. Second, it suggests the value of a truly generic case management capacity—one which can empower a single professional or team to marshal resources on behalf of a family across categorical systems and over time. To enable such an authoritative and responsive case management system, of course, further implies the decategorization of service resources—that is, the elimination of those categorical eligibility and authorization requirements that currently prevent timely and coordinated delivery of multi-system responses to multi-need families.[1]

In their most extreme formulation, the implications of family preservation practices probably point to a thoroughly reorganized service system. Many states now have a bureau, division, or department nominally responsible for the coordinated delivery of what are called "family services." In reality, however, the jurisdiction of state and local "family service" units encompasses only a fragment of the resources and services that are relevant to enabling an at-risk family to more adequately provide for the care, welfare, health, and development of its children. "Family service" agencies typically have no responsibility or authority over income support resources, public health services, housing, mental health services, or delinquency programs, despite the fact that the need for one or more of these supports is often at the bottom of a family's referral to "family services." If the response of family preservation to families in crisis constitutes a micro-model of an appropriate response to the support requirements of vulnerable families at all stages of need, then it surely points to a far broader organizational and resource jurisdiction than "family service" agencies currently possess.

A Concluding Implication for Social Policy

The entire preceding discussion of family preservation—and, indeed, family preservation itself—rests on a premise that has so far gone unmentioned and unexamined. The premise is that society bears at least a measure of responsibility to help parents and families meet the needs of their children. Behind this belief, of course, is a host of other values and convictions that children are genuinely entitled to grow up in a family; that families themselves are the critical social unit for the nurture and development of children; and that families, by and large, do the best they can to meet their children's needs.

At some level of abstraction, there is a broad consensus about the rightness of these views about families. Reliance on and faith in families remains a rule that gives order to much American social policy. At a more particular level, however, there appears to be an increasing willingness or need to admit exceptions to this rule. For many Americans, the commitment to families wavers when extended across ethnic and class lines and crumbles when applied to fragmented, neglectful, poor, abusive, or drug-dependent parents. In these contexts, we find it harder to affirm or even envision the benefits or value to family and much easier to see the deprivation and dangers these environments represent to children. Put another way, we find it easy here to make an exception to our general rules about families.

In a sense, family preservation represents a perspective that begrudges every such exception. It is an orientation that affirms the potential of almost all families and accepts a social responsibility to help even dysfunctional families endeavor to realize that potential. For these very reasons, it has its critics. Family preservation has been charged with reinforcing a misplaced idealism and encouraging a blindness to the unremediable pathologies that put too many children at risk (Barth & Barry, 1987). It has even been accused of distracting public agencies from their primary purpose to protect those in danger.

These are not mindless accusations, but in the long run they represent a truly shortsighted and unrealistic perspective. The fact is that there is no socially acceptable alternative for children aside from a reliance on families. Certainly no one remotely familiar with the actual circumstances of the nearly half-million children who are now living in shelters, group homes, hospitals, training schools, residential treatment centers, or temporary foster care could argue that these arrangements constitute an acceptable prospect for two or three times as many children in the decade ahead. And surely no one can plausibly or long defend a public policy that disowns responsibility for remediating family dysfunction when we know that the vast majority of placed children will sooner or later return to the families from which they were removed.

In the end, the fact that family preservation directs us to recognize families as the only practical resource for securing the interest of children may be its most important policy implication. It is, of course, a recognition that takes us beyond family preservation. Intensive in-home services to families at risk of disruption are, by themselves, neither an efficient nor a sufficient response to the rapidly changing circumstances of American families. To address these needs intelligently, the nation needs a comprehensive family policy that will direct more resources into the educational, health, housing, employment, drug, and support services that are absolutely required to equip more families to more fully guarantee the interest, safety, and health of its children.

Note

1. For a more extended discussion, see Center for the Study of Social Policy. (1988c). *Framework for child welfare reform.* Washington, DC: Center for the Study of Social Policy.

References

AuClaire, P., & Schwartz, I. (1986). *An evaluation of the effectiveness of intensive home-based services as an alternative to placement for adolescents and their families.* Minneapolis: University of Minnesota.

Barth, R., & Barry, M. (1987). Outcomes of child welfare services under permanency planning. *Social Service Review, 61,* 71-89.

Behavioral Sciences Institute. (1981). *First year Homebuilders mental health project report.* Tacoma: Behavioral Sciences Institute.

Behavioral Sciences Institute. (1986). Homebuilders cost effectiveness with various client populations. Federal Way, WA: Behavioral Sciences Institute.

Bruner, C. (1988). *Family preservation services in Iowa: A legislator's perspective on key issues.* Washington, DC: Center for the Study of Social Policy.

Center for the Study of Social Policy. (1988a). *1988 trend analysis.* Washington, DC: Center for the Study of Social Policy.

Center for the Study of Social Policy. (1988b). *Recognizing and realizing the potential of family preservation.* Washington, DC: Center for the Study of Social Policy.

Center for the Study of Social Policy. (1988c). *Framework for child welfare reform.* Washington, DC: Center for the Study of Social Policy.

County Welfare Directors Association of California. (1990). *Ten reasons to invest in the families of California.* Sacramento: County Welfare Directors Association of California.

Fraser, M. W., Pecora, P. J., & Haapala, D. (1988). *Families in crisis: Findings from the family-based intensive treatment research project.* Salt Lake City: University of Utah.

Fuqua, R., & Thieman, A. (1989). *Iowa family preservation project evaluation report: Year two.* Ames: Iowa State University.

Haapala, D., & Kinney, J. (in press). Avoiding out-of-home placement among high-risk status offenders through the use of home-based family preservation services. *Criminal Justice Behavior.*

Haugaard, J., & Hokonson, B. (1983). *Measuring the cost-effectiveness of family-based services and out-of-home care.* Oakdale, IA: Institute of Urban and Regional Research.

Hinckley, E., & Ellis, W. (1985). An effective alternative to residential placement: Home-based service. *Journal of Clinical Psychology, 14,* 209-213.

Johnson, K. (1987). *SRS substitute care and intensive family-based services in Vermont.* Montpelier: Vermont Coalition of Runaway Youth Services.

Jones, M., Magura, S., & Shyne, A. (1981). Effective practice with families in protective and preventive services: What works? *Child Welfare, 60,* 66-79.

Kinney, J., Haapala, D., Booth, C., & Leavitt, S. (1988). The Homebuilders model. In J. Whittaker (Ed.), *Improving practice technology to work with high risk families: Lessons from the Homebuilders social work education project.* Seattle: University of Washington.

National Resource Center on Family-Based Services. (1983). *Family-centered social services: A model for child welfare agencies.* Iowa City: University of Iowa.

Office of Evaluation, Florida Department of Health and Rehabilitative Services. (1982). *Intensive crisis counseling: An evaluation report.* Tallahassee: Department of Human Resources.

Pearson, C., & King, P. (1985). *Intensive family services: Evaluation of foster care prevention in Maryland, final report.* Baltimore: Maryland Department of Human Resources.

Pecora, P. J., Fraser, M. W., Haapala, D., & Bartlome, I. A. (1987). *Defining family preservation services.* Salt Lake City: University of Utah.

Tennessee General Assembly, Select Joint Committee on Children and Youth. (1988). *Taking care of children: Increasing costs of out-of-home services in Tennessee.* Nashville: Tennessee General Assembly.

U.S. Congress, House Committee on Energy and Commerce. (1988). *Medicaid source book: Background data and analysis* (Energy and Commerce Committee Print 100-AA). Washington, DC: Government Printing Office.

U.S. Congress, House Committee on Ways and Means. (1989). Background material and data on programs within the jurisdiction of the Committee on Ways and Means (Committee Print 101-4). Washington, DC: Government Printing Office.

Wald, M. (1988). Family preservation: Are we moving too fast? *Public Welfare, 46.*

11

Family Preservation Services:

Their Role Within the Children's Mental Health System

SUSAN W. YELTON
ROBERT M. FRIEDMAN

The growth of intensive home-based services, often called family preservation, has had a major impact on the public mental health system as well as the child welfare system. The purpose of this chapter is to describe the role of intensive family preservation services, such as the Homebuilders model, in the context of developments in the children's mental health system, and to discuss the implications of that role for the evaluation of family preservation services.

Status of the Children's Mental Health System

At the outset of the 1980s, as documented in a report done for the Children's Defense Fund (CDF) by Jane Knitzer (1982), the status of services for children with emotional disorders and their families was grossly inadequate. The report estimated that two-thirds of the three million (approximately) children and adolescents with serious emotional disorders in this country received no services. It further suggested that the services provided to those who did receive assistance were frequently inappropriate.

In most communities, the service options available were infrequent, office-based, outpatient treatment or hospitalization, with the consequence that there was an excessive reliance on hospitalization. Knitzer found that not only was there excessive use of hospitalization, but also that hospital stays were longer than necessary. Children were often not able to be returned home when they were ready to leave the hospital because of the lack of community-based services.

The CDF report went on to say that many states did not have a single full-time children's mental health staff person in their state office; only seven states had made significant progress toward developing a continuum of services; and collaboration between public agencies to meet the needs of children was the exception rather than the rule. Both the findings and the recommendations of the report were not unlike the results of a prior study conducted by the Joint Commission on Mental Health of Children from 1964 to 1969. That report, *Crisis in Child Mental Health: Challenges for the 1970's,* concluded that "as of today, the treatment of the mentally ill child in America remains uncertain, variable, and inadequate. This is true on all levels, rich and poor, rural and urban . . . only a fraction of our young people get the help they need at the time they need it" (Ribicoff, 1969). The Commission encouraged the development of coordinated, community-based, family-centered service systems, a recommendation that was further reinforced by Knitzer in 1982.

Since the early l980s, greatly assisted by the National Institute of Mental Health (NIMH), and particularly NIMH's Child and Adolescent Service System Program (CASSP), there has developed considerable interest in the needs of children with emotional disorders, and their families. States have begun to strengthen their capacity to provide leadership in this area; new service models have been developed that provide intensive service in home- and community-based settings; models of system of care have emerged; the role of parents has been redefined; and interagency collaboration has become more common. The state funding provided by CASSP has clearly made an improvement in the way in which services to children with severe emotional disorders, and their families, are delivered by states and communities.

The Child and Adolescent Service System Program (CASSP) was initiated in 1984 when Congress earmarked $1.5 million to develop a new initiative to improve service delivery for children with severe emotional disorders. The original appropriation provided for 10 state grants. By 1989 only three states had failed to receive a CASSP grant.

Based upon the philosophy that children and adolescents with serious emotional disorders, and their families, require a multi-agency approach, CASSP encourages the interagency coordination and planning of services, as well as the development of a stronger mental health component within the broader child serving system (which includes, for example, child welfare, juvenile justice, education, and public health). In order to best respond to the needs of the population, CASSP emphasizes the need for families to be included in the planning and implementation of such services and to act as a voice to support the development of an adequate and appropriate range of service options. Like the child welfare reform agenda, CASSP strives to reinforce policy initiatives which strengthen families. It recognizes that effective family functioning is not only in the best interest of children, but it is also essential for the welfare of our society as a whole. It is the basic unit through which a child receives and maintains social stability.

In a document prepared for NIMH by the Georgetown University CASSP Technical Assistance Center and the Research and Training for Children's Mental Health at the Florida Mental Health Institute (Stroul & Friedman, 1986), a set of values and principles was presented to serve as a foundation for improving services. Among the principles that are most relevant for understanding the role of family preservation services are the following:

1. Emotionally disturbed children should have access to a comprehensive array of services that address the child's physical, emotional, social, and educational needs.

2. Emotionally disturbed children should receive individualized services in accordance with the unique needs and potentials for each child and guided by an individualized service plan.

3. Emotionally disturbed children should receive services within the least restrictive, most normative environment that is clinically appropriate.

4. The families and surrogate families of emotionally disturbed children should be full participants in all aspects of the planning and delivery of services.

5. Emotionally disturbed children should receive services that are integrated, with linkages between child-caring agencies and programs and mechanisms for planning, developing and coordinating services. (Stroul & Friedman, 1986)

The emphasis on an array of services, treatment in the least restrictive setting that is appropriate, and active participation of families is critical. Also essential is the overall emphasis that the needs of children and families could be best served within the context of comprehensive, multi-agency, community-based systems of care. A part of this emphasis on systems of care is a recognition that many different services may be needed, but that there should be a balance in the system so that youngsters who might be effectively served in intensive outpatient services or day treatment, for example, do not end up being placed in out-of-home settings because that is the only way for them to receive services.

This concept of balance has even been operationalized in specific formulas intended to serve as guidelines to indicate both the absolute and relative amounts of different types of services that should be available (Behar, Holland, & MacBeth, 1987; Friedman, 1987). The Friedman model, for example, indicates that for every unit of out-of-home service that is available in a community, there should be a capacity to serve at least two families in home-based services and two in day treatment. In addition, there should be a capacity for four youngsters and their families to receive intensive, individualized case management services, according to this model, for every residential slot.

Unless there is a greater capacity to serve youngsters and families in the intensive, non-residential components of a community-based system of care, according to the overall system of care model, then a community will not be able to operationalize its commitment to family-focused treatment and treatment in the least restrictive setting, and youngsters will end up being removed from their home without having an opportunity to be served in intensive non-residential services.

Another significant development in the 1980s was the emphasis within the child mental health system on establishing children with serious emotional disorders, and their families, as the priority population. As states struggled with defining this class of youngster, there was an important shift in thinking. Traditionally, the "mentally ill" were defined as a class of persons who were "a danger to themselves or others." In most states, the diagnostic criteria for mentally ill children and adults were the same. As a children's agenda emerged, the uniqueness of children had to be taken into consideration. With NIMH providing considerable leadership, states began to rewrite, or define for the first time, a "severely emotionally disturbed" child.

The parameters that were suggested by NIMH in defining the population emphasize not only the presence of a diagnosable mental or emotional disorder but also an impairment in social functioning, a problem of at least one year's duration, and a problem that requires services from more than one agency (Stroul & Friedman, 1986).

Children Served in Child Mental Health
and Child Welfare Systems

As states began to identify their population of children with serious emotional disorders, it became quite evident that the children and adolescents the child welfare and mental health systems serve are often indistinguishable. Both systems report serious behavioral and emotional problems among children and widespread patterns of violence and disruption within the families. For example, a study of older children in foster care in Virginia, comparing case records of children entering care in 1975 with those entering care in 1985, concluded that the FY1985 children evidenced more emotional/behavioral problems than the earlier group (Virginia Department of Social Services, 1986). When mental health providers testified before Congress about the needs of emotionally disturbed children, they too reported that the children they were serving in clinics were more disturbed, more violent, and more substance abusing (U.S. House Select Committee on Children, Youth and Families, 1987).

Studies of children in out-of-home placement also point to shared characteristics among the population serviced by the two systems. For example, during the summer of 1986, Kentucky conducted a survey of children and youth who were receiving residential mental health services. Of the children sampled, 28.5% had a history of abuse; 29.9 % had a history of neglect; 30.6% had a learning disability; and 53.3% were status offenders.

In August 1987, Washington State Children's Interagency Committee developed a plan for the 31 emotionally disturbed children in out-of-state placements. They reported that 80% were victims of abuse and neglect and 60% had more than five out-of-home placements.

New York State's Family Based Treatment Program 1989 Annual Report indicates that the majority of the children placed with professional parents by mental health agencies are in the custody of the Department of Social Services (DSS). The report suggests that to serve the most disturbed youth in DSS custody in a mental health-funded Family Based Treatment home is not a duplication of effort by the mental health agency, but rather the creation of an alternative currently lacking for those youths in the system as a whole.

This is not to suggest that all children served by public mental health systems come from highly inadequate, if not abusive, families. Such is clearly not the case, and the potential for families to participate with professionals in developing service plans for their youngsters is being increasingly recognized (Friesen, 1989). However, out-of-home placement for youngsters in the public mental health system is often determined for a combination of reasons related to dependency needs as well as mental health treatment needs; and states are finding much similarity in those youngsters served in the most restrictive settings by the child welfare and children's mental health systems. These patterns have led to a new receptivity to cross-system collaboration, particularly those involving public child welfare and child mental health agencies (Knitzer & Yelton, 1989).

Comparison of Reform Agendas

Not only have child welfare and child mental health agencies begun to recognize the similar trends in their caseloads, but they have also begun to recognize that their reform agendas are complementary. PL 96-272, the Adoption Assistance and Child Welfare Act of 1980, set a framework for state child welfare administrators that has resulted in renewed emphasis on strengthening families and providing protection for individual children. Although the law mandates that "reasonable efforts" must be made to ensure that children are not unnecessarily removed from their parents, and that parents must be assisted in correcting the problems causing the removal if it proves to be necessary, the law does not require that a continuum of preventive/family support services must be available in each community, nor does it define a set of core services that should be available as alternatives.

In contrast to the child welfare emphasis on building protections for individual children, the mental health reform efforts have focused, at least in theory, on expanding a set of core services designed to keep children both in their own homes and in their communities. These include crisis intervention services, respite care, day treatment, intensive case management, and therapeutic foster care. There is also recognition that these services must be linked together at the community level to form a "system of care" that will permit children and families to get the necessary services from any agency, not just mental health (Stroul & Friedman, 1986).

As operationalized, system of care efforts generally involve: (a) strengthening the range of nonresidential services to balance the typically more readily available residential ones, (b) creating a cross-system case planning capacity to ensure that services work together for individual families, and (c) creating a cross-system, community-based management and planning mechanism to facilitate effective resource allocation, to identify service gaps, and to plan for new services. For a system such as children's mental health, which has had a history of permissiveness regarding services for emotionally disturbed children, this agenda is a major shift in policy.

Taken together, PL 96-272 and the child mental health reform efforts utilize complementary strategies, one focusing on protection, the other on the array of community-based, family-focused services. However, to this point, both have promised more than has been delivered. For child welfare, the reasons are complex, including limited federal leadership in following through on the agenda of PL 96-272, and the increased demands on the system as a result of higher rates of abuse, homelessness, substance abuse, and poverty. With respect to the children's mental health agenda, the vision is greater than the capacity to deliver, primarily because there is an inevitable resistance to change both by administrators and providers, and the resources required to provide the needed services have not been available. Nevertheless, there is considerable potential for the complementary agendas to create opportunities for communities to address the needs of their most troubled children and their families and for state administrators to address the mounting fiscal pressures on both systems.

As both child welfare and child mental health systems try to address the complex and similar needs of their caseloads, both are being strapped by the high cost of placements and lack of options for cost-effective alternatives. In many states, currently, two thirds or more of the children's mental health budget is allocated to residential or hospital treatment. The Invisible Children Project of the National Mental Health Association reports that about 5,000 children with emotional disorders were placed out of their own state each year in residential treatment programs (1989); and Friedman (1990) reports annual expenditures for out-of-state placements as high as $40 million in New Jersey, $23 million in Washington, D.C., and more than $10 million in a state with a small population like Wyoming.

Trend analyses of the child welfare system show increases in rates of foster care placements in recent years after a period of declining placement rates. The foster care population has increased 20% from 1985-1988 with states like California experiencing a 48% increase, Michigan 45%, and New York 75% (U.S. House Select Committee on Children, Youth, and Families, 1990). Missouri reports that, between 1985 and 1988, the cost of residential care increased 87% through child welfare and 84% through mental health. If the rate of increase in Missouri were to continue, by 1992 the placement system would have to serve and pay for an additional 1,100 children. A conservative estimate is that this would cost an additional $17 million (Citizens for Missouri's Children, 1990).

In addition to the rising cost of placements, the mental health system is questioning the effectiveness of out-of-home placements in residential treatment centers and inpatient hospital settings. To this point, there have been no studies utilizing adequate research designs to support the effectiveness of these placements, according to several reviews (Burns & Friedman, 1990; Curry, 1986; Friedman & Street, 1985; U.S. Office of Technology Assessment, 1986; Whittaker & Maluccio, 1989). In fact, a consistent finding of the research has been that post-discharge services and supports play a major role in the overall effectiveness of residential and inpatient treatment (Friedman & Street, 1985; Lewis, Lewis, Shanok, Klatskin & Osborne, 1980; Whittaker & Maluccio, 1989).

Role of Family Preservation Services

An examination of the role of family preservation services in the effort to bring about an improved children's mental health system must take into account the following principles, needs, and efforts:

- An increased emphasis on the need for a range of services that are integrated into a community-based system of care;
- A strong focus on family-focused services and on treatment in the least restrictive setting that is appropriate to a child's needs;
- A recognition that unless intensive, non-residential services are available in greater quantity than out-of-home services, then a community will not be able to operationalize its commitment to family-focused services and services in the least restrictive environment;
- A recognition of the right of parents to be active participants in identifying needs and in planning services, and of the value of parents as a resource in implementing the treatment plan;
- An emphasis on the need for agencies to work together in planning and providing services;
- Increasing costs of services in residential treatment centers and inpatient settings and in many cases continued waiting lists to receive such services despite increases in availability;
- Lack of research evidence to indicate the effectiveness of treatment provided in such settings.

From a conceptual, programmatic, and systems perspective, perhaps the most important program development to address these issues has been the growth of the intensive, home-based interventions known as family preservation. These interventions have demonstrated that intensive services can be provided in the home and do not require removal of the child from the home; that some families for whom removal of a child appears to be unavoidable can, in fact, be kept together; that services provided at a time of crisis can have enduring effects; and that families considered to be unworkable when treatment was based in office settings can, in fact, be involved in home-based treatment.

Given the fact that mental health services are typically provided in an office or hospital setting, the outreach focus of family preservation services has been even more of a departure from the predominant mode of providing services for the mental health field than it has for the child welfare field. It has been a challenge in terms of the locus of service and the intensity of service; and, with its emphasis on a family and ecologically oriented approach, it has also been a conceptual challenge to the mental health field.

From a systems perspective, the development of intensive, home-based models has provided policymakers with a programmatic option that allows them to operationalize their values and principles as they relate to family-focused services and treatment in least-restrictive settings. The development of this model has provided systems with a far more intensive option than traditional outpatient services.

As systems have moved to an emphasis on the need for a range of services, in addition to family preservation, there has been significant work on other models, such as day treatment ("Day Treatment," 1985; Stroul & Friedman, 1986), intensive case management ("Case management," 1986), therapeutic foster care (Hawkins & Breiling, 1989; Stroul, 1989), other types of mobile crisis services ("Crisis/Emergency Services," 1987; Goldman, 1988), and individualized approaches with flexible funding (VanDenBerg, 1990; Burchard & Clarke, 1990).

With all of these developments, one of the inevitable questions has been: How can we determine which youngsters and families should be placed in each type of service? This question was addressed by Friedman and Street (1985) in an article on admission and discharge criteria for different services in a continuum of care. In this article, the authors maintain that, at this point, there is no empirical basis for concluding that there exist assessment procedures that can validly address the issue of differential placements. Rather, Friedman and Street indicate that as the power and effectiveness of new service models, such as family preservation, increase, the field is learning that youngsters, for whom more restrictive services may have originally been considered necessary, do not, in fact, always need those services.

Instead, it is argued, that with the exception of rare emergencies involving a life-threatening situation, the best alternative is to initially serve youngsters and families in intensive, non-residential services before assuming, based on whatever type of assessment, that such services will be ineffective.

Recent research on the Homebuilders model of family preservation has identified certain subgroups of youngsters and families for whom the success rate in family preservation is lower than others (Fraser, Pecora, & Haapala, 1988). However, even with the lower rates for particular subgroups, the success rate is still sufficient to try youngsters and families in family preservation services, provided no harm is done during the process. As Fraser et al. point out, the challenge is to strengthen the power of the model with particular groups. It would be a mistake to deny accessibility to the service to individuals and families based on the findings.

What, then, is the role of family preservation services within a child mental health system with the types of values and conceptual framework that have been described? In our view, family preservation services essentially have four roles to play.

1. Protection—The first concern of all human service professionals must be protection and safety of their clients. Obviously, this is especially important with family preservation services since they are provided at a time of individual and/or family crisis. It should be recognized in this regard that the concept of risk is very complex. First, while leaving a child in a home that may potentially be explosive, or leaving a child who has threatened suicide in a home, clearly involves some degree of risk, so the process of removing a child from a home involves risk as well. This is the case whether the removal is to a shelter, foster home, or psychiatric hospital and is particularly true if the potential emotional harm of placements, as well as the physical harm, is recognized. Second, a major mechanism for protection against risk is to have well-trained staff that will be in regular contact, on a daily basis if needed, with the family. This reduces the need for removal in comparison to a situation where there may be a considerable time lag before a professional can return to a potentially explosive home. Third, the degree of risk can best be assessed, and often reduced, if staff are not only well-trained but also able to spend enough time with a family to assess a situation, to begin to defuse it, and to start the process of addressing problems. The training and the small caseloads of staff within family preservation programs makes this possible.

2. Assessment—Family preservation services provide an excellent opportunity to do an in vivo, ecologically oriented assessment, because they involve bringing the staff person into the environment of the family, rather than asking the family to enter the environment of the staff person. This provides a chance to learn about the family as a group: the strengths, interests, supports, and

needs of the individuals within the family; the cultural and neighborhood influences; the effect of friends, extended family, and other social institutions, like the schools. In a traditional approach to intervention, assessment precedes treatment. In a crisis situation, however, the processes are ongoing from the beginning.

3. Treatment—Another major role of family preservation is treatment. This involves defusing the initial crisis; identifying strengths and needs; building, in combination with the family, a treatment plan; supporting and assisting the family as it carries out the treatment plan; and monitoring the progress. The intervention seeks to benefit not just an individual child but also the entire family and to empower the family to effectively act on its own behalf. It is always the hope that the successful implementation of the treatment plan will alleviate the need for anybody from the family to be removed. However, this is not always possible, particularly given the priority focus on watching out for the best interests and safety of the people involved.

4. Linkage with Other Services—The final major role of family preservation is to link the family with other services that it may need. This is particularly important since the intensive home-based model is typically a short-term model. The linkages need to be established in a manner that empowers the family and utilizes natural supports as well as services from formal agencies.

It should be noted that family preservation services and other intensive nonresidential services are often spoken of as alternatives to residential treatment. In our judgment, this is an oversimplification of the role of family preservation in a system of care. At any single point in time, family preservation services may be used rather than residential treatment in an attempt to protect the child and family, assess the situation, provide treatment, and establish needed linkages. In this regard, if less intensive services have already been tried, or are considered unlikely to be effective, family preservation services may be considered a first step to be tried in almost all situations, except those involving serious, immediate danger. However, the use of family preservation services as an early intervention does not preclude the subsequent use of residential treatment. If the professional staff person considers that such residential treatment is required at any point, then he/she has a responsibility to communicate that to the family and to initiate such an action. While a system of care may embrace a philosophy of family-focused treatment and treatment in the least restrictive setting that is clinically appropriate, the use of residential treatment is not only acceptable but inevitable for a certain percentage of youngsters.

To describe family preservation services as an alternative to residential treatment may, in fact, be accurate only at a single point in time when a decision is being made about appropriate service. It is more accurate to describe family preservation as one of the first and most intensive efforts to be made to serve the family, with residential treatment being a needed subsequent service for certain families.

Issues Related to Use of Family Preservation Services in Mental Health Systems

While the use of family preservation services within mental health systems is increasing, there are certainly many issues that are being debated and obstacles that need to be overcome. One issue is the duration of service. Intensive family preservation services are time-limited (usually about six weeks in duration). The appropriateness of this is debated. While this issue has relevance in all systems that use family preservation services, it has particular relevance in the mental health field because of the lack of services in most communities for children with emotional disorders and their families.

One response to this situation is to propose increasing the duration of the service. An alternative response, however, is to add the necessary service components so that children receive case management, and whatever other services they need, after the time-limited intervention has ended. The relative efficacy of these strategies remains to be evaluated.

Another issue concerns the relationship between intensive family preservation services and other types of crisis and home-based services ("Crisis/emergency," 1987; Stroul & Goldman, 1990). It is not uncommon for communities to assume that if they have one of these services, they do not need the others, or to confuse one with another. There is clearly an important need for more conceptual and empirical work to better distinguish between different crisis and home-based services and to describe the components and interrelationships of overall systems of crisis and home-based services.

An obstacle to the provision of family preservation services within mental health systems is the long-held orientation to providing services in office settings. Our experience is that mental health providers who want to start home-based services are often not supported by their colleagues, and frequently find it difficult to find practitioners who want to work in the homes of clients and at odd hours.

Other issues that are being debated within mental health systems are whether fees should be charged for this type of crisis services, what the appropriate role of traditional diagnostic nomenclatures is, and what types of standards should be developed. These issues affect mental health systems more than child welfare because of the manner in which mental health services have traditionally operated. For example, many mental health agencies seek accreditation from the Joint Commission on the Accreditation of Health Care Organizations. The standards for accreditation from these organizations are oriented toward more traditional mental health services and may serve as an obstacle to family preservation services.

Despite these issues and barriers, there are indications of growth in family preservation services within mental health systems. While mental health does not have the same legal mandates as child welfare for reasonable efforts to prevent removal of a child from his/her home, with the emergence of the CASSP initiative and increased leadership from state mental health directors, states are requesting, and receiving, funding from their legislatures to provide these services to children with emotional disorders. For example, Pennsylvania currently has more than 22 such programs, and New York has three and will be increasing by five more in the near future.

Mental health departments are further requesting changes in Medicaid plans to allow for reimbursement of services provided in the home. Maine and South Carolina have proposed some very promising Medicaid rules, which would allow for the funding of family preservation services; and recent changes in Medicaid law concerning the Early Periodic Screening, Diagnosis, and Treatment program should further enhance the ability of states to fund this service through Medicaid.

Evaluation of Family Preservation Services

Given the type of system of care that is emerging in the children's mental health system, and given the role of family preservation within that system, what are the implications of this for evaluation of family preservation services?

First of all, there needs to be an examination of the role of family preservation as just described. If this role is accepted, then an evaluation should focus on the effectiveness of family preservation services in carrying out its role.

The first question may then address the degree to which families receiving this service are adequately protected. What is the rate of abuse and neglect while treatment is going on? Are there many serious incidents that take place during treatment, such as suicides and major crime violations? Furthermore, how do these rates compare with the rates of these events for youngsters who have been removed from their homes and placed in other settings? These are important questions that have only rarely be addressed in the evaluation literature on family preservation services. It should be noted that the authors, despite having extensive experience with family preservation services in many states and with the research literature on family preservation, are aware of only one incident where a child died while the family was receiving family preservation services. While the lack of abuse suggested by this type of anecdotal information is certainly encouraging, it clearly does not remove the need for more systematic study of this issue.

The next question should address the broader issue of the extent to which the process of intervention, including assessment, treatment, and community linkage, is able to help the family both improve its functioning and remain together. These issues obviously need to be addressed both in the short-run and on a follow-up basis after the initial intervention has been completed.

From the perspective of the role of family preservation in a system of care, it is important to look at two issues. First, to whom is the service being provided? Given the relative costliness of the service in relation to office-based outpatient treatment or regular child protective services, and given its focus on families in crisis where removal of at least one person appears imminent, is the service being provided to families who, in fact, have already been unsuccessfully served in less intensive services, and/or families where removal is genuinely imminent? This is important to determine as part of the overall assessment of effectiveness.

Second, in relationship to more restrictive and expensive services, do family preservation services have a high enough success rate with families, who might otherwise end up in more expensive and restrictive services, to justify their continuation? The precise level of success rate that needs to be achieved is not easy to determine. If, in fact, family preservation is a service that adequately protects the families it serves, does not have harmful effects, and is considerably less expensive than residential care, then even a 50% rate of helping families and keeping them together may be more than sufficient.

The next important issue to consider is the type of evaluation design to be used for purposes of assessing success rates. From a standpoint of internal validity, the best design would clearly be to randomly assign families either to family preservation services or the community services that would normally be used. Such random assignment designs are difficult to use in field research with families in distress. An appropriate alternative, however, is to use a quasi-experimental design in which a sample of families, who are eligible for family preservation services but do not receive such services because they are filled to capacity, are used as comparisons with families receiving such services. Such designs have, in fact, been used in several cases (AuClaire & Schwartz, 1987; Fraser et al., 1988; Sokol, 1988). In North Carolina, as described by Sokol, such a design was specifically used in a family preservation program operated within a mental health system of care.

This type of design permits an assessment of the rate at which families referred to the service, but who do not receive it, end up with at least one member being removed. Unfortunately, the studies, in which this type of design has been used, are too few and varied at this point to allow any firm conclusions to be reached.

Also, the research that has been done has often not involved large enough samples, adequate descriptive data on the samples, long enough follow-ups, enough information on the overall community and system in which the service is operating, or a wide enough range of measures to really assess overall family functioning. These deficiencies, however, do not detract from the value of this basic type of quasi-experimental design to evaluate the effectiveness of family preservation services.

It should be noted that, for a child being served by a family preservation program, to be removed from his/her home is only a failure in one sense, and that is in regard to the overall goal of trying to maintain all children with their families, if at all appropriate. In another sense, however, when such a removal is found to be needed, at least decision makers and clinicians can reassure themselves that, in keeping with the values of their system and the technologies and resources available to them, they have made a strong effort with intensive services before recommending the removal. In our judgment, the greater failure from a humanitarian perspective—based on the importance of a family to a child and the risks involved in removing the child from the family; from a cost-effectiveness perspective, given the cost of residential treatment and the lack of convincing data on its effectiveness; and from a system perspective, given the importance of system adhering to a clearly articulated set of values—is when youngsters are removed from their homes without benefit of the families' receiving intensive services designed to try to avoid this. It is unrealistic to aspire to maintain every child in his/her family. It may be more realistic, however, to aspire to ensure that before a child is removed, except for extreme emergencies, the child and the family will have the benefit of the most intensive, non-residential services available to them.

The test for family preservation services, in this regard, is not whether it is more effective than residential care, or totally successful in eliminating the need for residential care, or even whether it reduces the total need for residential treatment, given the increasing prevalence of risk factors, such as physical abuse and substance abuse. Rather, the test is whether family preservation services, given their important role in a system of care, are able to cost-effectively and safely support and assist families, many of whom might otherwise experience disruption, in their efforts to improve their functioning and to stay together.

Summary

This chapter has reviewed the status of the children's mental health system, discussed recent developments in the field, and described the role of family preservation services within community-based systems of care. The implications of this role for efforts to evaluate family preservation have been discussed, and it has been argued that family preservation needs to be viewed as much more than simply an alternative to out-of-home placement. Rather, family preservation services should be viewed as an effort to implement a safe, minimally restrictive, family-focused intervention that operationalizes the values of a system of care while providing a cost-effective service.

References

AuClaire, P., & Schwartz, I. (1987). Are home-based services effective: A public child welfare agency's experiment. *Children Today, 5,* 16-21.

Behar, L. B., Holland, J., & MacBeth, G. (1987). *Distribution of mental health service components and their costs within a comprehensive system for children and adolescents: The North Carolina plan.* Raleigh, NC: Department of Human Resources.

Burchard, J. D., & Clarke, R. D. (1990). The role of individualized care in a service delivery system for children and adolescents with severely maladjusted behavior. *Journal of Mental Health Administration, 17,* 48-60.

Burns, B. J., & Friedman, R. M. (1990). Examining the research base for child mental health services and policy. *Journal of Mental Health Administration, 17,* 87-98.

Case management. (1986). *Update, 2,* 10-12, 15.

Citizens for Missouri's Children and the Institute of Applied Research. (1990). *Interrupted lives: A study of out-of-home placement in six Missouri counties.* St. Louis: Citizens for Missouri's Children.

Crisis/Emergency services. (1987). *Update, 3,* 10-12, 19.

Curry, J. (1986). *Outcome studies of psychiatric hospitalization and residential treatment of youth: Conceptual and research implications.* Paper presented at annual meeting of the American Psychological Association, Washington, DC.

Day treatment. (1985). *Update, 1,* 8-10, 15.

Fraser, M. W., Pecora, P. J., & Haapala, D. A. (1988). *Final report of the family-based intensive treatment (FIT) research project: A two state analysis of factors contributing to the success and failure of family-based child welfare services.* Salt Lake City: University of Utah Graduate School of Social Work.

Friedman, R. M. (1987). *Service capacity in a balanced system of services for seriously emotionally disturbed children.* Tampa: Research and Training Center for Children's Mental Health, University of South Florida.

Friedman, R. M. (1990). *Children's and communities' mental health services improvement act of 1990.* Testimony presented to the Health and Environment Sub-Committee of the Energy and Commerce Committee, U.S. House of Representatives, Washington, DC.

Friedman, R. M., & Street, S. (1985). Admission and discharge criteria in children's mental health services: A review of the issues and options. *Journal of Clinical Child Psychology, 14,* 229-235.

Friesen, B. J. (1989). Parents as advocates for children and adolescents with serious emotional handicaps: Issues and directions. In R. M. Friedman, A. J. Duchnowski, & E. L. Henderson (Eds.), *Advocacy on behalf of children with serious emotional problems.* Springfield, IL.: Charles C Thomas.

Goldman, S. K. (1988). *Crisis services* (Volume II: Series on community-based services for children and adolescents who are severely emotionally disturbed). Washington, DC: CASSP Technical Assistance Center, Georgetown University Child Development Center.

Hawkins, R. P., & Breiling, J. (Eds.). (1989). *Therapeutic foster care: Critical issues.* Washington, DC: Child Welfare League of America.

Joint Commission on the Mental Health of Children. (1969). *Crisis in child mental health: Challenge for the 1970's.* New York: Harper & Row.

Knitzer, J. (1982). *Unclaimed children: The failure of public responsibility to children and adolescents in need of mental health services.* Washington, DC: Children's Defense Fund.

Knitzer, J., & Yelton, S. (1989). Interagency collaboration. *Update, 5,* 12-14, 23.

Lewis, M., Lewis, D. O., Shanok, S. S., Klatskin, E., & Osborne, J. R. (1980). The undoing of residential treatment: A follow-up study of 51 adolescents. *Journal of the American Academy of Child Psychiatry, 19,* 160-171.

National Mental Health Association. (1989). *Report of the invisible children program.* Alexandria, VA: National Mental Health Association.

Ribicoff, A. (1969). Preface. In Joint Commission on the Mental Health of Children, *Crisis in child mental health: Challenge for the 1970's.* New York: Harper & Row.

Sokol, P. (1988). Presentation to conference on collaboration between child welfare and child mental health, Denver, Colorado.

Stroul, B. (1989). *Therapeutic foster care* (Volume III: Series on community-based services for children and adolescents who are severely emotionally disturbed). Washington, DC: CASSP Technical Assistance Center, Georgetown University Child Development Center.

Stroul, B. A., & Friedman, R. M. (1986). *A system of care for severely emotionally disturbed children and youth.* Washington, DC: CASSP Technical Assistance Center, Georgetown University Child Development Center.

Stroul, B. A., & Goldman, S. K. (1990). Study of community-based services for children and adolescents who are severely emotionally disturbed. *Journal of Mental Health Administration, 17*, 61-77.

U. S. House of Representatives, Select Committee on Children, Youth, and Families. (1987). Hearings on "Children's mental health: Promising responses to neglected problems." Washington, DC: U.S. House of Representatives.

U. S. House of Representatives, Select Committee on Children, Youth, and Families. (1990). *No place to call home: Discarded children in America.* Washington, DC: U.S. House of Representatives.

U. S. Office of Technology Assessment. (1986). *Children's mental health: Problems and treatment—A background paper.* Washington, DC: Government Printing Office.

VanDenBerg, J. (1990). The Alaska youth initiative: An experiment in individualized treatment and education. In A. Algarin, R. M. Friedman, A. J. Duchnowski, K. M. Kutash, S. E. Silver, & M. K. Johnson (Eds.), *Children's mental health services and policy: Building a research base. Conference proceedings.* Tampa: Research and Training Center for Children's Mental Health, University of South Florida.

Virginia Department of Social Services. (1986). Unpublished report, Richmond, VA.

Whittaker, J. K., & Maluccio, A. N. (1989). Changing paradigms in residential services for disturbed/disturbing children: Retrospect and prospect. In R. P. Hawkins & J. Breiling (Eds.), *Therapeutic foster care: Critical issues.* Washington, DC: Child Welfare League of America.

Conclusion

KATHLEEN WELLS
DAVID E. BIEGEL

This book has presented previously unpublished research on family preservation services and has identified a number of research and policy issues raised by these and other investigations. Two important objectives of this effort were to promote a critical evaluation of the research literature on family preservation services and to develop a research agenda for the next generation of investigations in this area. Accordingly we note in this conclusion the ways in which we believe that the material presented contributes to the extant literature; we discuss the common themes that emerged across chapters; and we propose an agenda for future research on family preservation services. We focus on intensive family preservation services, although the analysis presented here is applicable to research on all kinds of family preservation service programs.

Work Presented in This Volume

Developers of intensive family preservation service programs have taken the lead in evaluating their practices (cf. Kinney, Madsen, Fleming, & Haapala, 1977). Not surprisingly, as we stated in the introduction to this volume, initial investigations were modest in scope. Typically they focused on one or two outcome variables, depended on small samples, provided little evidence with respect to the reliability and validity of measures, and employed nonexperimental designs (Hinckley & Ellis, 1985; Kinney et al., 1977). Those early studies concentrated on the proportion of children served who remained at home after receiving intensive family preservation services. The investigators stated that the majority of children served remained at home at service termination or at follow-up.

Although these findings provided hope that intensive family preservation services might be powerful interventions, the data were too preliminary and suffered from too many methodological problems to yield specific conclusions (see Frankel, 1988; Magura, 1981; and Stein, 1985 for discussion of problems in the knowledge base in family preservation service programs in general).

The empirical chapters in this volume by Feldman, K. Nelson, Pecora and his colleagues, Schwartz and his colleagues, and Yuan and Struckman-Johnson contribute to this literature by examining multiple outcomes of treatment; by exploring some family, child, and treatment correlates of success and failure in treatment; and by employing experimental and quasi-experimental designs.

The nonempirical chapters by Dore, Jones, D. Nelson, Schuerman and his colleagues, Tracy, and Yelton and Friedman, building on the work of Frankel (1988), Magura (1981), and Stein (1985), also contribute to this literature by raising questions about the impact of the social-political and service system context on program implementation and outcomes, the ideal role of intensive family preservation services within the child mental health, child welfare, and juvenile justice systems, and the most appropriate ways in which to conceptualize and assess the target population and outcomes for these services.

Taken together, these chapters indicate that intensive family preservation services prevent the placement of some children for some period of time.[1]

For example, Feldman found statistically significant differences between the placement rates of treatment and those of control families for up to nine months after termination. These statistically significant differences disappeared by 12 months, with 46% of treatment families and 58% of control families having experienced a placement by that time. Pecora and his colleagues found that 44% of treatment children and 85% of matched comparison group children experienced a placement 12 months after intake. Schwartz and his colleagues found that 56% of treatment youths and 91% of comparison youths experienced a placement between 12 and 16 months postintake. It is notable, however, that the average number of placements experienced by both groups was about the same in light of the fact that the first placement of the comparison group was counted as a placement.

These chapters also provide data and analysis, however, that make it clear we still cannot state the extent to which intensive family preservation services are effective. This is so for several reasons:

First, not all children who enter control or comparison groups are placed outside their homes. This situation makes it difficult to attribute the placement prevention rates found in treatment groups to involvement in intensive family preservation services alone.

Second, the differences in placement rates of children in intensive family preservation service programs and those in alternative services diminish over time. This means that intensive family preservation service programs may delay rather than prevent placement for some children.

Third, the predictors of placement reported in this volume suggest that the factors affecting placement may vary according to the child's age, the nature of the child's and the family's problem, and the characteristics of the service system of which the child and family are a part. This means that we may need to identify placement prevention rates for specific populations considered within the context of specific service systems.

In addition, we have no empirical data as to whether children and families who entered intensive family preservation service programs are safe from abuse and neglect during treatment or for specified periods after service termination. We have only sketchy evidence as to whether they are functioning better than would have been the case in alternative services. Indeed, one of the few studies to address this issue is the one by Feldman, and he found few differences in the functioning of families who received intensive family preservation services and those who received alternative services.

Common Themes

The common themes that emerged across chapters pertain to the most appropriate way in which to conceptualize basic concepts in research on intensive family preservation services.

Definition of Outcome

In view of the goals of intensive family preservation service programs, there is considerable agreement that prevention of placement is an appropriate indicator of programmatic success. The use of this measure poses the following problems, however: (a) Placement is not an unambiguous event because some placements may be desirable for some children; (b) not all children who enter programs would have been placed, thus it is difficult to determine the true success rate for a program; and (c) placements are affected by factors that are external to success or failure in treatment, such as the availability of institutional placements or aftercare services in a community. These factors may change over time so it is difficult to compare placement rates over time and across communities.

Indeed, some researchers argue for reconsidering an appropriate definition of success. Dore, for example, favors the introduction of outcome measures that are related logically to theories underlying intensive family preservation programs (e.g., resolution of referral crises, enhancement of parenting skills). In a similar vein, Jones advocates the introduction of process outcomes that might make research more useful to clinicians. It is clear, however, that we need to be able eventually to link clinical and policy outcomes in order to understand both individual and system-level change.

Definition of the Target Population

The definition of the target population for intensive family preservation services is linked ultimately to the desired role of such services within the child welfare, mental health, and juvenile justice systems. Researchers along with program planners and policymakers in the field lack consensus regarding the role of these services. Schuerman and his colleagues provide some anecdotal evidence that expectations about the purpose of intensive family preservation services vary widely. Some observers, such as D. Nelson, argue that services should be targeted to families with a child at risk of out-of-home placement who also meet criteria for entrance into programs. Others, such as Yelton and Friedman, believe that services should be available to a wider range of families.

Most observers agree, however, that even where consensus exists regarding criteria for the target population, referring agencies and programs find it difficult to apply these criteria consistently over families and over time. As Tracy notes, the methodology for making such decisions is not well developed.

Definition of the Intervention

Although there is some consensus as to the definition of intensive family preservation services (indeed, the Child Welfare League [1989] recently published guidelines to help define such services), observers acknowledge that there is only limited information about how programs have been implemented or how treatment works. The data provided by Feldman, Pecora and his colleagues, and Schwartz and his colleagues vary with respect to the impact of key components of intensive family preservation services on outcome.

Difficulties in Conducting Research in Intensive Family Preservation Services

Researchers conducting investigations in intensive family preservation services suffer from the same difficulties as do researchers of other human service delivery programs. These difficulties include problems in implementing and maintaining experimental designs, in obtaining reliable and valid data, and in procuring informed consent. These problems are exacerbated by the high staff turnover that characterizes some referring agencies and programs (see the chapter by Schuerman and his colleagues for a discussion of this issue).

Research Agenda

Despite the limited knowledge of to what extent and how intensive family preservation services work, many observers argue that the evidence warrants expansion of these programs. In addition, considerable optimism has been expressed that the innovative features of such services—the integrated response to the problems of families, provided for a brief period and delivered in families' homes—hold potential for reform of the systems serving children (Nelson, 1988). Yet if intensive family preservation programs are to be expanded or used as an aid to redesign these systems, these changes must be informed by the most accurate and fullest obtainable evidence regarding not only the efficacy of services but also the processes by which results are obtained.

Toward that end, we offer a research agenda for intensive family preservation services. This agenda was informed by discussions at the National Conference on Intensive Family Preservation Services, held in Cleveland in September 1989 (Wells & Biegel, 1990), by prior research in family preservation services, and by the work presented in this volume. The agenda is presented in two sections: the first details major unresolved issues and questions facing research in intensive family preservation services, and the second makes recommendations for future research in this area.

Major Unresolved Issues

We face three major sets of unresolved issues at this stage of our knowledge about intensive family preservation services:

1. Even though intensive family preservation services are intended only for children whose safety can be assured with the provision of services, we do not have empirical data to document whether children served are safe at home, or for how long; whether the emotional problems that triggered their referral to a placement service are resolved; whether these children remain uninvolved in delinquent behavior; or whether the postponement of entry into out-of-home placements that occurs for some children who have been served is even desirable. To ensure that children and families in the three major systems serving children are served well, research must address, more comprehensively than to date, the consequences of involvement in intensive family preservation services for children and their families.

2. We do not know what proportion of children approved for out-of-home placement meets the criteria for entrance into intensive family preservation services. If we are to expand these services to the populations for whom they could be most beneficial and if we are to clarify the needed balance between intensive and nonintensive services, research must help to determine what proportion of the population of children in out-of-home placement can be served by these programs.

3. We do not know whether the clinical hypotheses underlying intensive family preservation service programs are generally valid (e.g., "Families are in a crisis state at the entrance into intensive family preservation service programs," "A crisis creates an openness to change," and "An increase in a parent's parenting skills reduces their child's behavior problems" and so on); what configuration of services is most effective for which types of families; or how experiences postdischarge (including aftercare) affect functioning of children and families at follow-up. To ensure that such programs can be developed further, research must examine an array of organizational and clinical issues that carry import for both improvement and expansion of programs.

Recommendations for Future Research

With these issues and questions in mind, we make the following recommendations to guide future empirical investigations in this area:

1. Investigations are needed to determine what proportion of the population of children approved for out-of-home placement meets the criteria for entrance into intensive family preservation services. Such research will help

to address questions about the proportion of the population at risk of imminent placement that could be served and the resources that might be devoted to expanding these services.

2. Outcome evaluations are needed to assess the degree to which intensive family preservation services are meeting their principal goals, such as prevention of placement, maintenance of family environments in which family members are safe, reduction of the crises that led to the need for placement, and acquisition of skills that families need to stay together. We can determine the effectiveness of intensive family preservation services by comparing families in these services with those in alternative services or with those who receive no services. Such investigations could be used to test the efficacy of various models of intensive family preservation services as well as the effect of key service components, such as the intensity and the duration of services, on outcomes.

3. Prospective, longitudinal evaluations are needed to assess whether the outcomes that are achieved are maintained over time. Such research will help us to address questions such as "What child, family, and community characteristics are associated with the maintenance of outcomes of programs over time?" and "At what point in time after discharge do these outcomes diminish?"

The studies reported in this volume reveal that the proportion of children who received intensive family preservation services that remain at home diminishes over time. Indeed, about one year after service termination, the proportion of such children who remain at home is about half of those served. These data also suggest the need to evaluate the conditions under which children are placed (and sometimes replaced) and the consequences of these placements for their functioning and the functioning of their families.

4. Investigations are needed to assess the impact of the ecological context in which programs are operating on their implementation, functioning, and outcomes. Ecological features include the characteristics of the service system and the communities in which programs are operating, the informal supports and the placement and nonplacement services that are available, and how children are referred to those services. (See Weiss & Jacobs [1988] for a general discussion of an ecological approach to evaluating family programs.) Research of this type will help us to address questions such as "Are placement rates found due to programs or to changes in the available placement resources?" and "How does service availability affect clinical decisions regarding need for intensive family preservation services and placement services?"

5. Process evaluations of programs are needed to examine the clinical assumptions underlying the treatment models employed and the ways in which clinicians and their clients experience programs. We need such evaluations to provide information necessary to improve programs. This work can help us to answer questions such as "What components of treatment facilitate child and family change?" "Through what interpersonal processes do these changes occur?" and "How do the structure and the process of programs support or impede change?" Process evaluations should be conceptualized so as to include the subject, programmatic, and outcome variables that are believed to be relevant to basic clinical assumptions.

6. Comprehensive evaluations of the functioning of children (and of their families) at service termination are needed. Many providers of intensive family preservation services argue that crisis intervention services such as these should strive only for limited goals, but it is important to document the developmental status of children who are served (and the functioning of their families). This information would help to inform the kinds of interventions and/or social changes needed by children and families in this vulnerable population.

7. We need investigations of the costs of services, which take into account all services used by families during the receipt of intensive family preservation services and after termination (for a specified period). Such research would provide the data needed to reflect the costs of treating families, and would furnish a baseline by which to compare the costs of intensive family preservation services with the costs of placement services.

8. Investigations are needed to identify and examine the elements that impede and facilitate faithful replication of services in various contexts (e.g., public versus private agencies). Such research would inform efforts to expand services and to institutionalize them within public systems that serve a substantial number of children.

In addition, let us make three final remarks. First, research in intensive family preservation services would be advanced through the use of a range of designs (preexperimental, quasi-experimental, experimental, and correlational) and the use of both qualitative and quantitative techniques. While the selection of any particular design and technique would depend upon the research question under examination, we note that the literature contains not one investigation that relies on qualitative data. As a result, we have no systematically collected information on such crucial issues as to how programs develop, how intensive family preservation service workers experience their jobs, or even how families experience treatment. Qualitatively-based empirical investigations would inform not only practice but also theory.

Second, research in intensive family preservation services has tended to be atheoretical. The theoretical assumptions underlying treatment programs have not been tested. No attempt has been made to connect theories relating to treatment with theories pertaining to the causes and consequences of specific child and family problems. For example, K. Nelson provides evidence in chapter four that delinquent or antisocial youths do not fare as well as youths with other kinds of problems in intensive family preservation service programs as they are currently configured. Research in these services could be enriched by attention to the literature on antisocial behavior and juvenile delinquency (cf. Elliott, Huizinga, & Ageton, 1985; Patterson, 1980).

Third, we need to clarify expectations regarding duration of the effects of intensive family preservation programs. This step will help us to judge programs fairly and to delineate the nature of follow-up services that families need.

A Closing Note

Intensive family preservation services are important because of their emphasis on preventing the placement of children outside their homes, on keeping families together and empowering them to solve their own problems, and on teaching families the specific skills they need to meet their current crises. As Knitzer and Cole stated:

> In the broadest sense . . . [intensive family preservation services] represent an effort to shift the ecology of the service system for troubled children and families away from a placement orientation to one where home-based alternatives are equally available . . . perhaps most importantly, the family preservation "movement" has called attention to the possibility of success in a field where too often, either with or without evidence, the threshold assumption is that nothing works. (1989, pp. 27 - 28)

Research has played a vital role in the development of intensive family preservation services; it has the potential to inform the refinement and expansion of these services in the coming decade.

Note

1. It is difficult to compare placement rates across studies due to differences in the definition of placement, the unit of analysis (i.e., that is whether the data pertain to families in which any placement has occurred or to children placed), and the length of the follow-up period. Therefore, care should be taken when undertaking such an analysis.

References

Child Welfare League. (1989). *Standards for services to strengthen and preserve families with children.* Washington, DC: Author.

Elliott, D. S., Huizinga, D., & Ageton, S. S. (1985). *Explaining delinquency and drug use.* Beverly Hills: Sage.

Frankel, H. (1988). Family-centered, home based services in child protection: A review of the research. *Social Service Review, 62,* 137-157.

Hinckley, E., & Ellis, F. (1985). An effective alternative to residential placement: Home-based services. *Journal of Clinical Child Psychology, 14*(3), 209-213.

Kinney, J., Madsen, B., Fleming, T., & Haapala, D. (1977). Homebuilders: Keeping families together. *Journal of Consulting and Clinical Psychology, 4*54), 667-673.

Knitzer, J., & Cole, E. (1989). *Family preservation services: The policy challenge to state child welfare and child mental health systems.* Unpublished manuscript, Bank Street College of Education, New York.

Magura, S. (1981). Are services to prevent foster care effective? *Children and Youth Services Review,3,* 193-212.

Nelson, D. (1988). Recognizing and realizing the potential of "family preservation." In J. Whittaker, J. Kinney, E. Tracy, & C. Booth (Eds.), *Improving practice technology for work with high risk families: Lessons from the "Homebuilders" Social Work Education Project* (pp. 19-35). Seattle: University of Washington, Center for Social Welfare Research.

Patterson, G. (1980). Treatment for children with conduct problems: A review of outcome studies. In S. Feshbach & A. Fraczek (Eds.), *Aggression and behavior change* (pp. 83-132). New York: Praeger.

Stein, T. J. (1985). Projects to prevent out-of-home placement. *Children and Youth Services Review, 7*(2), 109-121.

Weiss, H., & Jacobs, F. (Eds.). (1988). *Evaluating family programs.* New York: Aldine.

Wells, K., & Biegel, D. (1990). *Intensive family preservation services: A research agenda for the 1990s.* Proceedings of the Intensive Family Preservation Services National Research Conference. (Available from The National Resource Center on Family Based Services, School of Social Work, The University of Iowa, Iowa City, Iowa 52242).

Intensive Family Preservation Services Research Conference Agenda and Conference Participants

7 p.m.	**Sunday, September 24th**	
	Reception	
Day 1	**Monday, September 25th**	
8:15 a.m.	Continental Breakfast	
8:30–9:00 a.m.	I. Introduction	
	A. Welcome	Samuel Kelman
		David Biegel
	B. Conference Plan	Kathleen Wells
	Conference Purpose, Focus,	David Biegel
	Products, Participants,	
	Structure	
	C. Introduction of Conference	
	Participants	
9:00–9:30 a.m.	II. Background	
	A. Evolution of Programs	Kristine Nelson
9:30–11:00 a.m.	III. Research Overview	
	A. Overview of Family	Kathleen Wells
	Preservation Services	David Biegel
	Research	
	B. Research on Alternative	Martha Dore
	Family Preservation	
	Service Models	

11:00 a.m.–Noon	IV.	<u>Broad Issues Pertinent to Evaluation of Evidence</u>	
		A. Social Science or Policy Science	Charles Gershenson
		B. Research and Clinical Paradigm Compatibility	
12:00–1:30 p.m.		Lunch	
1:30–4:30 p.m.	V.	<u>Small Work-Group Discussions</u>	
		Group 1: Client Characteristics	David Fanshel Elizabeth Tracy
		Group 2: Program Characteristics	Kristine Nelson Peter Pecora
		Group 3: Conceptualization of Outcomes	Mary Ann Jones Ira Schwartz
6:30 p.m.	VII.	<u>Dinner and Panel Discussion</u>	
		Panel Discussion: Family Preservation Services Research in Context	
		Panel Chair: Samuel Kelman	
		Panelists: Leonard Feldman, Peter Forsythe, Cecilia Sudia, Mario Tonti, and Ying-Ying Yuan	

Day 2:   **Tuesday, September 26th**

8:15 a.m.		Continental Breakfast	
8:30–8:40 a.m.	I.	<u>Introduction</u>	Kathleen Wells David Biegel
8:40–10:00 a.m.	II.	<u>Presentation of Research Synthesis</u>	John Schuerman
10:15 a.m.–Noon	III.	<u>Presentation and Discussion of Research Agenda</u>	Kathleen Wells David Biegel
		A. Perspectives	
		B. Divergences of Opinion	
		C. Questions and Concepts	
		D. Questions for Next Generation of Studies	
		E. Conclusions	
12:00 p.m.		Lunch	

Conference Participants

Neil Abell, Ph.D.	Assistant Professor Case Western Reserve University
David Biegel, Ph.D.	Henry L. Zucker Professor of Social Work Practice Case Western Reserve University
Betty Blythe, Ph.D.	Associate Professor University of Pittsburgh
Martha M. Dore, Ph.D.	Assistant Professor University of Pennsylvania
David Fanshel, D.S.W.	Professor Columbia University
Leonard Feldman, M.A.	Assistant Chief New Jersey Division of Youth and Family Services
Peter Forsythe, J.D.	Vice President Edna McConnell Clark Foundation
Charles Gershenson, Ph.D.	Senior Research Associate Center for the Study of Social Policy
Linda Greenan, M.S.W.	Director of Public Policy Child Welfare League of America
Selma Gwatkin, M.A.	Director of Parents and Children Together Program Bellefaire/Jewish Children's Bureau
David Haapala, Ph.D.	Executive Director Behavioral Sciences Institute
Mary Ann Jones, D.S.W.	Associate Professor New York University
Samuel Kelman, Ph.D.	Executive Director Bellefaire/Jewish Children's Bureau
Douglas Nelson	Deputy Director Center for the Study of Social Policy

Kristine Nelson, D.S.W.

Associate Professor and Acting Director
National Resource Center on Family-Based
    Services
University of Iowa

Peter J. Pecora, Ph.D.

Associate Professor
University of Utah

Tina Rzepnicki, Ph.D.

Assistant Professor
University of Chicago

Alvin Schorr, M.S.W.

Leonard W. Mayo Professor of Family and
    Child Welfare
Case Western Reserve University

John Schuerman, Ph.D.

Professor
University of Chicago

Ira Schwartz

Professor
University of Michigan

David Struckman-Johnson, Ph.D.

Associate Professor
University of South Dakota

Cecilia Sudia

Family Services Specialist
U.S. Administration for Children, Youth,
    & Families

Mario Tonti, D.S.W.

Director of Community Services
Bellefaire/Jewish Children's Bureau

Elizabeth Tracy, Ph.D.

Assistant Professor
Case Western Reserve University

Kathleen Wells, Ph.D.

Director of Research
Bellefaire/Jewish Children's Bureau

Jim White, M.A.

Research Analyst
Oregon State Department of Human
    Resources

Dale Whittington, Ph.D.

Research Associate
Bellefaire/Jewish Children's Bureau

Ying-Ying Yuan, Ph.D.

Vice President
Walter R. McDonald & Associates, Inc.

About the Authors

Philip AuClaire, Ph.D., is Program Analysis Supervisor and Grants Manager for the Hennepin County (Minnesota) Community Services Department. He received his Ph.D. from the Graduate School of Social Work and Social Research, Bryn Mawr College, Pennsylvania. He has taught at the School of Social Work, University of Minnesota and has served as Adjunct Faculty at the Hubert Humphrey Institute, University of Minnesota. He has published in the areas of social service evaluation, welfare reform and public attitudes concerning social welfare. Currently he is involved in evaluation of service programs for substance abusing pregnant women and chronically neglecting families involved with child protective services.

David E. Biegel, Ph.D., is the Henry L. Zucker Professor of Social Work Practice and Co-Director, Center for Social Work Practice, Mandel School of Applied Social Sciences, Case Western Reserve University. Currently, he is also serving as a Research Fellow, Ohio Department of Mental Health. Dr. Biegel received his Ph.D. from the School of Social Work and Community Planning, University of Maryland at Baltimore. Prior to coming to Cleveland in 1987, he was an Associate Professor of Social Work at the University of Pittsburgh School of Social Work and Senior Research Associate, University Center for Social and Urban Research, University of Pittsburgh. He has been involved in research, scholarship, and practice for the past 15 years and

255

the author of numerous books and articles, including *Aging and Caregiving: Theory, Research and Policy* (co-edited with Arthur Blum) and *Family Caregiving in Chronic Illness: Alzheimer's Disease, Cancer, Heart Disease, Mental Illness and Stroke* (co-authored with Esther Sales and Richard Schulz), both published by Sage. Additionally, he is co-editor with Richard Schulz of a new 10-book series, *Family Caregiver Applications,* also to be published by Sage.

Martha Morrison Dore, Ph.D., is Assistant Professor of Social Work at the University of Pennsylvania and Director of Social Work Research at the Philadelphia Child Guidance Clinic. She earned her doctorate at the University of Chicago School of Social Service Administration. She is currently principal investigator of a state-wide research and demonstration project in family-based children's mental health services funded by the Pennsylvania Office of Mental Health. She is also co-principal investigator on a study of the effects of participation in family day care services on abused and neglected infants and toddlers and their families. Findings from this study were presented at an invitational research conference sponsored by Temple University. In addition, she has recently received a grant from the UPS foundation for the study of public policy to continue her research in the area of adolescent pregnancy policy development. Recent articles on her research have appeared in *Families and Society, Child Welfare,* and *Social Service Review.* She is currently co-editing a book on family-based mental health services with Marion Lindblad-Goldberg, Director of Training at the Philadelphia Child Guidance Clinic, and Lenora Stern, Pennsylvania CASSP coordinator.

Leonard H. Feldman, Ph.D., is Chief of the Bureau of Research, Evaluation and Quality Assurance within the New Jersey Division of Youth and Family Services, which is the public child welfare agency of the state. He is a contributing author to *Preserving Families: Evaluation Resources for Practitioners and Policymakers.* He also teaches courses in research and statistics at Rutgers University School of Social Work. He is past chair of the conference planning committee for the American Public Welfare Association sponsored National Conference on Research, Demonstration and Evaluation in Human Services.

Mark W. Fraser, Ph.D., is Associate Professor at the Graduate School of Social Work, University of Utah where he directs the school's Ph.D. program. He received his MSW from the University of Denver and his Ph.D.

from the University of Washington. He has been a school social worker and family services director of a family program for the parents of deaf-blind, multiply-handicapped children. He also serverd as a consultant to the Homebuilders Program for approximately ten years. From 1982 to 1989, he served as the Director of the school's Ph.D. program. He has worked with a variety of public and private agencies. He is the author of numerous articles on family-focused treatment, delinquency, children's services, and substance abuse.

Robert M. Friedman is a clinical psychologist who has specialized in research and treatment of children and adolescents. He is currently Professor at the Florida Mental Health Institute, University of South Florida, and Director of the Research and Training Center for Children's Mental Health. The Research and Training Center is funded by the National Institute on Disability and Rehabilitation Research and the National Institute of Mental Health to develop an integrated set of research, training consultation, and dissemination activities to strengthen services for emotionally disturbed children. In addition to publishing and presenting more than 100 papers and articles, he has consulted with more than 40 states on improving services for children with emotional disturbances. He is co-author of a monograph, *A System of Care for Severely Emotionally Disturbed Children and Youth,* and co-editor of a book, *Advocacy on Behalf of Children with Serious Emotional Problems,* both of which are being widely used in many states to plan services.

David A. Haapala, Ph.D., is co-founder and an Executive Director of Behavioral Sciences Institute, a nonprofit corporation created to provide, promote, and study community-based family-centered services. He also cofounded the nationally recognized Homebuilders Program, which began in Tacoma, Washington, in 1974. He has authored numerous papers on program evaluation, social service delivery, and public policy. He has provided consultation to such diverse groups as Universal Studios, Hollywood, California; the Ute Mountain Ute Indian Nation, Tawaoc, Colorado; the Department of Juvenile Justice, New York City; and Community Services Victoria, Melbourne, Australia. Before his involvement in intensive family preservation services, he worked in a children's psychiatric hospital, a community mental health center, and maintained a private psychotherapy practice.

Linda J. Harris is a senior scientist with the Adolescent Health Program at the University of Minnesota. She is currently working on her Ph.D. in sociology at the University of Minnesota. Her research interests include the study of youth health risks, and the identification of factors promoting positive health and social outcomes for high risk youth. She has worked on several evaluation studies involving human services programs. She also has worked and published in the areas of educational achievement and computer literacy, juvenile justice research, diet and food practices, and public health nutrition.

Mary Ann Jones, BA, MSW, DSW, is Associate Professor at the New York University School of Social Work. For nearly 20 years she has been engaged in the evaluation of services to prevent the placement of children in foster care, and in the development of measures to assist in those evaluations. Formerly Director of Research at the Child Welfare League of America, she directed the first experimental study of preventive programs, a study of New York State's Chapter 911 preventive services programs published under the title, *A Second Chance for Families*. Subsequently, she conducted a five-year follow-up study of the original families to determine the longer-term effects of the experimental programs. This was published under the title, *A Second Chance for Families: Five Years Later*. She is also a member of the Wilder Settlement Panel, a three-member federal court-appointed panel charged with overseeing the implementation of the settlement decree in *Wilder v. Grinker*, which alleges racial and religious discrimination in the placement of foster children in New York City.

Julia Littell, is a doctoral student in the School of Social Service Administration at the University of Chicago and Senior Program Associate at the Chapin Hall Center for Children. She is the author of several articles on program evaluation and on community-based programs for children and families. In addition to her work on the family preservation evaluation, she is conducting research on the long-term effects of young people's involvement in extracurricular activities.

Douglas W. Nelson, MA, is Executive Director of The Annie E. Casey Foundation, which is the nation's largest philanthropy devoted to disadvantaged children, in Greenwich, Connecticut. Its principal mission is to support policy, programmatic, and research initiatives aimed at improving future outcomes for at-risk youth. Prior positions held include: Deputy Director of the Center for the Study of Social Policy, a Washington, DC-based nonprofit organization specializing in policy research and analysis across a range of domestic issues including health care, aging, long-term care, welfare, and social services to children and families; State Aging

Director, and Assistant Secretary of the Department of Health and Social Services in Wisconsin. He is a nationally known advisor and trustee as a result of his leadership and advocacy on behalf of family-centered, community-based responses to the needs of at-risk children, elderly persons and adults with disabilities. His widely published works include *Heart Mountain* (a social history of World War II relocation of Japanese Americans), studies and essays on aging, long-term care, housing, children and youth.

Kristine E. Nelson, DSW, is Director of Research at the National Resource Center on Family Based Services and an Associate Professor at the School of Social Work, The University of Iowa. She has been the principal investigator on several federally funded studies, including a six-state study of factors contributing to success and failure in family-based placement prevention programs and a study of chronically neglecting families in a large metropolitan area. Currently, she is principal investigator on a project demonstrating a family-based treatment model for chronic neglect, a study of the effect of length of service on case outcomes and costs in family-based services, and a study on family functioning of neglectful families. She has published in *Social Service Review, Social Casework, Children and Youth Services Review, Child Welfare,* and *The Journal of Sociology and Social Welfare,* and contributed a chapter, "Program Organization and Description," to *Preserving Families: Evaluation Resources for Practitioners and Policymakers,* edited by Ying-Ying T. Yuan and Michele Rivest. Before joining the University of Iowa, she worked in public social services, child welfare, Head Start, and program evaluation and planning.

Peter J. Pecora, Ph.D., holds a joint appointment as Manager of Evaluation and Research with The Casey Family Program, and Associate Professor at the School of Social Work, University of Washington. He began his social work career as a line worker and later served as a program coordinator for a number of child welfare organizations in Wisconsin. From 1982 to 1990, he was on the faculty at the Graduate School of Social Work, University of Utah, where he worked with the Utah Department of Social Services to implement intensive family preservation service programs and a new risk assessment system for child protective services. He has provided training in risk assessment and evaluation of family preservation service programs to social service staff in over six states. The co-author of three books on personnel management and program evaluation in child welfare, the results of his research have been published in *Administration in Social Work, Child Welfare, Social Service Review,* and other professional journals.

Tina Rzepnicki is Assistant Professor at the School of Social Service Administration, the University of Chicago and Faculty Associate at the Chapin Hall Center for Children. She has written articles on permanency planning and co-authored three books, including *Decision Making in Child Welfare Services: Intake and Planning*. Currently Co-Principal Investigator on the Illinois Family First Evaluation, her primary research interest is in the design and testing of innovative services for child protection cases.

John R. Schuerman is Professor in the School of Social Service Administration at the University of Chicago, a Faculty Associate at the Chapin Hall Center for Children, and the Editor of *Social Service Review*. He is author of *Research and Evaluation in the Human Services* and *Multivariate Analysis in the Human Services*. Currently he is engaged in an exploration of the use of expert systems in child welfare decision making.

Ira M. Schwartz is Professor and Director of the Center for the Study of Youth Policy at the University of Michigan's School of Social Work. He joined the faculty at the University of Michigan in 1987, after being a Senior Fellow at the University of Minnesota's Hubert H. Humphrey Institute of Public Affairs. Between 1979 and 1981 he served as the Administrator of the Office of Juvenile Justice and Delinquency Prevention, U.S. Department of Justice. He has also directed criminal and juvenile justice agencies in the states of Illinois and Washington and has worked extensively in both the public and the private sectors. He has written numerous articles on juvenile justice and is the author of *(In)Justice for Juveniles: Rethinking the Best Interest of the Child*, published by Lexington Books.

David L. Struckman-Johnson, Ph.D., is Associate Professor of Psychology and Computer Science at the University of South Dakota. He has been involved in evaluations of rehabilitation for drinking drivers, motorcycle rider education, driver improvement courses, seatbelt use, university image, condom advertisement effectiveness, and legal services for Native American elders. Most recently, as a consultant to Walter R. McDonald & Associates, Inc., he has assisted in the evaluation of a major intensive in-home services project in California.

Elizabeth M. Tracy, Ph.D., is Assistant Professor at the Mandel School of Applied Social Sciences, Case Western Reserve University, where she teaches social work practice methods courses and coordinates the Child Welfare Practice Demonstration Project. She has also served as facilitator for a National Family Preservation Educators Working Group funded by the Edna McConnell Clark Foundation, which is developing curriculum materials for the teaching of family preservation practice in graduate schools of social work.

Kathleen Wells, Ph.D., is a social psychologist and Director of Research at the Bellefaire/Jewish Children's Bureau in Cleveland, Ohio, where she developed the clinical research program. The program focuses upon treatment of severely emotionally disturbed youth. It involves the conduct of empirical investigations and research symposiums intended to improve agency programs and to contribute to knowledge in the field. She has published numerous papers concerned with mental health and welfare services for children, youth, and families, as well as the development of clinical research programs. Currently she is engaged in child mental health policy, residential treatment and family preservation services research.

Susan W. Yelton, MSW, is Project Director on the Edna McConnell Clark Foundation grant to the Research and Training Center for Children's Mental Health, Florida Mental Health Institute, at the University of South Florida. She previously worked for the State of Florida for more than 20 years, guiding program development and administration in both child welfare and child mental health. She provides technical assistance to many states in policymaking for implementing systems of care. Her multifaceted expertise in all areas of children's service systems is also being utilized for federal issues of funding for these systems.

Ying-Ying T. Yuan is Vice-President of Walter R. McDonald & Associates, Inc., a human services management consulting and information systems development firm. She received her doctorate degree from the Department of Social Relations, Harvard University. For the past several years, she has focused her attention on the assessment of human services delivery systems at the local, state, and federal levels and the relationship between evaluation and program planning. From 1986 to 1990 she was the principal investigator of a major evaluation in intensive in-home services in California and is currently serving in that role for the State of Connecticut Department of Children and Youth Services. She is co-editor, with Michele Rivest, of *Preserving Families: Evaluation Resources for Practitioners and Policymakers,* published by Sage.